MASSIVE ATTACK OUT OF THE COMFORT ZONE

THE STORY OF A SOUND, A CITY AND A GROUP OF REVOLUTIONARY ARTISTS

Melissa Chemam

The author would like to warmly thank her friends for their help: music journalist and writer Bertrand Dicale for his work and efforts in making this book possible, as well as David Armstrong, Anne Cazaubon, Amy Racs and Marjorie Hache for their constant support.

This book is an adaptation of the orginal version published in French by the author with Editions Anne Carrière. She wants to express her gratitude to them for enabling this project.

Massive Attack: Out of the Comfort Zone.
The Story Of A Sound A City And A Group Of Revolutionary Artists
First published 2019 by Tangent Books and PC Press

Tangent Books/PC Press
Unit 5.16 Paintworks, Bristol BS4 3EH
www.tangentbooks.co.uk
www.pc-press.co.uk

ISBN 978-1-910089-72-9

Author, Translator, Editor: Melissa Chemam

Design: Joe Burt

Cover image courtesy of Robert Del Naja

Copyright: Tangent Books/PC Press All rights reserved

Published under licence from Editions Anne Carrière, France

A CIP record of this book is available at the British Library.

Printed by Short Run Press in the UK on paper from a sustainable source.

"People can change anything they want to. And that means everything in the world. People are running about following their little tracks – I am one of them. But we've all got to stop just following our own little mouse trail. People can do anything – this is something that I'm beginning to learn."

Joe Strummer (1952-2002), member of The Clash, in *The Future Is Unwritten*, documentary film by Julien Temple, 2007

"I was a really lousy artist as a kid. Too abstract expressionist; or I'd draw a big ram's head, really messy. I'd never win painting contests. I remember losing to a guy who did a perfect Spiderman".

Jean-Michel Basquiat, American painter

"We're natives of the massive territory and we're proud
Get peaceful in the dance, no death or glory in the crowd
The problem ain't a different kind of skin Tricks
I love my neighbour I don't wait for the Olympics"

In 'Daydreaming', *Blue Lines*, by Massive Attack

Contents

Chapter 1
Follow The *Blue Lines* Road

"I was lookin' back to see / If you were lookin' back at me / To see me lookin'
back at you"... Here is one of the most famous lines from 'Safe From
Harm', Massive Attack's third single released in 1991, from their debut
album, *Blue Lines*.

The album came out at a time of radical change and soon epitomised
a lot of core cultural evolutions about to start. 1990-91 was a turning
point politically in the United Kingdom and worldwide. On November
28, 1990 the "reign" of the Iron Lady, Margaret Thatcher, who had been
the UK's Prime Minister for more than eleven years, came to an end.
This was followed by the fall of the Soviet Union and, *de facto*, the end
of the Cold War. And from mid-1990, with the preparation for the First
Gulf War, the United States' main enemy increasingly became "the
Middle East".

Meanwhile, in England, this aforementioned young band from
Bristol had to shorten their name from "Massive Attack" to a simple
"Massive", to avoid any association with the ubiquitous tabloid slogans
about the war. Their album, though, *Blue Lines*, reinvented a sum of
cultural elements that merged together during the previous decade in
their hometown, and brought in a sonic revolution that was about to
have a huge influence on popular culture. The late 1980s had already
displayed the influence of American hip-hop on British youth, but
Blue Lines also carried reggae and soul music influences, new sampling
techniques, genuine rap lyrics and powerful vocals from different
collaborators, in both a sound system and a collective approach. The
band opened a new, more ambitious path for British music.

Formed in 1988 in Bristol, Massive Attack were a trio of DJs and
vocalists known as Daddy G (28 years old), 3D (23), and Mushroom

(21) – real names Grant Marshall, Robert Del Naja and Andrew Vowles. They launched their project after years spent in the collective known as the Wild Bunch, mixing reggae, punk and hip-hop. They were intimately and culturally rooted in the west of England. Their first album especially featured eloquent guest vocalists: Shara Nelson, a soul singer from London, the reggae legend from Jamaica Horace Andy, as well as rappers from Bristol Adrian "Tricky Kid" Thaws and Claude "Willy Wee" Williams.

Blue Lines was released in the UK on April 8, 1991; it reached number 13 in the UK Albums Chart, an unprecedented event for a band from Bristol, a location then relatively unknown culturally to the rest of the country. The press was mesmerised by the record and dealt with it as it would for a piece of classical music. It was described as the "album of the decade" by many reviewers and a "sonic revolution for dance music".

And more than 25 years after its release, *Blue Lines* remains a masterpiece and a highly relevant opus that hasn't aged in any way, praised from England to the USA, via Europe and Latin America.

The first single, 'Daydreaming', was released at the same time as Elton John's 'Sacrifice' and Madonna's 'Vogue'. It offers references to a nocturnal easy-going lifestyle, full of creativity, ethnically and musically diverse, provocative and underground.

With two first hits, 'Unfinished Sympathy' and 'Safe From Harm', the record presented a new sound, a new form of urban "DIY" creativity and a new way of producing music in Britain: without instruments, without a lead singer, offering long tracks without a chorus, inventing its own referencing world with a machine reusing other sounds – the sampler. Moreover, it offered multiple musical and visual directions and combined them in a unique way for the first time, fusing rap, soul melodies and reggae basslines. Massive Attack's technique and style were soon to become a major influence in Bristol then worldwide.

The album also summed up parts of Bristol's history and musical heritage. It became the manifesto of its counterculture. Bristol was, at that time, isolated from London's main concerns, it was rarely featured in national headlines, and was remote from industrial and cultural hot spots such as Liverpool, Manchester or Glasgow. Bristol suffered from unemployment as much as the rest of the UK at the end of the 1980s but was not on the country's priority list, because it was smaller, quieter, less populated and culturally unknown outside of its area. Bristol relied less on the factory work than the Northern English cities, so appeared less hurt by the deindustrialisation process. It had historically been more of a hub for trade, from the sixteenth century, and a key centre in relations with the Americas – a port of departure for the first voyages exploring the "New World".

After the First and the Second World War, Britain encouraged people from its Commonwealth to come and help rebuild the country. And, like other large cities, Bristol was a destination for people arriving from the Caribbean. The city became a hub for Jamaican food and reggae music. Multicultural, humble, green and inclusive, it later thrived around the ethos that had come out of the punk movement since the 1970s, which meant that young people adopt a 'Do it yourself' attitude rather than asking for permission or support.

Mixing their musical revolution with this underground feel and a very sharp sense of artistic presentation, Massive Attack quickly inspired, in Bristol and beyond, a whole new generation of musicians and artists: their own collaborator Tricky; Geoff Barrow and his upcoming project, Portishead; James Lavelle and U.N.K.L.E; the Icelandic singer based in London Björk; and later on Gorillaz, Goldfrapp, Boards of Canada, Burial, as well as artists such as James Blake and Nils Frahm.

Almost three decades after the making of *Blue Lines*, after undergoing many changes and challenges and reinventing themselves for the stage, Massive Attack are still breaking records, pioneering technological revolutions and reaching the top of the charts, inspiring ever-evolving sounds and working in many dimensions of the music business. They also epitomise a unique form of multuculturalism at its height. From 1990, their background and the quickly evolving world around them inspired the band's themes – positivity, social awareness and a special gaze on political issues – themes developed in their lyrics, stage productions, and an iconoclastic visual universe.

What did Massive Attack manage to create that makes the collective so unordinary? How did the three self-made musicians attract collaborators as prestigious as reggae veteran Horace Andy, Tracey Thorn from Everything But The Girl, Madonna, David Bowie, Elizabeth Fraser from the Cocteau Twins, Sinéad O'Connor, Damon Albarn from Blur and Gorillaz, Thom Yorke from Radiohead, soul singer Terry Callier and many more? How do they manage to still capture the attention of emerging musicians like Mercury Prize Winner from Scotland Young Fathers and New York's hip-hop heroes Run The Jewels, as well as one of the greatest documentary filmmakers in the English-speaking world, Adam Curtis?

The answer, according to me, is in their journey. Independent spirits and iconoclasts, attached to England as much as avid travellers, Grant Marshall and Robert Del Naja still embody their city's rebellious ethos. Robert, the graffiti artist who created the band's visual identity and wrote their first and main lyrics, also developed one of Massive Attack's strongest dimensions – an engaged and meaningful discourse about their era – a special observation of the world that reveals the artist's ability to reflect and even define his time. Enriched by many collaborations and foreign experiences as much as a deep social involvement with other artists and thinkers on four continents, he also remains rooted in his own cultural environment, in his hometown. This is where I started to look into this journey. I came to Bristol from Paris, France, after years of reporting in America, Europe, Middle East and Africa, and decided to write this story.

Chapter 2
Rebellions And Riots

The core members of Massive Attack, when they started making music, were three young men from England's West Country, born between 1959 and 1967, all sons of immigrants. They grew up in Bristol where they met regularly from 1980, a time of upcoming social change. So, without a doubt, the city came to define their upbringing and early influences. Robert Del Naja regularly stated that "the city reflects the amounts of efforts, ideas, love and time people put into it[1]"; and that's why he has stayed. With a unique history in the UK, the city's culture was a core element in their first artistic experiences. Let's have a look at this specific history to understand why.

The Romans settled in nearby Bath; some remains can be found in Brislington and Blaise, as well as a Roman port on the River Avon at Sea Mills. Bristol was founded as an English town by the end of the tenth century by Saxons, around a bridge on the river Avon, at the corner of the river Frome, in the South West of England. The ideal location, 120 miles from London, in a lush green fertile land and at the end of an estuary, near the shores of the Irish Sea but also protected by the gorge and hills, soon attracted the then-ruling Normans, before other populations. Its name comes from the old English word *Brycgstow*, which means "the place by the bridge".

It quickly became a connecting place in England, linking routes for traders going from France to Ireland notably. In 1247, when a more solid bridge was built, Bristol started to become a major port city, its population increased, manufacturing companies opened and the small town soon incorporated the southern boroughs of Redcliffe

---

1   For instance in an interview with the BBC, on April 27, 2010

and Bedminster. It was therefore redefined as a county of its own in 1373. Reaching over 20,000 inhabitants by the mid-fourteenth century, Bristol became England's third-largest town, after London and York.

From England to America

After 1492, with the start of the exploration of the "new world" launched by Christopher Colombus, Bristol's port became the main English access from London to America. In 1497, sponsored by the King Henry VII, the Italian navigator Giovanni Caboto – known in England as John Cabot – departed from Bristol on the *Matthew*. Cabot reached the northern area then baptised as "Newfoundland", in what is now known as Canada. According to some local historians[2], Bristol merchant Richard Ameryk could even have been the inspiration behind the name given to the continent, America... Although official history retains the name of the Florentine explorer Amerigo Vespucci as the proper source of the name. Cabot was followed by other navigators, financed by Bristol's wealthy traders, and for decades the city remained defined by this American calling...

Bristol gained an autonomous status in 1542 and increased its wealth with the development of the English colonies in North America. Like Liverpool, it became a platform in the triangular trade between Europe, America and Africa, which included a replacement of Irish and English slaves by African slaves, deported from their continent to America[3]. This is probably what would mark Bristol's history the most, and therefore its artists emerging from the 1970s.

First Liverpool's then Bristol's merchants started to fight to obtain the right to access the trade in sugar and slaves, lengthily monopolised by London. Bristol's pivotal *Society of Merchant Venturers*, founded in 1552 by entrepreneurs, acquired its incredible wealth through the trade of slaves for sugar, cotton and rum. During the eighteenth century, the organisation purchased major ships and buildings in Bristol, and started to control a large part of the city's economy and politics, a domination

2 Including Alfred Hudd, professor from Bristol who wrote an essay on that matter in 1908, entitled *Richard Ameryk and the Name America*

3 On this topic: *The Black Presence in Slaving Port: Bristol 1688-1835*, by Madge Dresser (reproduced by French publisher Ellipse, in English, in 2009)

that would last for decades. Between 1698 and 1807, 2,108 ships left Bristol for Africa, charged with enslaved Africans, taking them to the Caribbean and America. And more African people began to travel to England from the sixteenth century; some stayed in Britain from the eighteenth century[4].

One of Bristol's most famous and controversial historical figures is Edward Colston (1636 – 1721), a merchant and elected Member of Parliament who enriched himself through slave trafficking, epitomising this troubled part of England's history. In 1680, he took the helms of the *Royal African Company*, controlling most of the English slave trade. In 1694, the *Society of Merchant Venturers* protested against the monopoly over slaves of the London-based *Royal African Company* and obtained its suppression four years later. In the years 1730s and 1740s, Bristol's revenue coming from the slave trade exceeded London's.

Colston founded schools and hospitals in Bristol, and is commemorated by a statue and in the names of streets, avenues, squares, schools, a tower and the city's main auditorium, the Colston Hall. Most of the glorious Georgian houses of West Bristol's area of Clifton have been built with money from the triangular trade. But a few decades later, with the industrial revolution starting in Britain, Liverpool became England's most dynamic centre of production, especially for textile, and Bristol's commercial glory would only decrease from then. Although many Bristolians prefer to remember Colston as a benefactor, there is a growing movement to portray him as a leading figure in the slave trade, as more evidence of the extent of his role comes to light. To underline the role of his inhuman activities in his wealth, some musicians refuse to play in the Colston Hall, first and foremost Massive Attack. Yet, in 2017, the Hall's trust members announced that it would be renamed when reopened after building work.

Such an expansion, stamped by colonisation and slave trade, will deeply shape Bristol's cultural landscape. Nowadays, its mixed-race population carries an ambiguous and painful heritage, having historical links with a vast number of African slaves, dockers or servants.

---

4   On this issue, you can read *Black and British, A Forgotten History*, by David Olusoga, Pan MacMillan, 2017 and check the work of Pr Simon P. Newman at the University of Glasgow

Intolerance for intolerance

What changed Bristol and turned it into the city we know today is the reaction to these historical developments. From the eighteenth century, the city became an active centre for advocacy against the slave trade. From 1780, many Bristolians took part in the abolitionist movements, through religious organisations notably, like the Quakers and Methodists. One of these first militants was Thomas Clarkson (1760-1846), born in Cambridgeshire, who visited London, Liverpool and Bristol for his research on slavery in Britain. In 1787, he used Bristol's Seven Stars pub, in Redcliffe, as a base for most of his work.

Members of the *Bristol Journal* published extracts of his writing. In 1788, Bristol therefore became the first city outside London to set up a committee for the abolition of the slave trade. It saw the first petitions to end slavery circulating, as well as some slaves getting the protection of some powerful families.

A few years later, abolition was finally obtained in two steps: in 1807, the transport and exchange of new slaves was forbidden in the British colonies, but current slaves remained owned by their masters; and in 1833, the British Parliament voted a law for the emancipation of all slaves, assuring a "compensation" for the masters' "loss", according to the legal text[5]...

To try and commemorate this part of British history, Bristol inaugurated *Pero's Bridge* in 1999, on the Floating Harbour, in remembrance of Pero Jones, born around 1753, and who died in 1798. Pero had arrived in Bristol in 1783, from the island of Nevis, in the Caribbean, as a valet for rich landlord John Pinney (1740–1818). The bridge faces some of the city's main artistic institutions: the Watershed cinema, the Arnolfini Gallery and the M Shed Museum.

In 1793, Bristol witnessed one of its most significant riots as the Corporation began to feel the effects of the impending loss of revenue from the slave trade. The *Bristol Bridge Riots*, as they're known, erupted against a plan to impose a tax at the bridge crossing. In 1831, the Queen

---

5   More on the issue in Dr Madge Dresser's research: *Remembering Slavery and Abolition in Bristol - Slavery and Abolition* (University of West England, 2009) and *The Black Presence in a Slaving Port: Bristol, 1688-1835* in *L'Abolition de l'esclavage au Royaume-Uni (1787-1840): Débats et dissensions* (Editions Sedes, Paris, France)

Square Riots occurred amidst a debate on cities' representation in Parliament, during the era of industrialisation.

During the nineteenth century, the city went through a notable industrial development, partly engineered by Isambard Kingdom Brunel, the mastermind of the SS Great Britain ship and Clifton Suspension Bridge, inaugurated in 1864. The city's population went from 66,000 to more than 300,000 in a hundred years. Brunel opened the Temple Meads train station, which linked London with America via Bristol at the time of major transatlantic ships and massive emigration. Bristol's wealth was on the rise again, but the number of poor workers as well. Then in February 1932, the Old Market Riots erupted when the police tried to crush a demonstration decrying unemployment. Other types of protests would also occur repeatedly in the last decades of the twentieth century.

According to the local writer, poet and historian Dr Edson Burton, the result of this boiling history is that authority, in Bristol, is now something that people are hardly tolerant of. "Most of what has been achieved culturally here and what Bristol is known for, has happened against or in spite of the civic, polite culture," he explains[6]. Bristol does have "intolerance for intolerance", according to Edson. We are talking in Bristol's M Shed Museum, in February 2015, after one of his conferences on the role of Black soldiers in the First World War. "People have now discovered that it's a city that built its wealth on slavery and that has not been talked about enough. They discovered that in situations of depravation and so on, it becomes a means to galvanise protests. I would be careful about romanticising the melting pot of the city, but Bristol is really about the quality of relationships. The city is more democratic, not so pro Monarchy, and rebelled against slavery[7]".

Meanwhile, during the nineteenth century, Bristol's population became more and more diverse, receiving newcomers from British colonies from all around the globe, especially from the Caribbean. And these new citizens, as well as their relatives in the islands, made a large contribution to the country's history with the First World War.

6   In an interview with the author in Bristol in February 2015
7   Ibid.

Hundreds of soldiers from Barbados, Grenada, Jamaica, Trinidad and other colonies were sent to fight the Triple Alliance's forces in Germany and Central Europe from 1914. These descendants of former slaves believed in the slogans calling them to defend their "motherland". According to the Memorial Gate Trust, founded in 1998 to study and highlight the role of the soldiers from the Commonwealth, 15,600 men from the British Caribbean served in the imperial army during WWI. Two thirds of them were from Jamaica[8]. The islands also sent commodities such as cotton, sugar and rice to help the army and the people of England.

The wars, the soldiers and the Commonwealth

Bristol was also at the centre of fighting during the war and thousands of soldiers from the Commonwealth transited via the western city to reach the battle zones. Most of them were sent back to their hometowns at the end of the war, often without any pension. But some of them remained in the port city. While in 1914, Britain counted around 10,000 "black" people; by 1918 they were 30,000, according to historian Stephen Bourne[9].

After the war, Bristol suffered from a severe lack of housing, due both to building destruction and to an influx of inhabitants. And in 1919, Prime Minister David Lloyd-George launched a new housing programme, for the former soldiers notably. In Bristol, they were developed in new suburbs such as Hillfields, Sea Mills, Shirehampton, and Knowle West, where Adrian 'Tricky' Thaws was born in the 1960s.

But soon enough, with the start of World War II, Bristol was even more shattered by fighting and destruction. From November 1940 and until May 1944, the port city was heavily bombarded by the German *Luftwaffe* – the Nazi air force – as it was the site of Bristol Aeroplane Company. The effects of bombings and fighting are still visible to this day on Bristol's walls and streets. The destroyed areas, especially in the north and east of the city, in Saint Pauls or Easton, were slowly

---

8   For more on this issue: *West Indian Blacks and the Struggle for Participation in World War I*, Journal of Caribbean History, par G. Howe (1994) and *The British West Indies Regiment, 1914-1918*, par C.L. Joseph, in Journal of Caribbean History (1971)
9   See his book *Black Poppies – Britain's Black Community and the Great War*, The History Press (2014)

rebuilt, but suffered from increasing poverty in the 1950s. Ironically, the gorgeous villas erected with the slave money in Clifton are still standing.

To help rebuild the most destroyed cities, the government called on more immigrants from the Caribbean, Asian and African colonies, while the war also brought a few dozen American "Black" G.I.s to Bristol.

New workers arrived in the 1940s and 1950s from Barbados, Dominica, Jamaica and Nevis, including Grant Marshall's parents. They were encouraged to settle in the suburbs of St Pauls and Southmead, in the north of Bristol. The city's new and poorer council housing was also pushed towards the South, with the construction of areas like Hartcliffe. In July 1948, the British Nationality Act gave them access to the territory and to citizenship. In the 1960s, in Bristol's areas of St Pauls and Montpelier, the population from the Caribbean brought a Jamaican feel to the neighbourhoods. Immigrant workers also came from Ireland and Italy. The number of mixed marriages started to rise. The city's new inhabitants are increasingly pushed to the South, with the construction of new buildings.

Time of social change

The new generation born in Bristol in the 1950s and 60s was therefore incredibly more diverse than the previous one. Montpelier and St Pauls, for instance, started to become culturally deeply Caribbean. Most of these families are Jamaican or Barbadian. A lot of them also had relatives in Harlem and in New Jersey, in the USA. They quickly brought their culture to Bristol, which included ska music then reggae that would never leave the place. But if this culture was flourishing, for many it was also causing discrimination. It was harder for Caribbean young men to find housing in the early sixties than for local English guys, as it used to be harder for Irish men in the 1920s. Gangs of so-called 'Teddy Boys' regularly attacked young "black" men.

To improve their situation, families on City Road, in St Pauls, started organising "welcome" meetings for newcomers and later on specific church congregations. They finally founded the West Indian Association in 1962 to defend their rights. They take on, for instance, the Bristol Omnibus Company because it refuses to employ Caribbean, Asian or African workers. In 1963, the Bristol Bus Boycott lasts for almost four months. The movement was led by a young social worker, Paul Stephenson, born in 1937 to a Jamaican father and an English mother. The Bus Company eventually backed down and agreed to employ non-white workers on August 28, 1963, the same day that Martin Luther King Jr. delivered his 'I have a dream' speech at the Lincoln Memorial in Washington. The Bristol Bus Boycott mobilised all around the country to obtain a change in the legislation. And this victory remains a huge turning point in Britain's history of equal rights.

The *Race Relations Acts* was consequently implemented in December 1965, to address racial discrimination[10]. The Acts outlawed discrimination "on the grounds of colour, race, or ethnic or national origins" in public places and prompted the creation of The Race Relations Board, in 1966, to receive any necessary complaints under the Act. It was strengthened two years later with the *Race Relations Act 1968*, which extended the legislation's remit to cover employment and housing. The same year, in January, Adrian Thaws was born in Knowle West, south of Bristol (later to be known as Tricky), just a few months after Robert Del Naja's family moved to Bristol, and settled in the St Andrews area.

And July 1968 saw the launch of the most Jamaican of the city's cultural events: St Pauls' Festival (later renamed St Pauls Afrikan Caribbean Carnival), celebrating African, Portuguese, and West Indian traditions as developed in Britain, while the Caribbean islands had progressively gained their independence during this decade. One of the Carnival's founders is Roy Hackett, who also participated in the Bus Boycott.

Born in Jamaica in 1928, Roy held a British passport and travelled to England to work in 1952. When he first came to Bristol to visit friends, he started looking for a place to live, while there were still often, on the windows of houses with rooms to rent, signs saying "No Blacks, No Gipsies, No Irish and No Dogs". He co-founded the Commonwealth Co-ordinated Committee (CCC) in 1962, which would run St Pauls'

---

10   On the issue can be read *Black and White on the Buses, Bristol*, by Madge Dresser (Bristol Broadsides, 1986)

Carnival for a decade.

A musical land with an unorthodox spirit

At this time, St Pauls' passion for reggae echoed Bristol's core love of music. While Britain experienced a thriving development of popular music, in the 1960s, the city is a hotspot for jazzmen. The local concert venues received influences from ska and rocksteady, also coming from Jamaica. In 1966, a completely different type of band also invaded Bristol's pubs: the Wurzels. Formed by Tommy Banner, Pete Budd, John Morgan, Sedge Moore, and singer Alan John Cutler – known as 'Adge', born in 1930 in Portishead, Somerset. The Wurzels' first single, 'Drink Up Thy Zider' was released in 1966, mixing folk music, West Country influences and a passion for their country traditions.

Meanwhile in St Pauls, new clubs opened, including the Carnot, Charlotte and Top Cat, inviting the first 'disc jockeys' to mix reggae records with funk music, classics of Elvis Presley and of course the Beatles. A very special Bristolian mix that would come to define the city.

"I think that with reggae culture, there is in Bristol a 'Do It Yourself' spirit, a rebel spirit," underlines Edson Burton when I asked him how this scene came about. "And I think it's because, historically, it's a city, which is fragmented between where power lies, who has power, and other groups of people who don't have any access to power and feel that there is no relationship. There is an 'outsider-ness' and a fragmentation. In some ways that has also generated a creative space. It's a key thing in the rebel culture of reggae, of course of the Rastafarian movement, and to punk culture. It's about breaking walls, moving away from conservativeness[11]".

In the early 1970s, this exchange and encounter of diverse subcultures was only emerging. The second part of the decade would bring it to a next level...

From the 1990s, Massive Attack would be able to both reflect and change these times. They invented a form of collective creativity, never centred around the face or voice of single frontman, but enriched by

---

11   In an interview with the author in Bristol in February 2015

multiplicity and diversity. This ethos was directly influenced by Bristol's love for sound systems born out of its reggae culture, and enriched further by emerging movements. And the best way to understand the roots of Massive Attack's cultural revolution is to look back at this background and at Bristol's history from the mid 1960s.

Chapter 3
Underground Revolutions (1965-1982)

From 1960, England was culturally booming. And its series of artistic explosions were soon baptised the *Swinging Sixties*. *Time* magazine actually penned the phrase *Swinging London* in 1966 to describe the energy that was characteristic of new movements in popular music, in films and in the fashion industry. With the 'Made in Liverpool' Beatles, the Who, the Rolling Stones, Kinks, the Small Faces, Pink Floyd, and soon David Bowie, British culture became celebrated all over the world.

This is the England in which Robert Del Naja was born, in Brighton on January 21, 1965, to an English mother, Ann Rosemary Peters, and an Italian father recently arrived from Naples, Franco Del Naja. The family moved to Bristol in 1967 and settled in the area named St Andrews. Not so far from this neighbourhood, Grantley Evan Marshall was born on December 18, 1959. His parents had come from Barbados and settled in Long Ashton, a Bristol suburb. A few years later, on November 10, 1967, Andrew Lee Isaac Vowles was born, to a Dominican father and an English mother who brought him to Bath in the early 1970s, then to Bristol's suburban area of Fishponds.

Mixed childhoods
Franco Del Naja arrived in England from Italy in the early 1960s and settled in Brighton to work in the hospitality trade. He met Ann, born in Brighton in 1941, they married and soon after their son's birth, the family moved to Bristol, where Franco started to work in a restaurant, in the city centre. A year later, Robert's sister, Sarah, was born.

Robert grew up in St Andrews, north of Montpelier, spending his first years mostly around the local park. He was first sent to a catholic school, St Bonaventure's, but faith-based schooling didn't really work for the young boy. He was disturbed by the obligation of confession and the regular church services.

From five years old, he developed a passion for comic books and drew his favourite heroes at home as in school: "I was obsessed by artists like Jack Kirby and John Romita. My school exercise books were literally covered in superhero sketches. The comic shop was my gallery I guess," Robert said[12]. He also drew himself and his family but expressed eclectic choices of colours: he painted his own hair green and his Christmas trees brown. "My mum thought I was a bit eccentric[13]." A test later revealed that he was colour-blind.

He switched to Sefton Park Primary School, near St Andrews Park. With Franco busy working day and night in a pub, his son spent most of his family time with his mum, whom he describes as the most open-minded person, and also passionate about music. She listened to Roxy Music, the Moody Blues and of course the Beatles. In September 1969, when *Abbey Road* was released, Robert was four years old and this record is part of his daily life, as well as *Sgt. Pepper's Lonely Hearts Club Band*, out in 1967.

Franco was an excellent cook and considered all over Bristol as one of the most charming publicans. It demanded hard work though, leaving little time for family life, spending most of the day out. He took his son to Italy only twice, once when as a kid with the whole family, the second time, just the two of them after Maradona had helped Napoli to the Italian title for the first time in their history. They went on a tour of the backstreets of the city, where Franco had grown up, a place his son came to love for its energy and the mysterious symbology, he told me[14]...

Franco was also a football fan and supported his hometown's team, Napoli, as well as Bristol City, one of Bristol's two teams. He regularly took his son to the Ashton Gate stadium and Robert started watching football regularly. At the end of primary school, he entered Monks Park School in Southmead, four kilometres away from St Andrews, where he mingled with children from all over the city, in a very diverse

---

12   In an interview published in *Fact* magazine in March 2014
13   In his book *3D and the Art of Massive Attack*, published by The Vinyl Factory, in July 2015
14   In Bristol in February 2015

environment.

Grant Marshall lived through a similar experience. Son of immigrants, he was exposed to many other cultures in the Sixties. His parents were known for their marvellous collection of Jamaican reggae records from Bob Marley, Coxsone Dodd, Lee 'Scratch' Perry, Leslie Kong, Duke Reid, Joe Gibbs and King Tubby. A few of his dad's friends were DJs and they organised Sunday parties for their neighbours. They also discovered new records of Jamaican ska and Anglo-Jamaican blue beat as soon as the albums came out in Bristol and sometimes even earlier, thanks to their relatives in Jamaica.

"We used to throw parties at the house," Grant recalled in an interview with the label !K7 Record in 2004. "I remember there was an old geezer we used to know, this guy called Sunny in Bristol, he had this sound system and at the time sound system wasn't about big speakers and stuff but you had the most powerful gramophone. When my parents came over in the late 50s from Barbados and there was a lot of West Indians in Bristol, there wasn't anywhere for them to go. The British culture hadn't really catered for the new influx of West Indians... There wasn't any social infrastructure for them. So they made their own parties you know what I mean, called Shabeen's and Blues parties and you used to get the whole neighbourhood turn up on Fridays and Saturdays at somebody's house. Parties would be in the basement where people played dominoes and stuff like that, there would be a bar on another floor, just take the whole house over for a party for the weekend this is where all of these people with their big sound systems used to come and bring them – bass in your face from the time I was six and stuff like that, it's amazing, it really was."

Reggae was booming in the city but also in London. In June 1976, Bob Marley and the Wailers visited Britain, as part of the *Rastaman Vibration Tour*, and came to play in Bristol, at the Colston Hall.

But a few years later, with the end of the economic expansion, immigration became a source of tension in political debates and the British government implemented laws to restrain it. "Quite a lot of my dad's friends didn't qualify for that and some of them had to go back," Grant later explained. "Even my dad and mum were going around trying to make sure that they were all right[15]."

For Andrew Vowles, who arrived in Bristol as a young boy, the city always seemed very unwelcoming. "Bristol is a racist place – but it's undercover," he stated once[16]. "There was a documentary on telly about a black guy and a white guy both looking for accommodation and it just summed up people's attitudes. People won't shout at you down the street but there's a really horrible undercurrent of racism down here," added Andrew. "I lived in Bath for a bit and that was just outright up to your face racism. I was only little at the time, in fact, it was so bad that it's the reason my mum had to bring us to Bristol."

The boys would later be able to escape this undercurrent in Bristol's music underground scene. From a very early age, Andrew became a fan of American rhythm and blues and of Pink Floyd. And his life changed with the discovery of hip-hop music. Just like Robert's life changed, a few years earlier, when he discovered punk music in 1976.

Bristol and the punk revolution

After the first oil crisis in 1973, which caused a sudden increase in crude oil and petrol's prices worldwide, England radically changed. Unemployment and inflation doubled in a few years. In 1976, the country's revenue per habitant dropped drastically. Under James Callaghan's cabinet, the end of 1978 was baptised the "Winter of Discontent" by the *Sun's* columnist Larry Lamb, inspired by a quote from William Shakespeare's *Richard III* (*"Now is the Winter of our Discontent / Made glorious summer by this son of York"*)[17]. Many strikes blocked the main cities. Consequently, public spending was limited and cultural infrastructure the first to suffer. The situation was worsened by the election of a Conservative government, to be led by Margaret Thatcher, after the Tory victory in the general election on May 4, 1979. The country was progressively ravaged by mass unemployment and a cultural void. This soon encouraged the birth of countercultures.

This is when the "Punk" movement started to bloom in the UK,

---

15 In an interview with *Dazed and Confused* magazine, published in February 1998
16 Ibid
17 On this topic, watch Channel 4's documentary series: *Secret History: Winter of Discontent* (Brook Lapping Productions for Channel Four, 1998)

almost at the same time as in the US, where, from 1967, appeared bands like Iggy Pop and the Stooges, Suicide (formed in New York by vocalist Alan Vega and instrumentalist Martin Rev in 1970), the New York Dolls (founded in 1971), Television with their frontman Richard Hell (from 1974), as well as the Ramones (created in 1974). Patti Smith also gloriously emerged from New York in 1975 with her unforgettable debut album *Horses*.

In London, simultaneously, the Sex Pistols launched British punk in 1975, led by Johnny 'Rotten' Lydon, with the help of their manager and producer, the now legendary Malcolm McLaren. He had worked with the New York Dolls and brought some of their energy with him back to England. The Sex Pistols started touring late 1975 and the movement literally exploded in the summer 1976, when the Clash were formed by John Graham Mellor – known as Joe Strummer, Mick Jones (on lead guitar and lead vocals), Paul Simonon (on bass guitar and vocals) and Nicky "Topper" Headon (on drums and percussion). The Damned also formed the same year in Croydon, in South London, and released the first British punk single: 'New Rose', in October 1976. A month later, the Sex Pistols put out their first single, 'Anarchy in the UK', and appeared on *Thames Television* in December. The same year, punk bands joined the *Rock Against Racism* campaign, launched to fight xenophobia in the country through concerts.

Very quickly, all these bands had a major influence in Bristol. At 14 years old, Robert Del Naja became an obsessive fan of the genre, especially of the Clash. In March 1977, the band released their first single with the now legendary song 'White Riot', short and intense, with its soon-to-become typical three chords played in a very fast style. It was written in the summer 1976, after Joe Strummer and bassist Paul Simonon took part in the riots at the Notting Hill Carnival. *"Are you taking over / Or are you taking orders? / Are you going backwards / Or are you going forwards?"* The lyrics encourage white youths to find the right cause to riot, as black people in the UK already have.

The punk motto – "Do It Yourself" – incited many young boys to start their own band. For Annie McGann, former lecturer in creative writing at Bath Spa University and a key witness of Bristol's music scene from the mid-1970s, "youth there had a real passion for Bob Dylan and American folk music and rapidly adopted punk music[18]." Annie came from London to Bristol in 1976 and later started to work with the Glastonbury Festival, launched in nearby Somerset in 1970. "I moved in with students while finishing my studies in theatre and that's what they were listening to, folk music then punk".

The whole energy of punk music embraced Bristol when a group of friends decided to create their bands at only 16 years old: in 1976, Nick Sheppard founded the Cortinas with Jeremy Valentine; in 1977, Mark Stewart started the Pop Group. Mark and Jeremy lived on the same street; Mark and Nick, both born in 1960, met in school. At that time, Bristol was a rough place and the boys grew up trying to avoid getting beaten up by the skinheads' gangs. Mark impressed with his height; Jeremy with his rugby skills. Music allowed them to escape the horizon of youth violence. In London, they got to see one of the first Clash concerts – at the ICA, in 1976, where Patti Smith and her band were in the audience – and a few weeks later a Ramones gig.

The Cortinas started with covers from the Stooges and the New York Dolls. They played regularly in London venues, including in the Roxy Club, where the Sex Pistols and the Clash started. The Cortinas' first single was released on Step Forward, a label run by the Police's managers, Miles Copeland and Mark Perry. They wrote very politically charged lyrics, like in their notable single 'Fascist Dictator'. In July 1977, the Cortinas were invited to record a session at BBC Radio 1's Maida Vale studio, with the famous DJ and broadcaster John Peel. They played their tracks 'Defiant Pose', 'Television Families', 'Having It', and 'Further Education'.

In January 1977, the Cortinas supported the Stranglers and headlined the Roxy in March and April, supported by the Models. In June 1977, they had their first headlining show at the Marquee Club. They also supported Blondie and Chelsea. Their unique album, *True Romances*, was released by CBS Records in 1978, getting a lot of reviews. Wilson Neate of Allmusic wrote: "Having begun life under the spell of '60s

---

18   In an interview with the author in Bristol in February 2015

R&B and garage rock, the Cortinas soon emerged as Bristol's premiere punk band, injecting a speedy, shouty, confrontational edge into their sound for their first two singles ('Fascist Dictator' and 'Defiant Pose')". But the band soon split up. In 2001, their debut single, 'Fascist Dictator', released in June 1977, was included in Mojo Magazine's list of the "best punk-rock singles of all-time".

Mark Stewart was joined in the Pop Group by Gareth Sager, who's from Edinburgh, John Waddington, Bruce Smith, and Simon Underwood. Also in 1977, Geoff Alsopp, Dan Catsis and Tom Nichols formed the Glaxo Babies, rapidly joined by singer Rob Chapman and instrumentalists Tony Wrafter, Charlie Llewellin, Tim Ayelett and Alan Jones. In 1978, they signed with a local label, Heartbeat Records, and released the EP *This Is Your Life* in February 1979. Dan Catsis soon after joined the Pop Group.

Other UK punk bands included Wire, formed in London late 1976; Stiff Little Fingers, from Northern Ireland, formed in 1977; Gang Of Four, based in Leeds; and Crass in Essex. The Dead Kennedys emerged in America in 1978 and had a huge influence on Bristol's youth. Bristol's first *Rock Against Racism* music concert was held at Trinity Centre in 1978 and featured local punk band the X-Certs, as well reggae bands Misty in Roots and Reality. Stiff Little Fingers released their first album, *Inflammable Material*, in 1979 and played in Bristol at the Colston Hall. They were the first band Robert Del Naja went to see play live. "That had a big impact on me," he recalls in his visual art book, published in 2015[19]. "I was 14. I fell in love with that album; it's such a powerful record. The sleeve always stood out. In amongst all my punk records nothing was quite as graphic as that, as simple."

Yet rapidly, punk evolved in the UK and in January 1978, the Sex Pistols split. Other bands adopted a "new wave" style, like the Police, formed in London in 1977, or reggae influences. Music journalists declared that punk had dissolved; some even wrote that "punk is dead"...

But after a trip to Jamaica, Johnny Rotten formed Public Image Ltd in May 1978 with guitarist Keith Levene, bassist Jah Wobble, and

19   *3D and the Art of Massive Attack* (Vinyl Factory), by Robert Del Naja

drummer Jim Walker, known as PiL. And soon enough a new genre was baptised "post-punk". A genre that started to explode in Bristol. "The transformation of John Lydon from the Pistols to PiL also had a big impact on me musically and stylistically," explained Robert. "Turning the band literally into a brand was a brilliant statement during Thatcher's Britain[20]."

Public Image Ltd's second album, *Metal Box*, was released by Virgin Records on 23 November 1979. It is one of Robert's favourite records, 'Poptones' being one of his favourite songs.

The legacy of Mark Stewart and the Pop Group

As new bands formed, split up and merged with others, one of them became particularly influential: the Pop Group. A tall, energetic and impressive young teenager, Mark Stewart quickly stood out, thanks to a powerful and deep voice and a talent for political texts. "Bristol is a small town," insists Mark, who now lives in London, the first time we talk in 2015. "Most of its musician have become friends; we started in the same clubs[21]."

Mark produced mixed tapes of his favourite tracks, compiling different genres, from punk to reggae, in order to get inspiration for new experimentations. He was galvanised by ideas mostly, visions and messages that he brought to his band's instrumentalists to work around. "Without punk music, people like me would have spent their life in a factory," says Mark. "This music gave us a crazy confidence, punk was a revolution, a kind of cultural 'Prise de la Bastille', which opened the range of our creativity and forced us to reinvent our political ideas or framework of thinking as well as our type of relationships. The Clash, the Pistols and their 'No Future' slogan were all brilliant and their anger became a positive energy[22]."

In Bristol, the Pop Group opened many doors. Most of the young people who would come to define the city's music in the 1980s and 1990s met at one of their shows in 1978 or 1979. The Pop Group soon

---

20   In *3D and the Art of Massive Attack* (Vinyl Factory)
21   In an interview with the author in June 2015, between Bristol and London
22   Ibid

found more inspiration in reggae music, used different sound effects and embodied a sense of rebellion that was quickly embraced by their fans. Their lyrics were politically aware and socially charged, at a time when the nomination of Conservative leader Margaret Thatcher at the head of the government in May 1979 was a reason to despair for many young Brits. This situation was soon to be darkened by the election of Ronald Reagan as the President of the United States of America in November 1980 and the increase in tensions of the so-called Cold War with the Soviet Union. Both Thatcher and Reagan were directly targeted in Mark Stewart's lyrics.

The band released their first single in March 1979, 'She Is Beyond Good and Evil', with Radar Records, and a first album, named Y, a month later. The record had a huge impact in Bristol notably at Revolver Records, in Clifton, a meeting point for hardcore music fans. The Pop Group, later signed by the Rough Trade label, released a second single, 'We Are All Prostitutes', followed in 1980 by a second album, For How Much Longer Do We Tolerate Mass Murder? The same year, they performed as part of the Campaign for Nuclear Disarmament protest at London's Trafalgar Square, in front of a crowd of 500,000 people.

But after too many internal disagreements, they decided to split in 1981. Members of the group started to collaborate with other local and London bands. Mark spent some time travelling, mainly in New York City, and later formed his own band, Mark Stewart & the Maffia. His first album, Learning to Cope With Cowardice, was released in 1983 by On-U Sound Records, influencing many musicians from Tim Saul in Bristol to Trent Reznor in Pennsylvania.

At the same time, Mark's friend Nick Sheppard joined a new band in Bristol, the Spics, with his guitarist friend Mike Crawford. The young Scottish man settled in the city in his teenage years. "The first wave of new music to come out of Bristol was really from post-punk," says Mike, when we meet in February 2015, in Stokes Croft, near St Pauls and Montpelier. "It did not last long but it did put on fire the young ones who would later become influential musicians. At the time, we did not have any structure; we even had to create our own label to release an album. It was part of the punk ethos, the 'Do It Yourself' idea[23]."

These young musicians also spent their evening in reggae clubs in St Pauls, like the Bamboo Club, created in St Pauls in 1966 by Tony Bullimore (1939-2018), a sailor married to a West Indian immigrant, where young DJs mixed Jamaican EPs. The club housed a restaurant, a theatre workshop, a football team, and was soon billed as "Bristol's Premier West Indian Entertainment Centre". It was also headquarters of the Bristol West Indian Cricket Club. Its top floor hosted the music venue, where the DJs played reggae and American soul music. Famous bands came to perform, including Bob Marley and the Wailers, Jimmy Cliff, Ben E. King and Tina Turner. There, guitar players like Mike and Nick crossed path with reggae fans as Grant Marshall, Miles Johnson and Rob Smith. The club unfortunately burned down in 1977, just before the Sex Pistols were due to play… Bullimore also opened The Granary club at Bristol's Granary building in the early 1970s, and became a race relations' advocate.

In the same area, a young singer and clarinet player, Janine Rainsforth, formed the band Maximum Joy with Tony Wrafter, who had just left the Glaxo Babies. They found rapid success with their first five singles and in less than a year they also released a first album, with Y Records, *Stretch*. They were compared by the press to bands like the Slits and Gang of Four.

Janine grew up in St Pauls, where her mother, a poet, and her stepfather, a factory worker and amateur actor, settled at the beginning of the 1970s. "And I have great memories from St Pauls," says the charismatic Janine when I interview her at the Watershed. "It was a diverse and friendly neighbourhood, even if our financial possibilities were dreadful. It was a time of conflicts, nuclear threats and mass unemployment. But St Pauls was a place of integration, especially during the Carnival, where a lot of gigs against racism were organised. In the background though, the country was ridden by the National Front's speeches. Workers' strikes were recurrent. Families like mine were suffering from power cuts; our garbage were sometimes not

23   In an interview with the author in Bristol in February 2015

collected for days... And of course, our music was influenced by that context, and also by African sound and jazz music. I was a big fan of the band Television. Music quickly represented a new form of hope for us, of independence. And our lyrics were from the start a reflection of all that, polemical and provocative[24]."

Bands formed all over Bristol from 1980, including the Blue Airplanes, started by Gerard and John Langley with guitarist Angelo Bruschini, Lunatic Fringe (with Adrian 'Age' Blackmore, Nick Horn, John Finch and a singer called Birdshit – they were later joined by Bear Hackenbush then in 2012 by Simon Hobbs), Chaos UK, Disorder, Chaotic Dischord, distributed by the local label Riot City.

Meanwhile, Mark Stewart travelled from London to Brooklyn, then Berlin and Vienna. Former members of the Pop Group joined Maximum Joy, the Slits, Pigbag. In 1981, the drummer Bruce Smith formed Rip Rig + Panic with bass player Sean Oliver and Mark Springer. And they were soon joined by a very young and very talented Swedish-American singer, based in London: Neneh Cherry.

Born Neneh Mariann Karlsson in 1964 in Stockholm, to a Swedish mother and a father from Sierra Leone, she was raised by her mum with her stepfather, the great American jazzman Don Cherry, who got her early into his music world. Neneh was singing backing vocals with the Slits. Bruce Smith met her when Don Cherry enrolled her on his tour in Great Britain. She and Bruce got married soon after; Neneh was only 17 years old and showed an outstanding, unmissable talent. Lively, gorgeous, joyful, she was also gifted with a marvellous voice and an incredible energy.

A few months later, Neneh divorced Bruce but remained a close friend of Mark Stewart's and comes regularly to Bristol. That's where she met DJ Miles Johnson, a childhood friend of Bruce's, who was gaining a reputation as one of the most promising DJs in St Pauls, along with Grant Marshall. A year later, in 1982, Miles and Grant formed a DJ collective: the Wild Bunch, which would help define another musical trend in Bristol, based on hip-hop culture, and revolutionise Bristol's

24   In an interview with the author in Bristol in January 2016

music scene...

Meanwhile, in the autumn 1983, Nick Sheppard replaced Mick Jones in the Clash and accompanied the band on the tour that followed the release of their album *Cut the Crap*, in 1985. In 1993, he moved to Australia and Bruce Smith, on his side, went on to become Public Image Ltd's new drummer.

Noisy teenagers

Bristol, 1979. Punk, reggae and 'new wave' were the musical diet of Bristol's aspiring musicians. When Thatcher came to power, Robert Del Naja was only 14 years old, but already liked to live outdoors, spending his time in the park with friends or exploring pubs. His parents had high hopes for his studies, but the boy was not very interested in school. He was too distracted, too anxious and restless. He embodied the rebellious teenager, hated imposed rules, and lived with and for music. He wasn't particularly easy to get on with, he admits. He often missed school, slept out at night and got into juvenile drinking and glue sniffing.

Worried that he might get caught up with bad influences, his parents decided to leave St Andrews and move into Franco's new pub, the Adam and Eve, in Hotwells. To try and help him develop his strong talent, drawing, his parents wanted to send him to art college but he had never been academic. His mother struggled to keep him home, and more than twice the police brought him back after catching him with booze and glue. As the political climate started getting gloomier, he joined the dole queue, and punk and its discourse became the horizon of his youth. Robert listened to Bauhaus, Crass, the Pop Group, Dead Kennedys, Stiff Little Fingers, Public Image Ltd and the Clash.

They used alternative vocalists like Mikey Dread and the graffiti artist Futura 2000. Mikey Dread, aka Michael George Campbell (1954-2008), was a Jamaican singer, producer and broadcaster, considered as one of the most influential performers and innovators in reggae music.

In 1980, Bristol was particularly sensitive to tensions. On April 2, riots erupted in St Pauls, when the police entered the *Black and White*

Café, where jobless West Indian kids spent time playing games and scratching records. "It's the media which did baptise the 1980 events as 'riots', for sure, not the protesters," insists local historian Roger Ball[25], who wrote a thesis on the issue. "The events started in St Pauls, then spread to other neighbourhoods, and young Irish, English, East Europeans, Poles were involved in it, which the official history doesn't always mention," he adds.

Anger spread to London in 1981, especially to Brixton, the southern part of the capital with a strong West Indian and African population, then to other cities. The 1980/81 events become the largest social movement in the United Kingdom since 1945. "But if 'white' and 'mixed race' boys participated in the uprisings, police were more repressive against black youth," says Roger Ball[26].

According to the Bristolian historian and author Edson Burton, "if St Pauls is often presented as a 'black' neighbourhood, it is a shortcut. Since the 1960s, it has been a mixed area of different working class groups from diverse communities, including Irish, Scottish, English, Italian families, and others. The neighbourhood never had a high school, so the young people had to continue their studies elsewhere and mix with the rest of the population. Which gave to this generation a sense of solidarity and brought the different cultures closer[27]."

Thus, punk and hip-hop influenced this youth concomitantly. If Ray Mighty and Grant Marshall grew up with the sound of reggae in their own homes, they recognised themselves in the punk's ethos and energy. This crossover was the product of endless weekends hanging out at Virgin records, drinking cider, sniffing glue. This was a rite of passage for groups of teens in Bristol, and Robert grew up painting his leather jackets, dying his hair, experimenting with DIY piercing, collecting 7" colour vinyl and getting chased by skinheads. He got into reggae at gigs and pubs or through pre-release imports on Picton Street or at Revolver and US 12" electro imports in London...

Caribbean and English boys met at the punk gigs as well as in the

25   In an interview with the author in Bristol in March 2015
26   Ibid
27   In an interview with the author in Bristol in February 2015

clubs, going to rap break dance nights and drinking Special Brew. These experiences filtered their taste and outlook, taking them through a whole social and musical journey of discovery.

From reggae to disc jockeys, dub and hip-hop music

This culturally mixed society, angry at the values of Thatcher's Britain, allowed Grant Marshall, who grew up to the sound of reggae, to quickly recognise himself entirely in the punk movement.

Reggae gave birth to a deeply rooted sound system culture in the city, particularly in St Pauls, which would a few years later also pave the way for a love of hip-hop. In Grant Marshall's family, Friday evenings and Sunday afternoons were times for partying and dancing. A habit that soon turned the young man into a future DJ. Grant got a job at Revolver Records in the Bristol area named the Triangle, near Clifton, and his life soon revolved around music.

Since 1968, St Pauls' Carnival, held in early July, had been attracting visitors from all over the city. Local residents hosted their cousin from East and South Bristol for the weekend. For Chris Johnson, later to be known as DJ Krissy Kriss then Kinsman, born in Southmead in North Bristol in the mid 1960s in a family of five kids and a single mother, "the Carnival became a real pilgrimage. Even if the place had a territorial logic, and gangs were circulating there, no one wanted to miss it and it remains among my best memories in Bristol[28]." It gradually attracted English, Irish, Polish, Welsh and Italian working-class families. Shows and extracurricular projects developed on its fringes.

In the late 1970s, St Pauls' Carnival became a hotspot for a new generation of DJs. Dennis Richard, Martin Star, Seymour, Superfly came to play disco and funk music. Nightclubs like Top Cat, Granary, Carnot and Charlotte's organised parties for the evenings, with ska, dub and reggae music. DJ Derek, aka Derek Morris, emerged as one of the first English DJs to popularise reggae music outside of St Pauls. Born in 1942 to a working-class family, he soon developed a passion for all sorts of Jamaican music. He sadly passed away in 2016 and is considered by

---

28   In an interview with the author in Bristol, in May 2015

Grant Marshall as an idol and a "national treasure".

At the time, Bristol's best-known reggae band was probably Black Roots, formed in St Pauls in 1979 by eight musicians of Jamaican origin. "Reggae has always been about conveying a message," says their guitarist, Jabulani Ngozi, when I come to see him in his home in Bristol in 2016. Born in Saint Andrew, in Jamaica, he moved to Bristol at the age of 11 in 1965. "It took me at least two years to adapt. It was so different, and difficult. Schools in the neighbourhood did not even have a book or a pen to offer to students like me. We lived with the constant interrogation of a possible return. Then we all experienced unemployment, we spent our days playing dominoes in the cafes of St Pauls. One day we went to listen to Burning Spear at the Colston Hall and reggae gave us a reason to live. He made us understand that we had something to offer to life. At that time, St Pauls was considered a ghetto, though there was no risk, there was no violence; but the media described it as a lawless neighbourhood[29]."

The favourite record store of the members of Black Roots was Mr. Pews' shop, on Picton Street, between Stokes Croft and Montpelier, specialised in reggae music. It became the meeting point for young people.

"If their parents live with the idea that at worst they have the option to return to Jamaica or Barbados, for the second generation the feeling of belonging to England is very strong," says Edson Burton. "But this feeling is at first rhetorical and reality reveals the disjunction between promise and reality. Black children still do not benefit directly from the same opportunities as others, the poor from those of the richer families[30]."

Most of the immigrant families tried to ignore these challenges and to focus on integration. "We had our group that we all moved with, so there was always some sense of safety," explained Grant Marshall in one of his rare interviews on the issue[31]. "But there was always that thing, you know, of someone out there ready to bash your head in if you stepped

29 In an interview with the author, in St Andrews, Bristol, in January 2016
30 In an interview with the author in Bristol in February 2015
31 While on tour in Dublin, published in the *Guardian* in January 2016

out of line. Going back to where we were with Massive Attack and the Wild Bunch, it was always a mixed-race thing, so we were always going into circumstances where it could go either way. Either Robert could get beaten up for being in the wrong place because he's in a Jamaican club with me, or I could get beaten up for being a black bloke in a punk club. So we were always treading water in that respect."

Reggae became a safe haven to escape this reality. "Reggae roots is not a music that can be learned, it is a physical and divine force that comes to you," insists Jabulani Ngozi[32].

Black Roots began by rehearsing some songs from Bob Marley and the Heptones in local pubs, and in 1981, they organised two concerts of roots reggae, on the principle of donation. The venue was packed. They soon released their first EP, *Bristol Rock*, on their own label, Nubian, consisting of four tracks: 'Bristol Rock', 'Tribal War', 'The Father' and 'The System'. The EP was noticed by journalist and popular DJ on BBC Radio One, John Peel, which helped the band release their first album, *Black Roots*, in 1983, and to start a bigger career. In 1984, they were invited by UB40 as the first act of their European tour. Black Roots then signed a contract with the French label Makasound, specialising in roots reggae.

Black Roots helped popularise reggae beyond social barriers. "Even in the post-punk scene, we all dived into reggae," says guitarist Mike Crawford, "whether it's at The Dug Out, on Park Row, or in clubs like the Bamboo Club in St Pauls, we were all there together[33]." Bands like Talisman, Restriction and the Radicals followed, as well as Joshua Moses, famous for his song 'Africa Is Our land', Buggs Durrant and female singer Sharon Bengamin. Double Vision and Torpedo soon mix reggae with ska. The X-Certs, a punk band formed in 1978, also delved into reggae from 1981.

Reggae was quickly followed in the early 1980s by hip-hop in the Bristol underground scene. It brought a whole new urban culture to the city: with DJs (disc jockeys), turntables, raps and MCs – masters of ceremony – but also break dancers – aka "b-boys and b-girls" – and the

32   In an interview with the author, in Saint Andrews, Bristol, in January 2016
33   In an interview with the author, in Bristol, in February 2015

art of graffiti. Some West Indians in St Pauls had relatives in New York and discovered American hip-hop records way before most Britons. The figure of the DJ became an inspiration for many young boys. In its underground venues, around 1980, Bristol already had a mix of punk, funk, reggae, etc. Hip-hop music shook the mainstream. And a new generation was soon ready to emerge.

Alternative venues for underground phenomena

1981. In Revolver Records, on Bristol's Triangle, at the corner of Park Street and Queen's Road, most of young music fans gathered in order to get vinyl records and discover new sounds. The owner was known for his broad tastes and his welcoming attitude towards those with a small budget... "A treasure trove," says Mark Stewart. "I learned more in that cavern of aural wonders than I ever did at school[34]."

The staff at Revolver had eclectic tastes ranging from free jazz to funk, reggae of course, but also country music, ska and hip-hop. They fostered a friendly, welcoming, anti-elitist attitude. Their main goal, it seemed, was for customers to leave the shop with a stack of vinyl that has nothing to do with what they came for. A student in Bristol in 1970s, music journalist Richard King spends more hours at the record store than at the University library and soon works there, for three years, describing it as an easy source of soft drugs[35].

Amid tottering vinyl towers and cigarette mist, the shop has a subterranean feel. Revolver became a focal point for young music enthusiasts from all over the region. "What is characteristic of Bristol at this time is that the city is small enough for all these influences to cross," says historian Edson Burton. "Black youth were also listening to Bryan Adams and ZZ Top and this culture became part of their history[36]."

Grant Marshall was 20 years old when he joined Revolver's team in 1979. He was so good at finding new sounds that he swiftly became a DJ himself, in local venues in Montpelier. Around 1980, he started teaming up with another young DJ, Miles Johnson, born in St Pauls to a

---

34   In an interview with the *Guardian* published in April 2014
35   In his book, *Original Rockers*, published in 2015 (Faber)
36   In an interview with the author, in Bristol, in February 2015

Jamaican family, and known as DJ Milo. They performed as an evolving DJ collective soon to be baptised the Wild Bunch.

Revolver also became a regular spot for Robert Del Naja, along with Plastic Wax Records on Cheltenham Road. "By 1981, tracks like 'Radio Clash' and 'The Magnificent Seven' had awakened me to rap and funk," recalled Robert. "This new direction was influenced by hip-hop acts of the time, like the Sugarhill Gang and Grandmaster Flash. When *Combat Rock* was released in 1982, it featured 'Overpowered by Funk', a collaboration with a NY graffiti artist called Futura 2000 on vocals[37]."

Robert started buying electro 12-inch records in Revolver and befriended Grant. He was 17 years old, and never left his parents' house without a Sony Walkman – the device was launched in the UK in 1979, changing many teenagers' life. When Robert first noticed a Wild Bunch poster behind the counter, he timidly asked two-metre high super-cool Grant: "Who are the 'Wild Bunch'?" And the stylish bloke behind the counter turned around and said: "I am the Wild Bunch."

At Revolver, Grant also befriended Nellee Hooper, passionate about music, whom he introduced to Miles Johnson. Nellee was a huge punk fan and owned a large collection of vinyl. Born in Barton Hill, in East Bristol, he later moved to Clifton and was known all over the city. Miles introduced him to reggae, dub and soul music. And Robert crossed path with Nellee and Miles regularly... at the dole office, queuing to receive their unemployment money. They all started to go out together in a club attracting all sort of music fans: the Dug Out on Park Row, a road that connects Clifton with St Pauls. Cheap and open-minded, the club was the ideal place for youngsters with no money.

The Dug Out soon became Bristol's core underground melting pot. Its central location enabled the meeting of two worlds: St Pauls' "Little Kingston" and Clifton's jazzy and folky crowd – for the love of music. From 1979, the venue hosted DJ nights, bringing in very diverse types of music, including hip-hop. The success of these DJs encouraged the owner to organise proper hip-hop nights, with young MCs and rappers, in a very relaxed atmosphere. DJs like John Stapleton and Miles

---

37 In his art book, *3D and the Art of Massive Attack*, The Vinyl Factory, 2015

Johnson, Daddy G, alias Grant Marshall, and Nellee Hooper formed the new generation of night-time heroes from 1982.

The West Country's "Studio 54"

"For Manchester in the 1990s, it was the Hacienda. For New York in the 1970s, it was Studio 54. And for Bristol in the 1980s it was the Dug Out - the legendary club, which became the spiritual, as well as the physical, home of the city's music scene," according to the BBC on its web page about the club.

With another venue named Trinity Centre, a former church turned into a cultural centre near Old Market, the Dug Out became one of Bristol's most multicultural hubs. Punk and hip-hop music sometimes met on the same nights. When the young boys and girls received their dole money on Thursday, they were surely to be found at the Dug Out a few hours later. Mark Stewart was also a regular visitor when he was not in London or New York.

"The Dug Out attracted pretty girls from Clifton and young guys from St Pauls," says Annie McGann[38]. She was living near the club, with her husband, actor Paul McGann, friend with many rock and jazz musicians, as well as Mark Stewart and the DJ Adrian Sherwood. "The venue had great music and an underground atmosphere with a real diversity. We all felt equal in the dark, wherever we were from," Annie adds, "and the place became a must at the beginning of the 1980s, despite its sticky and dirty floor. Drinks were cheap, people could smoke whatever they wanted and DJs were brilliant because they were ready to experiment. Also, that's one of the rare clubs where young black people were totally welcome."

DJs and hip-hop fans formed crews, posses and bunches, informal groups of disc jockeys, rappers and break-dancers. The posses became rivals and competed for the best beats and wittiest lyrics. From one night per week, hip-hop finally took over the Dug Out three to four nights a week around 1983, when another element of the culture got incorporated: graffiti. Grant sneaked a few new friends into the Dug

---

38   In an interview with the author in Bristol in February 2015

Out, including Robert Del Naja, Chris Johnson and Claude Williams known as Willy Wee.

"DJs who started out at that time had many dreams. Some, and I'm lucky to be part of them, have made it come true," says Chris Johnson[39]. Influenced by one of his brothers, Chris became a reggae, soul music and R & B fan from an early age. He discovered hip-hop at the Southmead Youth Club, one of the rare cultural and sporting places for miles around, where youngsters meet to play basketball. When he evokes his childhood in a housing estate, he remembers that "everyone knew each other and even if there were not many black families, there was mutual help. I have good memories of my youth for that, even if, outside my neighbourhood, I sometimes heard racist insults: 'nigger', 'black', etc[40]." Soon known as Krissy Kriss, the young DJ regularly joined the 2 Bad Crew.

A young photographer immortalised the Dug Out's best nights. Working under the name of Beezer, Andy Beese was born in Bristol and taught himself photography, but his black and white images of the place are radiant and as classy as pictures from a Martin Scorcese movie. "Around 1981/82, I went out all the time in the clubs of Bristol because my buddies began to become disc jockeys," says Beezer. "We did not have a penny, people were broke, it was Thatcher's years; so to earn my living, I started selling vinyl records, including punk records. I worked with the Clash to distribute their flyers. That's how I met everyone in Bristol, including in St Pauls. We also met in Redcliff, near Temple Meads Station, Clifton and then at the Dug Out[41]!" Soon, Beezer met with Grant and Milo and their crew became the centre of his photographic work.

"From then, Bristol became a real incubator for new talents," says Gill Loats, one of the rare female DJs at the Dug Out[42]. "The club was very different from other nightclubs, where girls wore tight-fitting dresses to go and pick up boys. We came to the Dug Out for the music and for the drinking, not to be seen! One could also talk about music,

39   In an interview with the author in Bristol in May 2015
40   Ibid
41   In an interview with the author from Japan, where he now lives, in February 2015
42   In an interview with the author in Bristol in March 2015

thanks to its configuration. Several small rooms followed one another, with spaces to dance, but also for conversations and exchanges about musical innovations," remembers Gill. "Because I was the only 'girl' DJ, my pals from St Pauls lent me their reggae vinyl. This is how the Dug Out became one of the few clubs where young public school boys, Clifton's ladies and black youth from working-class neighbourhoods rub shoulders and dust."

Other places that were influential for Bristol's music scene by 1982 are Plastic Wax Records and the club Thekla, on a boat in the Floating Harbour. From 1974, Bristol had its own music festival in Ashton Court and soon, the city started to feel the major influence of nearby festivals such as Glastonbury and WOMAD (*World of Music, Arts and Dance*) Festival, which was first held at the Bath & West Showground in Shepton Mallet in 1982. It was backed by former Genesis singer Peter Gabriel and Thomas Brooman, drummer with the Media and the Spics, also one of the founders of the *Bristol Recorder* magazine, a combination of vinyl record and magazine devoted to Bristol's music and cultural life.

Bristol's passion for punk is recognisable on Massive Attack's third album, *Mezzanine*. But for now, in the mid-80s, the crew that epitomised this melting pot was the Wild Bunch, mixing a passion for reggae with a strong hip-hop trend.

Chapter 4
The Wild Ride (1982-86)

In 1982, Bristol was still quite tribal. Young people moved in groups, following trends: punks, skinheads, mods, rude boys and new romantic kids. And hip-hop was starting to break the barriers between them.

While mods epitomised Swinging London, following every evolution in the fashion world and listening to modern jazz, working-class skinheads were recognisable with their military style and love of ska and rocksteady music. The term "rude boy" comes from Jamaica and brands the fans of 2 Tone ska, and especially the band the Specials. In Bristol, Tricky was one of their biggest admirers. New romantics were influenced by arty musicians, like David Bowie, Roxy Music and Kraftwerk.

Through these tendencies, the youth wanted to express a form of creativity and look for their own individuality. In Bristol, all these groups were also represented.

At the Dug Out, most DJs liked to mix different genres in their playlists. They were fond of record shops in the capital, especially Groove Records, in Soho, where they found fresh 12-inch. These Extended Plays (or EP), longer than singles (7-inch or 45 rpm), were DJs' favourite records as they contain longer or remixed versions of a track and rare items. The DJs also shared different influences and interests beyond music, including a passion for cinema and soon graffiti.

From reggae to hip-hop: superstar DJs
1982 was a great year for the blooming hip-hop scene in the US then soon in the UK. In New York, Grandmaster Flash and the Furious Five released their track 'The Message', an immediate hit. The band formed in the 1970s in the Bronx around Joseph Saddler, aka Grandmaster

Flash, born in 1958, whose family migrated to the United States from Barbados, in the Caribbean. The DJ is still considered as a pioneer of hip-hop DJing, cutting, and mixing.

In Bristol, the Dug Out was a venue where these young DJs came to improve their style, be in competition with each other, but with a sense of stimulation and fun. They came with their own records and their goal was to be remembered as the best night of the week.

Grant Marshall and Miles Johnson were getting tips from cousins and friends living in New York and were among the first to play Grandmaster Flash's EP. They mixed under the name the Wild Bunch, inspired by a western movie by Sam Peckinpah, released in 1969. The "bunch", as the terms "posse" and "crew", describes a collective of disc jokeys, masters of ceremony and breakdancers playing hip-hop, rapping and dancing. The Wild Bunch expressed their passion for music and films by playing extracts from film soundtracks during their events.

One of the first Wild Bunch nights was in 1980 at the Green Room, a club near the city centre, attended by the usual crowd of friends and DJs, including their soon-to-be third member, Nellee Hooper, whose vinyl collection rivalled Miles'. They regularly met in St Pauls and at Grant's place.

Miles Johnson was born in St Pauls in a Jamaican family and started mixing in clubs as DJ Milo from 1979. He was a real encyclopedia of sounds for funk, soul, disco, reggae and even folk music that his mother liked to listen to.

"I grew up listening to a wide range of different music at an early age," Miles states on his website. "The likes of Joni Mitchell, Joan Baez, Carole King, the Kinks, the Beatles, etc. From my mother. And 60s reggae, Sam and Dave, Otis Redding, James Brown, Aretha Franklin, from my father. Later I would go to school outside of my natural environment and meet new friends and the music they listened to like Deep Purple, Pink Floyd, T-Rex, Roxy Music in the early days and later the punk scene. I feel lucky to be born in such a time where we were able to enjoy such a wide variety of new music."

Miles could also talk for hours about any western and American films from the 1970s. Tall, handsome, charismatic, impressive and confident while behind his decks, he inspired respect and could get any door in any club to open. He was also always stylish, had a passion for fashion and later worked as a model.

He regularly went to the Princes Court Club in Bristol, to listen to DJs, never missed St Pauls Carnival and was a regular in Clifton house parties. He travelled to London to discover new bands and was quickly obsessed with hip-hop but also electronic music, garage and acid-house. In Bristol, he discovered post-punk thanks to his best friend, Duncan, and was a fan of Public Image Ltd and Wire, just like Nellee Hooper and Robert Del Naja.

"Everything influenced me at the time," said Miles, describing his DJ activities[43]. "It was an extension of what I think a lot of bedroom DJs were doing at the time, which was pause button mixes on cassette extending the favourite part of songs on your basic home stereo. The whole concept at the time was sacrilegious to musicians and I understand it now, but it was pure punk in ethic to me."

Paul Hooper, nicknamed 'Nellee', was born on March 15, 1963, and grew up in Barton Hill, in South East Bristol. Very sociable, at school he got on well with people from a variety of backgrounds and quickly knew pretty much all areas of the city. He shared with the young West Indian guys the same passion for "black" music, from soul to ska and reggae. He was also very confident and full of projects. With his long wavy hair, jeans jacket and a serious gaze, he knew how to impress a crowd when behind the mixing deck. He swiftly became a sort of impresario for the Wild Bunch.

With Nellee, Miles formed a "new wave" band for a while, in which he played drums. In early 1982, he moved to London and when he returned to Bristol, Nellee got him back on track in some DJs sets and he was featured as a DJ in St Pauls Carnival.

Grant was by then a pillar of the Carnival, just like his parents' friend Sunny was in the 1960s when he used to regularly set a sound system at his house for any kind of party[44]. Grant's place on St Michael's Hill

---

43 In the book *Art and Sound of the Bristol Underground* by Chris Burton and Gary Thomson (Tangent Books, Bristol, 2009)
44 As Grant Marshall told !K7 Record in an interview in 2004

and the record shop he worked in during the day, Revolver, became the Wild Bunch' headquarters. On weekends, the group met at his place, to smoke marijuana and listen to new records, inviting new friends.

At the Dug Out, they met with younger aspiring DJs, like Claude Williams, soon known as MC Willy Wee, and Chris Johnson, aka DJ Krissy Kriss. As DJs, they didn't make much of a living but their influence was already undeniable in 1983, pioneering a new form of underground sound and genre. From then, what they really wanted was to add two dimensions to their mix: raps, the voices of the whole movement, which would transform DJs into musicians, and graffiti, as a visual representation to their hip-hop sound.

3D – when the graffiti scene emerged

By that time, Bristol, like London and Paris, was already submerged by an invasion of tags on its walls, mainly signatures and names, written free-hand. In the summer 1983, a first real 'mural' appeared in Hotwells, near the river Avon, signed by the pseudonym "D.D.D.". Murals, with their distinct painting style, formed and decorative letters but also drawings, were taking graffiti to the next level, according to many artists choosing to paint them. The Bristol mural was entitled 'Graffiti Stylee' and was a piece done at night by 18-year-old Robert Del Naja, soon to become the city's main graffiti artist, under the tag of 3D.

After leaving school and only passing a few exams, Robert was unemployed and his world evolved around the sound of David Bowie, Stiff Little Fingers and of course the Clash, completed with hip-hop and electronic music from 1980. Graffiti art provided him the perfect excuse to be artistic without having to be academic. The genre also perfectly suited his rebellious temperament.

Since his favourite band, the Clash, had introduced him to the graffiti artist Futura 2000, his whole world had started to make sense and all his interests to converge. Futura 2000 (real name Leonard Hilton McGurr, born in Brooklyn in 1955, in an Irish-American-French family) started painting illegally in New York's subway in the 1970s, before exhibiting with Keith Haring, Richard Hambleton and Jean-Michel Basquiat. Futura designed the sleeve for 'This is Radio Clash', released in 1981. The band featured references to graffiti and breakdancers in their video. And the same year, the Clash enrolled Futura for their tour. He is even featured singing on a track with Joe Strummer, 'Overpowered by Funk', on their album *Combat Rock*, released in 1982.

By then, Robert was still living in his father's pub, helping him once in a while, but still had no firm idea of the occupation he'd like to embrace after the summer, when he started graffiti... He didn't go very far from home, down by the river, came back the next day, with a camera he borrowed, to take a photograph of the mural. It featured the expression 'Graffiti Stylee' in a typical wording / lettering fashion, with a drawing of a ghetto blaster. And the mural rapidly bemused the dwellers. This new activity didn't please his parents however.

From the start, music was to him very visual, accompanied by sketchbooks and paint. It became his most powerful means of expression. Being colour-blind, he developed his style and references in his own personal way, labelling his spray cans with the names of the colours, for recognition under street night-lights. He also started introducing visual inspirations from comics, western, science fiction, films noirs and crime movies in his sketches. At the Dug Out, where he already spent three to four nights a week, he could also access the club's television room, where kids could watch channels like MTV, launched in 1980 in the UK, and discover new films and music videos.

Bristol was a difficult place to party back then, members of the scene told me. A Saturday night out could involved what they called "a good fight" and the guys wanted to avoid it. There weren't many other places that would play good music, where they wouldn't get into a ruck. So the Dug Out was the place to be. Most of the boys could walk home from the club or 3D would stay out hours to paint in the city centre, Montpelier, St Pauls and Clifton.

3D's graffiti quickly attracted fascination from other kids; some aspiring graffiti artists started following him; some photographed his murals. He was soon joined by other crews, the Z-Boys and FBI. Among them, his friends Ian Dark and Oli Timmins, and an even younger aspiring graffiti writer known as Inkie. Born in Scotland on September 1, 1970, Tom 'Inkie' Bingle moved to Bristol with his parents in 1976.

Inkie would later become one of Bristol's street art heroes in the mid-1990s...

In a few months, through the summer of 1983, 3D, also simply called 'D', became the city's first confirmed graffiti artist. But by that time, his main dream was still to produce art for record sleeves, like his hero, Futura, and to mix art with music.

And the visual meets the sound

The blooming hip-hop culture of Bristol took on another dimension when the graffiti artists and the DJs came together. DJ crews wanted to have stylish artists to produce their flyers and invitations to their parties. This is when 3D started to become a direct part of the Wild Bunch. Being friends with 3D, Grant, Nellee and Milo soon wanted his graffiti to represent the collective. On flyers as on walls, from Park Street to Marlborough Street, in 1984, the Wild Bunch was then visible everywhere in town.

On walls, 3D often drew the posse's name in orange and blue bright letters, accompanied by faces, ghetto blasters or microphones. For their events, he drew typical hip-hop styled or film characters, in black and white mainly, and chose catchy lines to be featured on their photocopied flyers. He sometimes created flyers for other crews as well. "I saw D do some of his first ones," remembers DJ Ed Sargent from 2 Bad Crew. "The design of flyers was a very important part of the whole package[45]."

From there, 3D developed a link between graffiti's wording and writing lyrics. He was writing vocals, something new for the Wednesday at the Dug Out, which was very selective. The Wild Bunch wouldn't let anyone on the mic apart a few people like Gary Clail, who ended up with Mark Stewart & the Maffia and Tackhead, sometimes Mark Stewart himself. Daddy G, who was the king of reggae style toasting, Claude (Willy Wee) had a more New-York-style MC thing going on. And then there was D.

Mark Stewart was back in Bristol with his new band, and he and Grant, known as simply 'G' to his friends, shared the same connections, the same age and the same passions. G's rap was influenced by the Jamaican style of *toasting*, which described the 1960s types of lyrics found in reggae music, which was hugely influential on the first rappers in America and in Britain.

The Wild Bunch soon needed some permanent MCs to bring in their own lyrics and Willy Wee and above all 3D proved to be their best writers. D's friendship with Nellee, Grant and Miles, as well as his unique artistic style and his brilliant lyrics, took him to the centre of this underground scene. He rapped behind the DJ decks aside Grant and Milo, sometimes duetting with Willy Wee.

MCs wrote about their daily life, a form of storytelling rap, always looking for humour, good puns, and beautiful rhymes. Like in New York, their texts came to embody the oral history of their era, of an underground group and a marginal social class who could not get heard anyhow else in Thatcher's Britain.

The Wild Bunch's style mixed a form of rebellion, an eagerness for underground sound, with a sense of humour and self-mockery. Their members were really good at blagging, promising a good deal or seducing people to get their way into any party, any project. And graffiti became an integral part of this universe, made of soft provocation and a sense of derision.

The same year, 1984, a film about the American graffiti world was shown in Stokes Croft: *Wild Style*. It was produced by Charlie Ahearn and released in the USA in September 1982. The film features central figures from the New York graffiti scene, including Lee Quiñones – interpreting the main character named Zoro, but also Fab Five Freddy, Lady Pink, the Rock Steady Crew, the Cold Crush Brothers, Queen Lisa Lee of Zulu Nation, Grandmaster Flash and Zephyr.

"In Bristol, we flocked to see the seminal hip-hop film *Wild Style*," recalled Robert Del Naja[46]. It is centred on the encounter between Zoro, a graffiti writer from the Bronx, and Virginia, a young female journalist living in Manhattan. For the Bristol audience, the film only shows how much 3D and his crew were ahead of their time creatively, heroes of

---

46   In a column he published in the *Guardian*, on October 14, 2013, for the 25th anniversary of Jean-Michel Basquiat's death

a new generation of artists. Hardcore hip-hop fans came to the Arts Centre Cinema several times to watch the film again, according to Inkie. The centre would later become "The Cube Microplex", an alternative cinema.

"In those days, pre-internet and before the mass exposure of hip-hop, you had to dig deep to find tunes and graffiti art," Del Naja added. "It made everything you did find all the more precious. There would be a little bit on the radio, a magazine, then a tantalising snippet on video maybe. And the name Basquiat kept popping up[47]."

The young artists were also influenced by the release of *Subway Art*, a collaborative book published by American photographers Martha Cooper and Henry Chalfant, which documented the early history of New York City's graffiti movement. Published in 1984 in the USA, it soon arrived in the UK and became an important inspiration.

3D pursued his painting on walls with the Z-Boys in Bristol's city centre – one of his famous murals featured his tag and a masked character on the wall of the Virgin record store in the Broadmead shopping centre, where he used to hang out on weekends with punk friends. He also painted in St Pauls and in Clifton. Mixing the wording technique with proper drawing, his murals often depicted a story, added messages and used humour. D was also offered to come and paint pieces for shops and bars and was getting paid for it.

But for British authorities, graffiti was only a form of vandalism and the police arrested the writers when caught painting. The interdiction only made the whole game more appealing for most graffiti pioneers. He wanted to create something that people would talk about and that was interesting, Robert told me when I came to Bristol. Stopping so soon was not an option. Even if the rest of the society did not realise it, graffiti, just like DJing, was part of a social and artistic experiment for these young creative personalities that would evolve into a much greater movement.

After comics, films, punk music and American early graffiti, Jean-Michel Basquiat's work became a major source of inspiration for Robert

47   Ibid

Del Naja. Born in Brooklyn in 1960 to a Haitian father and Puerto Rican mother, Basquiat started drawing graffiti under the name of S.A.M.O. (for Same Old Shit), in 1976, having abandoned school at 15, run away from his home and slept on park benches in New York in the early 1970s, before dedicating himself to painting large canvases. Hardly a few years later, in 1984, his paintings were exhibited at the MoMA, Museum of Modern Art, in Manhattan, when Robert discovered his work more deeply. And he marvelled at Basquiat's "epic, powerful works such as The History of Black People and The Dutch Settlers[48]."

Anglo-American influences

Robert researched the works of other American artists such as Andy Warhol and started doing collages and paintings himself. He was interested in industrial symbolism, commercial packaging and label design, and he started cutting stencils. Basquiat completely embodied the link between the energy of the street and the strength of the art world, permanently questioning his own approach and remaining provocative.

"He painted in a raw and confrontational way that was beautiful and effortless," said Robert. "He abused the canvas with chaotic composition and intense primary colours. It wasn't just his imagery but the juxtaposed cultural references: media saturation, brand communication, power, poverty, African history, colonisation and exploitation. Everything was labelled for consumers and the words seemed part manifesto and part hit list. It was a slap in the face[49]."

3D mixed these references with the patterns he had always admired in comics and films, from Jack Kirby and Frank Miller to Martin Scorcese's Taxi Driver and Ridley Scott's Blade Runner, released in September 1982. Robert De Niro remained one of his favourite actors. He represented him in many of his stencilled graffiti, one remaining iconic: on the wall of the Special K Café, owned by Kosta, Grant's flatmate, which became the Wild Bunch' daytime headquarters.

In 1984, stencils were considered as a very inferior version of graffiti

---

48 In the Guardian, on October 14, 2013
49 Ibid.

by most artists and the ones who used them were shown little respect. But Robert was fond of the technique, which, ten years later, would revolutionise the art of graffiti. One of his first stencils was quoting the phrase 'God Is Love', that he saw daily on the front of the local church, near his dad's pub, printed on one of his T-shirts, to 'annoy' his family[50]... He had been collecting stencils since the release of the Clash's single 'Straight to Hell', in 1982, which included one, and he quickly started making his own. As he wanted to use graffiti to transmit messages on the city's walls, stencils immediately proved their efficiency.

3D felt graffiti art had the power to transmit raw messages, as a response to mass advertisements and billboards. One of his most revered murals was 'It's No Great Crime', painted in 1984 in St Pauls, as a statement on the art of spraying itself. In flashy yellow letters, the words appeared on a blue and green background, surrounded by a bloodlike red outline and, on the left side, a revolver, upright. It was so legendary for Bristol graffiti fans that it was reproduced in 2011 on the same wall as a homage, by the artist named Paris. On Campbell Street, a little further into St Pauls, 'The Longest Day' represented graffiti writers with spray cans, one of them with a star masking his left eye, the five-pointed star becoming one of 3D's signature patterns.

But illegal street painting became increasingly more difficult. The police started to focus on it. 3D was arrested for the first time on August 22, 1984, in St Pauls, not taking it too seriously. But he was arrested again while painting on May 23, 1985, in Clifton, with his friend Ian Dark from the Z-Boys crew. A third arrest could get him in jail. But he didn't intend to stop completely. Illegal painting was more appealing and thrilling and he still painted for the Wild Bunch. And in the summer 1985, the British art world began to pay attention to the graffiti movement.

That summer, 3D started painting one of his most famous murals, 'The Day The Law Died', on Jamaica Street, near Stokes Croft, which featured on the cover of the *Venue* magazine, in a photograph taken by Beezer. "I wanted to immortalise anything 3D had painted," says Beezer.

---

50   See the book *Children of the Can: Bristol Graffiti and Street Art*, by Felix 'FLX' Braun (Tangent Books, Bristol, 2008)

"I realise now we were living in a deeply multiracial environment that was quite unique. We didn't see colours[51]."

The pink and blue mural was painted on a big wall, five metres high, representing Robert De Niro on the left side, armed with a cartoon gun. This mural can be counted among the artworks that will help graffiti become considered as a real artistic movement in the UK.

Graffiti entered the gallery

In 1985, Bristol's galleries and curators could not help but noticing the boom of the graffiti movement. A few people then suggested to Jeremy Rees, the founder of the Arnolfini Gallery, on Narrow Quay, by the Floating Harbour, to organise an event. Through contacts, the project was submitted to 3D. That was how the Graffiti Art exhibition came about, the first graffiti exhibition in a gallery organised in the UK. 3D asked his mates to join: the Z-Boys, Fade, Jaffa, and the Londoner Pride. The show opened on July 19 with a big party where break-dancers performed with the Wild Bunch – Grant, Nellee and Milo joining 3D.

In the audience were Mark Stewart, many aspiring artists, as well as young DJs including the duo Smith & Mighty, Tricky, and Geoff Barrow, a 15-year-old music fan who came by bus from the nearby town of Portishead... The journalist Phil Johnson filmed the event. Among the guests from the rest of England was Goldie, a graffiti artist from Birmingham, who met Nellee Hooper in a party at the Redhouse, a disused warehouse recycled into a club in St Pauls.

Goldie (born Clifford Joseph Price in 1965 in a Jamaican/Scottish family but soon put in foster care) had spent months in Miami and New York, and brought with him two graffiti artists from the Bronx: Bio and Brim, members of a collective known as TATS CRU, close to the American hip-hop hero Afrika Bambaataa and his Zulu Nation crew. Wilfredo 'Bio' Feliciano and Brim Fuentes were probably the first New York street artists to come to the UK to discover the local scene and they developed a close friendship with Goldie, who was also an aspiring DJ. The opening night ended with a party led by the Wild Bunch in

---

51   In an interview with the author from Japan, in March 2015

Stokes Croft.

3D developed a creative friendship with Goldie. They started spraying together in Woverhampton. British graffiti was taking off. While 3D was on the cover of the July edition of the local magazine *Venue*, painting his recent mural The Day The Law Died, Bristol's youth was more enhanced than ever by his achievements. New graffiti writers emerged around Inkie, the FBI crew and the Z-Boys: Nick Walker, Oli-T, Chaos, Cheo, FLX, Lokey, Tuco and others.

"Young boys took buses from the nearby suburbs just to be able to see 3D's murals for real, including me and probably Banksy!" remembers Steve Lazarides, later to become Banksy's manager and a powerful gallery owner[52]. In one of his rare interviews, with the pop culture magazine *Swindle* in 2006, Banksy himself declared: "When I was about ten years old, a kid called 3D was painting the streets hard (…). He was the first to bring spray painting to Bristol. I grew up seeing spray paint on the streets way before I ever saw it in a magazine or on a computer. 3D quit painting and formed the band Massive Attack, which may have been good for him but was a big loss for the city."

The Wild Bunch at a high

In 1985, the Wild Bunch was the favourite crew at the Dug Out. They played on Wednesdays and Thursdays, sometimes with 2 Bad Crew. When you start going to a place all the time, then you become part of that scene, summarises Robert Del Naja, humbly, years later. In a couple of years, the collective had definitely reached a new level. And they wanted to produce their own music and to put it on tapes. The same year, 1985, they recorded their first demo, 'Tearing Down The Avenue', an energetic, joyful track, on which 3D raps. They performed it live at warehouse parties.

The crew also opened up to a new member that year: Andrew Vowles, known as DJ Mushroom. He was 17 when he became a member of the Wild Bunch. He was still a young teenager when he came to the Dug Out for the first time, thanks to Grant Marshall, to listen to the

52   In an interview with the author from London in January 2017

collective. "I'd try and go down to the Dug Out but I was only 15 and the doorman, Chippy, used to tell me that I was far too young so G had to sneak me in," Mushroom told *Dazed and Confused* in 1998[53]. "Those were wild times. I think Glastonbury was wilder when I first started going too. There were people with megaphones shouting 'Acid!' and 'Get your hot knives here!' really loud. I remember going to see Lenny Kravitz. I don't know where he is now but I do know that he was an all-time genius."

Mushroom met Daddy G at Revolver and made a big impression with his knowledge of American hip-hop. And he got inspired to believe in the possibility to produce a proper British hip-hop culture when he saw a piece in Hotwells, in 1983, stating 'Graffiti Stylee'... He didn't know at the time that the writer was 3D, aka Robert Del Naja.

Mushroom was totally mad for music and a lot of his inspiration came from Milo Johnson. Milo made regular trips to Japan and New York and brought back tapes, clothing and electronic gadgets – he had strong tastes. Mushroom became the living emblem of the Wild Bunch, he was this kid who actually seemed to embody hip-hop itself, the way he behaved and dressed.

Andrew/Mushroom brought a new energy and additional sounds to the Wild Bunch. He received his nickname at Special K's, Kosta's café, at the corner of St Michael's Hill and Perry Road, from the hours he spent playing on a video game named *Centipede*, in which avatars would fight mushroom-figured monsters... The café increasingly became the Wild Bunch daytime meeting point. Its walls were covered with 3D's graffiti, indoors and outdoors. Aspiring graffiti writers came to meet him and show him their drawings and sketches, just as young DJs came to exchange mix tapes and ideas about music. A young rapper, nicknamed Tricky, was also a regular and soon wanted to write lyrics with 3D.

The Wild Bunch particularly liked to organise private house parties by then and St Pauls was the ideal location for them. For the Carnival, they installed a huge sound system and mixed for hours, day and night. "The best nights were with the Wild Bunch and Newtrament, like the

---

53   In an interview with the three members of the band published in the magazine's February 1998 edition

one in the Saint Pauls' Carnival, on Campbell Street," says graffiti artist Chaos[54]. "I remember 3D, Pride and Inkie painting on Campbell Street while the Wild Bunch was playing." Nick Walker and DJ Krust were also regular members at their parties.

These nights became the collective's main events in 1986 when the Dug Out closed... Criticised by neighbours, watched over by the police worried about drug dealing, still struggling in a time of mass unemployment, the club couldn't survive. DJs found their way into Montpelier and St Pauls, where many buildings remained disused. If their parents were not very supportive, these young DJs and MCs were considered as superstars by their audience.

Then, the sound of the Wild Bunch was noticed outside Bristol. A version of 'Tearing Down The Avenue' was broadcast on London Weekend Radio, LWR, an underground network specialising in "black music". The main presenter, Tim Westwood, chose the track for his Saturday morning show on hip-hop. They were encouraged to produce other demos.

Meanwhile, the police's pressure on St Pauls' youth reached another height in September 1986, when the area was stormed again, as well as Hartcliffe, in an antidrug action named 'Operation Delivery', according to diverse police archives[55]. The local residents decried police brutality and constant discrimination on their neighbourhood. Local Member of Parliament William Waldegrave had to intervene to persuade the police to scale down their policy of containment.

However, the underground music scene was writing another version of St Pauls' history... "Before then, British youth culture in the 80s had been tribal and divided. Hip-hop changed that," insisted Robert Del Naja in a 2013 interview[56]. "It broke down class and race divisions in a way punk and the ska movement had tried and failed to do," he continues. "The Wild Bunch spent three years putting on warehouse parties and underground jams, using graffiti art to spread the word. The

---

54 In *Art and Sound of the Bristol Underground*, Op. Cit.
55 See diverse media including the *Independent*, in an article published on January 2, 1996. On the issues: *Bristol: Ethnic Minorities and the City 1000–2001*, by Madge Dresser and Peter Fleming, pp. 146–149 (Phillimore & Co Ltd, 2007).
56 With the *Guardian*, in an article published on October 14, 2013

parties attracted a cross-section of the young population: middle class and working class, black and white."

Lost in translation

As the police and the community took stock of the effects of the uprising, the Wild Bunch were already coming out of the nest. Nellee and Miles performed regularly as DJs in London and organised a few parties for the whole collective. Unlike Grant, 3D and Mushroom, they were keen to leave Bristol. Through Bruce Smith, an old friend of Miles, they were introduced to Neneh Cherry at a time when she was all over the London underground scene. Bruce and Neneh had met when performing with Rip, Rig & Panic in Bristol then London. Close to the fashionable monthly magazine *The Face*, she encouraged charismatic Miles to pose for them.

Thanks to Mark Stewart, Neneh already knew the performances of the Wild Bunch. She then got to know the members better and loved their energy and talent. In the spring of 1986, she encouraged them to perform... in Tokyo. Miles was totally fascinated by Japanese culture and wanted the collective to travel there for several months. He organised parties and DJ sets, tried to negotiate recordings and even planned a video shoot. He travelled to Tokyo in May to confirm the events, where he immersed himself in the stylish booming pop culture, collecting sneakers and vinyl. The rest of the Wild Bunch joined him for a couple of months.

Their budget was obviously quite tight. 3D and Grant borrowed money from their parents to start with, and Miles found them a cheap house in a suburban area of the Japanese capital. The group experienced a complete culture shock, at this time where England had never seen any manga, karaoke or sushi restaurant. They discovered a flow of new technology and gadgets. Unexpectedly, Robert also got to see more paintings by Jean-Michel Basquiat at the Akira Ikeda Gallery. A few parties were organised for the boys to perform, including a special night on May 26, at the club Cleo Palazzi II in Tokyo, a so-called "post-modern concept bar". The poster designed for the event introduced the team: 3D, "the Cool Breeze, graffiti outlaw supreme", DJ Nellee, MC

Willy Wee, DJ Milo, Papa G "the soul daddy".

But after a month, 3D was disillusioned. The money wasn't coming and the events were not numerous enough to keep them busy. Every night they had to get out in free bars, where, American or Europeans people in the fashion or music industry were given free drinks. But 3D didn't get on with it. The culture just seemed very alien to him. They were staying in the outskirts of Tokyo in this very traditional house with a doubtful French landlord and they got kicked out by some heavy gangsters one night... The house, with paper-thin walls and only one bathroom, was hardly suitable for these young Englishmen and the area didn't inspire Grant either, who believed it was full of yakuza gangs. "D and I were literally chased out of the place!" declared Grant Marshall, years later[57].

Difficulties arose increasingly and revealed the collective's profoundly different personalities, leading to tensions. 3D could not handle the situation anymore. One night, he was so unhappy that he got into a taxi with all the money he had left and went to the airport. He left a letter, saying 'sorry guys I've got to go'. D had panicked and wanted to be home. The journey, which promised to be a new beginning for the collective, instead provoked its implosion. Once back in England, the other members of the group officially excluded 3D. Then Nellee and Miles were even more determined to leave Bristol and move to London.

The crew kept its name in order to capitalise on their formative years, when Nellee and Miles performed events in London for instance, but practically it ceased to exist in its former Bristol form. It remains legendary to this day though, in England but also in Japan, where records shops still collect some of their rare EPs.

While Nellee was no longer in Bristol enough to enhance new projects, Grant decided to follow a career in DJing. Mushroom started to acquire some recording equipment. And for 3D, for whom music and art rhymed with collaboration and social engagement, the future seemed grim. But the three young men would not give up this easily.

---

57   In an interview with the Australian radio ABC, on March 15, 2010

Chapter 5
The Sons Of Massive Territories (1986-88)

Though he was one of the pioneers of the newly formed British graffiti artistic movement, midsummer 1986, Robert Del Naja was dreaming about music more than he was about art. But, back from Japan, he felt excluded from this musical world. The Wild Bunch had dissolved through their strange experience in Tokyo and Grant Marshall was tempted to join Nellee Hooper and Miles Johnson in London. Though he was the main voice and the lyricist of their now dormant collective, 3D had no direction to rebound. Not yet.

In order to reimburse the money he borrowed from his father for the journey to Japan, Robert had to take a job and found a position at BBC Bristol's canteen. He felt helpless and isolated. "It was a fucking nightmare," he later admitted[58]. "I had to wear little blue overalls and go to Kwik-Save and pick frozen meat and stuff. It was almost like an exercise of self-disesteem, where I'd walk up the road in this blue overall with a box of frozen food thinking, 'I was in Japan once, I was in a band'... I was in ruins, total ruins."

To remain sane, he kept on moving into new artistic directions. Around him, a new underground scene had emerged in Bristol and though the police fought against graffiti writers, the artists then had legal ways to express themselves, in pubs and through commissioned artwork. 3D's murals were still the most popular in town, inspiring the new emerging artists.

D's friend and former Dug Out club manager Dave McDonald offered him a space to paint at the Montpelier Hotel, a pub in the neighbourhood of the same name. For two years, the place became

58   In *Straight Outa Bristol*, by Phil Johnson (Hodder and Stoughton, 1996)

a sort of a gallery for his ever-evolving art. He decorated the pub's walls in exchange. For his indoor work, Robert Del Naja explored the possibilities with stencils and imposed a new style.

"I was literally trying to follow 3D everywhere," remembers Inkie, who is five years younger, when I meet with him at the Arnolfini Gallery in 2015. "I even managed to invite myself to his birthday party, 'cause I knew it would be unforgettable[59]!" Very tall for his age, witty and amicable, Inkie soon belonged to D's group of friends. "At the time in Bristol, we were still cut off from London," he adds, "we were living in our bubble, so we shared a lot, ideas, projects, good spots, and we helped each other. Everyone knows everyone in the city, or at least your mother or your cousin[60]!" Inkie became famous for his gorgeous profiles of female faces, surrounded by long, black, wavy hair.

A year older, born in 1969, Nick Walker took the nickname of 'The Vandal' and drew portraits of himself on giant walls all over the city. Inkie and Nick formed the Crime Inc. Crew in 1986 with FLX. To all of them, 3D's art, politicised, informed and clever, was an inspiration.

From Bristol to the Bronx, and vice versa

3D was the first Bristolian artist to attract the interest of New York artists: Brim and Bio, from the TATS CRU Inc. They introduced him to BG183, Nicer, HOW, and NOSM. Together with Goldie in Birmingham, they set up the Trans-Atlantic Federation, with a motto "United In Crime", and started spraying together in different locations in England.

They built links with other artists, like T Kid, Vulcan and Mode2, who was from Paris but painted mostly in London. They organised a first show in Birmingham, where Brim, Goldie and 3D got involved in the shooting of a film documenting what started to be named the "street art" movement. The film, entitled *Bombin'*, was directed by Dick Fontaine, who shot between 1986 and 1987 in New York and in England. Fontaine had produced a first film on the underground American scene in 1984, *Beat This: A Hip-Hop History, featuring Grandmaster Flash, Afrika Bambaataa and Brim.*

59   In an interview with the author in Bristol's Arnolfini Gallery, in June 2015
60   Interview with the author in June 2015 in Bristol

The documentary filmmaker followed Brim from the Bronx to England, via London, Oxford, Birmingham and Bristol. 3D and Brim were interviewed together during a graffiti contest in Birmingham, then with Goldie in his nearby neighbourhood of Wolverhampton. Brim explained that he found England more open to the art movement than New York, where it would be impossible to paint freely on outdoor walls in the daytime with permission. 3D was encouraged to show his sketches before he started his mural and mentioned 'The Day The Law Died', that he painted the previous summer, but insisted that he didn't intend to paint "anarchy statements"; to him, graffiti was simply a new, generational means of expression that could not be stopped, whether the police wanted it or not.

The artists also mentioned their love of music and the link between graffiti and hip-hop. Brim described Afrika Bambaataa and Grandmaster Flash as the voices of "his people in the Bronx", African-American and West Indian people. In one scene, 3D appeared rapping at a party in Bristol, attended by the members of the Transatlantic Federation. Goldie evoked the mix tapes he received from 3D, especially one containing the LP *Decoy* by Miles Davis and *Taxi Driver*'s score, later admitting that it took him years "to completely understand this type of music[61]", that would become very influential on him.

The film showed how graffiti had already become politicised. In one of the last sequences, D, Brim and Goldie were watching the news at Goldie's home in Wolverhampton and they criticised the police's attitude towards inhabitants of a poor area where they were patrolling. Starting from a fascination for Brim and his Bronx counterparts in graffiti, the film then dug into the English underground art scene.

Bombin' was broadcast in 1988 on different British television networks. Robert Del Naja was credited for designing the opening sequence, in which the young artists explored together some walls in an underground corridor ahead of an explosion. The title, *Bombin'*, and the scene are references to the graffiti expression—"to bomb", which describes the act of spraying many surfaces very rapidly with the same

---

61   In his book, *Nine Lives* (Spectre, 2003)

tag, in the same zone, according notably to Martha Cooper's book, *Subway Art*. The bomb also became at that time a metaphor of the idea of an artistic explosion.

Posses and crews on fire

While the Wild Bunch was almost inactive, Bristol's DJ culture was booming. Other posses formed such as Dom T and the 2 Bad Crew, City Rockas, Crime Inc., Def Con – with DJ John Stapleton and artist Ian Dark, FBI Crew, Krissy Kriss, the famous duo Smith and Mighty and Fresh 4. The latter were based in Knowle West, in South Bristol, and formed by DJ Flynn, Suv, from Ashton, and Judge, from Totterdown. They met for the first time at the Eagle House Youth Centre then jammed from 1985 on Saint Luke's Road, near Bedminster and Temple Meads. They were joined by DJ Krust, real name Kirk Thompson, born on July 26, 1968. They reckon they were inspired by the Wild Bunch and the FBI crew. In 1989, Fresh 4's single 'Wishing On A Star', a cover version of the Rose Royce hit, co-produced by fellow Bristol pioneers Smith and Mighty, would become one of the important exports of the city's sound. It was described by the press as a "fusion of heavy bass lines, hip-hop beats, soulful vocals and new takes on classic songs".

As Def Con, John Stapleton and Ian Dark performed at the Western Star Domino Club and the Tropic Club, in St Pauls, from 1985. They were influenced by funk and hip-hop from New York, Grandmaster Flash and Kurtis Blow. They heard their records at a party hosted by... the Wild Bunch.

DJ Ed Sargent, from 2 Bad Crew, reckoned that it was a special time for Bristol – full of new, excellent DJs and rappers, in a socially diverse environment. According to street artist Chaos, toward the end of the 1980s, Bristol had some of the best parties, attracting DJs from London.

From 1987, Smith & Mighty were the triumphant crew. Rob Smith and Ray Mighty formed the duo in 1986. Raymond Mighty is from St Pauls, where his Jamaican father and his friends spent a lot of time in blues club, Ray tells me[62]. In 1980, he was caught up in the St Pauls riots

---

62   In an interview with the author in August 2015

and almost arrested. He was earning a living working with drug dealers when music saved him from these activities. In 1984, he joined the indie funk band Sweat, as a keyboardist, influenced by Elvis Presley, as well as rock, funk, reggae… and punk music. At the Dug Out, he befriended Grant Marshall and Tricky. His casual look, with long dreadlocks and sparkling green eyes, made him quite noticeable.

In 1985, Ray met with Rob Smith, a young guitarist looking to join a band and play more reggae. He dropped an ad at Revolver Records. They saw each other regularly in St Pauls. "My band, Sweat, started to dismantle by then," remembers Ray Mighty. "And Rob and I had the same musical tastes, so we formed a duo. I was playing keyboard and Rob the guitar; first mostly playing covers then we started to adapt songs in rap versions[63]." They were also very much interested in dub and electronic music.

In 1987, Smith & Mighty made their name known in Bristol in clubs like Western Star Domino, Tropic, the Moon Club, Green Rooms, Rummer and Dockland Settlement. They worked with a sampler and started recording some first demos. They even turned down a proposal from Virgin Records, refusing to settle in London. They were happy working in Bristol with friendly young DJs: Krissy Kriss, Jackie Jackson, MC Kelz, Lynx, etc. Developing a passion for sampling, in 1988, they released two first singles: 'Anyone' and 'Walk On By', and produced 'Wishing On A Star' for Fresh 4.

London calling and Bristol rebirth

Meanwhile, in London, towards the end of 1986, Nellee Hooper and Miles Johnson were performing as a DJ duo, in the Krush Groove club, sometimes inviting Daddy G to join. They were noticed by the magazine *Blues & Soul*, which wrote about African-American music for the British audience. The track they played to introduce the Wild Bunch was 'Tearing Down the Avenue', with 3D on the mic, rapping mainly about his graffiti adventures, and quoting one of his nicknames, used largely in Tokyo: 'The Cool Breeze'. This demo was the main tool Nellee

---

63   In an interview with the author in August 2015

used to present the sound of the Wild Bunch to the DJs and rappers he met in the capital, including Jazzie B and the members of soon-to-be-formed Soul II Soul. In 1988, the band signed a deal with Virgin Records and released a hugely successful first single, 'Back to Life (However Do You Want Me)'.

Nellee and Milo thus got a chance to meet with producers at Fourth & Broadway, a label founded in 1984, linked to Island Records. Fourth & Broadway was eager to produce a single by the Wild Bunch and liked their idea of the wide collective, using samples to produce a different style of hip-hop, still including rappers. They were ready to sign them with a first contract. But in order to produce new demos, Nellee and Milo seriously needed a lyricist and rapper. Against all odds, the duo decided that they finally wanted to work with 3D again... to write lyrics. According to Grant Marshall, he was the one who convinced them to bring D back. Robert remembers them showing up at his door one morning...

That was how 3D reintegrated the Wild Bunch. In 1987, he brought his American friends Brim and Bio to their parties in Bristol, and the collective seemed reborn. That's when Brim gave them the nickname 'Massive Attack'. He used to call them an "underground massive attack", because they were putting on parties and it was kind of chaos... Brim liked to describe their jams as "real underground" or "massive attacks". The adjectives "massive" and "underground" had already appeared regularly on Wild Bunch flyers designed by 3D.

3D's graffiti artwork also reached a high point in 1987. His style was evolving; he was using more stencils, his lettering changed, and his choices of colours too. He was experimenting and met with more artists from different European capitals. "We were regularly travelling from Bristol to Amsterdam and Paris, and this is when a graffiti network started to form around John Nation and the Barton Hill Youth Club," says Inkie.[64] "John was a social worker back then but he really encouraged a second generation of graffiti writers with his space."

Illegal spraying was still considered as vandalism but it remained

---

64   In an interview with the author in June 2015 in Bristol's Arnolfini Gallery

a must for the graffiti writers. "I'd prefer to call it positive vandalism," 3D explained to *LM* magazine, which interviewed him in 1987. "Graffiti art has had a bad press, and some kids don't help by just going round spraying their names on the walls, but all I'm doing is brightening the place up. There are worse things happening." The magazine printed half a dozen photographs of him in front of his murals. But the police made things almost impossible, even for him. The tagging had become epidemic at that time, according to some of the artists, and had very little to actually do with art or risk.

In 1987, he was also offered to exhibit for the first time in London, at the Black Bull Gallery, in Fulham. 3D's stencils then evolved into paintings and posters; he was interested in broader forms of visual arts. He used more references to cultural icons, like Andy Warhol did, to Robert De Niro still, then Mike Tyson, the Mona Lisa, Marilyn Monroe and... Margaret Thatcher, notably in a piece named 'Maggie Monroe', painted in 1988, where his stencilled representations of Marilyn were progressively transformed in Thatcher's face. His art, like his lyrics were always politicised or at least socially aware.

3D also used industrial patterns and worked on collage and photocopy images to cut and paste them into his artwork. He became passionate about polar opposites and the contrasts of colours that he had been studying since working on correcting his colour-blindness. When "street art" began to enter the mainstream, 3D's visuals had already evolved. And he got more motivated by the thought of painting on canvas and create potential record sleeves for the Wild Bunch...

Some of the other Bristolian artists started to print work in order to make a living with their art. And Bristol really made its mark outside of the West Country when, in 1987 still, Cheo, from the Barton Hill Youth Club, was placed second at the National Graffiti Championship. In May 1989, with Inkie, he came second at the World Graffiti Championship held in Bridlington, in Yorkshire. The event was attended by artists from all over the world, from New York to Paris and Scandinavia, including JonOne, one of the most famous graffiti writers from Harlem, born in 1963 and already widely known. For Nick Walker, who planned his move to New York, "3D remains the one who opened the way for us, a pioneer, in street art and in music[65]."

3D was by then more involved with the Wild Bunch than ever. They recorded in 1987 a final version of 'Tearing Down The Avenue', pressed on vinyl, which included on its B-side a cover of 'The Look of Love', a song composed by Burt Bacharach and written by Hal David for the British singer Dusty Springfield (1939-1999). The song appeared in the James Bond movie, *Casino Royale*, in 1967. The choice of this song came from Miles, and it changed everything. He chose to slow the whole rhythm and it later really affected everyone in Bristol: Smith & Mighty, and later Portishead and Tricky.

The Wild Bunch asked a young singer called Shara Nelson to reinterpret it. They knew her from Adrian Sherwood's posse. Sherwood is a famous DJ from London, born in 1958, whom Miles got to know through common friends. Her demos would later become the main vocals that 3D, Grant and Andrew Vowles would use for their next projects.

An EP was pressed, as a promo 12-inch, by Fourth & Broadway, with 'The Look Of Love' (featuring Shara Nelson) and 'Tearing Down The Avenue'. The latter was played on underground radio stations in London, the anchorman presenting the bunch and their "new bassline", featuring 3D, "regarded as one of the top graffiti artists in the UK".

It was followed in 1988 by another EP containing two tracks: 'Friends and Countrymen', a hymn to a multicultural society interpreted by Milo and 3D with a few background vocals, and 'Machine Gun (Down By Law)', rapped by 3D. The EP was entitled 'Friends and Countrymen'; the cover shows four of the band members in Bristol (Milo, Nellee, Mushroom and 3D). It introduced the Wild Bunch more widely in England. Neneh Cherry, who had been following the collective for a couple of years by then, through Mark Stewart and Bruce Smith, became interested in working with them. At 24 years old, Neneh was preparing a first album, *Raw Like Sushi*, with her producer, Cameron McVey. And she was looking for collaborators.

Back in Bristol, the Wild Bunch also worked with Smith & Mighty,

65   In an interview with a French weekly magazine, while exhibiting in Paris, in March 2015

who had launched their own label, Three Stripe Records, in 1988, based in Ashley Road, in St Pauls. "We also recorded some demos in London," explains Ray Mighty, "but we didn't really enjoy working outside Bristol. In London, everything has to be done too fast, production is expensive, we chose to remain home where the atmosphere was much more amicable, whether with Grant and the Wild Bunch or others DJs, we always helped each other[66]."

On January 30, 1988, Smith & Mighty and the Wild Bunch participated to the Anti-Apartheid Party, at the Brunel Shed in Temple Meads train station, with 2 Bad and Def Con. The concert was in support of South African militants condemning the situation in their country.

In 1988, the Wild Bunch seemed completely resuscitated when Nellee finally decided to settle in London. He soon joined Jazzie B and Soul II Soul, who had signed to Virgin Records. They were working on their first album, *Club Classics Vol. One*, due out in April 1989. The band received immediate acclaim and were nominated at the Brit Awards. Their producer, Nellee Hooper, reached the success he had been dreaming about for years. His newfound fame attracted many projects, which led him to work with the outstanding Icelandic singer Björk. Madonna, Janet Jackson, Sinéad O'Connor, Sade and the Smashing Pumpkins soon followed.

Meanwhile, Miles Johnson chose to pursue his own dream and moved to Japan, where he got married and worked as a DJ, between Tokyo and New York. He felt that it was not possible to succeed in producing hip-hop in Great Britain. The fame of the Wild Bunch followed him. In Japan, the collective is until now regarded as a unique part of music history. Disappearing in a swift swirl of change in 1988, the heritage of the Bristol collective has remained legendary. And their musical explorations led to new revolutions.

Multiple Attacks

From 1988, encouraged to open his own path in music by all these events and by friends including Neneh Cherry, 3D worked on new demos with

---

66   In an interview with the author in August 2015, between Paris and Bristol

Mushroom. That was how in 1988, without any official statement, 3D and Mushroom definitely separated from Miles and Nellee. Helped by Neneh and her husband Cameron McVey, they formed their own new collective: Massive Attack. The name was inspired by a mural painted by Brim from the TATS CRU on the wall of the Malcolm X Centre in Bristol in the mid 1980s.

Meanwhile, Smith & Mighty produced 'Any Love', created by Daddy G and featuring a young singer known as Carlton. They used a new label named Massive Attack Records. The track was a cover of the song by Rufus & Chaka Khan (a funk American band formed in Chicago in 1973). The EP was distributed by Overdue Music, via the Cartel, a platform created in the 1980s to gather small labels. The Cartel distributed records of many new wave bands, from Joy Division to the Cocteau Twins, including Depeche Mode, Pigbag and the Smiths.

Grant chose to work with Carlton McCarthy, aka Carlton, a fellow Bristolian from a West Indian background, who sang and didn't rap. One of the versions recorded for the EP featured a rap performed by Daddy G, mentioning "the Wild Bunch Crew" and "Massive Attack". This version of the song slowed down the original rhythm, to make the whole song feel "rawer".

Milo has to get the credit for that, according to 3D, the whole style of classic covers over stripped back beats and production. It was his idea and it changed everything for everybody, Massive, Smith & Mighty, Fresh Four, Bomb the Bass and Portishead. It became its own genre. 'The Look of Love' and 'Any Love' were the first recorded examples of Bristol's slow tempo.

Around the same time, D was also writing with Adrian Thaws, aka Tricky, the youngest MC in his group of friends. Born in Knowle West on January 27, 1968, at 20 years old, Tricky was already well known in the underground scene, all over town, and was living with different friends, including at some point with Mark Stewart. Music literally saved Tricky from a very tough childhood, his father having left his mum soon after his birth, and his mother committed suicide a few years later.

"Knowle West, for me, it's Bristol," Tricky tells me years later when

I meet with him at the Bataclan in Paris[67]. "It's where I come from and it means a lot to me, even if I know it's not a place where people go out when in Bristol. People saw me grow up there and it's where I go when I come back to Bristol. I go there for a drink, to see my people and my family. It's my home". His father is Jamaican, and his mother, Maxine Quaye, mixed-raced but Adrian was raised by his English grandmother, in what he describes as a "white ghetto". His mother could have been linked to the family of jazzmen from Ghana related to Scottish musician Finley Quaye, according to the latter. Suffering from epilepsy and asthma, Adrian joined gangs at an early age and started dealing soft drugs from the age of 12. But compared to some of his neighbours and relatives, he was lucky to never get too involved in heavy trafficking. Most of his uncles regularly ended up in prison throughout his adolescence.

"I grew up in a very mixed family," he continues, "so I never knew racism. At our table sat my blonde half-sisters and Black, Jamaicans, Asian cousins, etc. I don't see these colours[68]." He became passionate about music at a very young age, loving both reggae and punk, and adoring one band particularly, the Specials, formed in Coventry in 1977, who embody to his eyes a perfect mix of Jamaican and English musicians.

Tricky met with Willy Wee around 1985 and got introduced to the Wild Bunch. "It was a great time for us all," he insists, "we didn't care about money back then, only about making the best music possible. We didn't think about incomes or bills. I lived on my cousins' sofa for a while, then I had a flat for a few months and later slept in friends' living room or in a squat. It was total freedom and my life revolved around music[69]."

From 1988, Tricky became really close to 3D. They shared the same passion for hip-hop and were both rappers. They spent their early evenings writing lyrics, before going out. In a few different record companies, the Artists and Repertoire (A&R), division of a record label

---

67   In an interview with the author in France in February 2015
68   Ibid
69   Ibid

responsible for talent scouting, were curious about hearing more from Massive Attack. And a new phase began.

Turntables and samplers

From 1988, Bristol started to overcome the years of mix tapes, when DJs were putting into recording the sounds they used to play on the decks, mastering the art of sampling. Re-recording and selecting sounds and extracts of music became a means of creating the DJ's own music, after year of formative constitution of playlists.

Sampling revolutionised experimental music from the 1970s and was, a few years later, popularised by hip-hop music. In 1988, in New York, hip-hop band Public Enemy, formed in 1982, used a huge amount of samples on their second album, *It Takes a Nation of Millions to Hold Us Back*, and this new way of constructing music massively influenced the former members of the Wild Bunch.

Newly formed at the beginning of that year, Massive Attack were meeting regularly in St Pauls, around Daddy G's new flat, on Campbell Street. Robert Del Naja still lived in Hotwells but spent most of his time at the Montpelier Hotel, painting, and travelling to London, especially to Soho and Ladbroke Grove, to look for records, go to the clubs and explore the underground scene.

The name Massive Attack shows a form of continuation from the spirit of the Wild Bunch, but their goal was henceforth clearly to exist on records, not just to play sound system parties or organised DJ sets. By then, the underground scene of house parties was deeply affected by police control in Bristol.

The band's first years were also very influenced by the technology available to them. Not working from a basis of instruments, they produced their music via tape recorders, mixing tables and samplers, especially the Casio FZ1, which came into the UK from Japan around 1987. Samplers became a kind of magic wand for DJs to produce a different form of music, putting their ideas and rich tastes into new sounds and musical creations. The sampling technique soon fascinated 3D, Mushroom and Grant.

The group, for instance, didn't have many microphones; they had to use only one for almost every voice recording, or to record vocals on a tape machine while the sampler was used to mix music. Massive Attack's music came firstly from a playlist of tracks, built up in progress, during an alchemical research in an ocean of sounds coming from their mental library, consolidated in a decade of underground practice in parties and clubs. A recipe for success.

Neneh Cherry, the godmother

Neneh Cherry and Cameron McVey were soon enabling Massive Attack's early steps, while working on Neneh's own first album, *Raw Like Sushi*, produced by Cameron with Jonny Dollar (real name Jonathan Peter Sharp). Neneh was herself influenced by her own diverse experiences with bands going from her jazzman stepfather, Don Cherry, to the punkish Slits, whom she toured with for a couple of years. To add a hip-hop feel to some of the track of her first album, she wanted to work with 3D and Mushroom on a few compositions. Nellee Hooper is also credited on the album, on the vibraphone.

Mushroom did a bit of programming for the album and performed some scratching on a few of her songs: 'Buffalo Stance', 'Kisses on the Wind', 'The Next Generation' and 'So Here I Come'. He even appeared in the promo video for 'Buffalo Stance', spinning vinyl behind his deck. 3D wrote the middle rap section of 'Manchild': *"Just turn around and ask yourself is this communication / Accentuate the positive and give some illustration / See Manchild, you're no one, you turn the microphone on'*, he penned, ending the rap with the famous phrase: *"I believe in miracles and words in heavy doses"*...

Neneh's single 'Buffalo Stance' was released in November 1988 and reached number three the UK Singles Chart. Soon after, 'Manchild' reached number five. The album came out in May 1989 on Virgin Records and entered the UK Albums Chart at number two in June. 3D and Mushroom also produced a remix of 'Manchild', featured on one of Neneh's EPs, credited as Massive Attack.

In a few months, Neneh Cherry became one of the major voices in the British hip-hop scene and enjoyed a wide success. She stood out among the lot of young female pop stars, with a deeply personal style and a singular, incredible voice. She was nominated at the Brit Awards in the UK and at the Grammy Awards in the USA in 1990. Her album was certified gold in Canada, Switzerland and the Netherlands. Soon after, she launched the production of her next album, *Homebrew*, to be released in 1992.

Around the same time, the members of Massive Attack started recording in Peter Gabriel's Real World studios, near Bath. They met Billy Cobham, did a lot of remixes there, notably of his own 'Games Without Frontiers', with Peter re-recording vocals and piano, and a remix of Nusrat Fateh Ali Khan's song 'Mustt Mustt', maybe the most important and influential mix of its era in crossover.

The Pakistani musician and singer Nusrat Fateh Ali Khan (1948-1997) released the album also named *Mustt Mustt* in 1990, the first fusion collaboration between the Qawwali singer and guitarist and producer Michael Brook, on Gabriel's Real World Records label. The late American singer-songwriter Jeff Buckley in 1993 described Nusrat Fateh Ali Khan as "my Elvis". Massive Attack's remix became a club hit in the United Kingdom, being the first song in Urdu to reach British Charts.

After their collaboration, Neneh knew that Massive Attack only needed a bit of discipline in order to produce their own first album. Her producer and soon-to-be husband, Cameron McVey, known as Booga Bear, listened carefully to the band's first demos and encouraged them to cultivate their heritage from Bristol. The three DJs also regularly worked with him in his house in London, in Kensal Rise, mostly in order to find some encouragement. "We were lazy Bristol twats," Grant Marshall later said[70]. "It was Neneh Cherry who kicked our arses and got us in the studio. We recorded a lot at her house, in her baby's room. It stank for months and eventually we found a dirty nappy behind a radiator. I was still DJing, but what we were trying to do was create dance music for the head, rather than the feet." Meanwhile, as Grant's track with Carlton, 'Any Love', had an underground impact in England, a few Bristol bands were getting attention from Londoners, notably via Smith & Mighty and their Three Stripe label.

70   To the *Observer* in June 20, 2004

Cameron knew the importance of keeping them in Bristol, felt Robert Del Naja. With the success of Smith & Mighty, it showed something. He set them up with the Coach House studio, then Neneh and Cameron relocated to a house just outside Bristol to manage it all, to get them to actually finish a record.

This was how Massive Attack's first album, *Blue Lines*, started to take shape. Some of its first notes came about in Neneh Cherry's child's bedroom... Like the song 'Hymn of the Big Wheel'. "I always loved the guys from Massive Attack," Neneh said years later, "but I didn't help them with their contract. I only provided them with cereals and Red Stripe![71]" The rest of the album was born in Bristol, in Andy Allen's Coach House Studio, on Richmond Hill Avenue, in Clifton. Cameron also involved Jonny Dollar on the production of the album.

But the process remained very spontaneous, sometimes even disorganised. They were sleeping on friends' floor and hating each other and walking out and disappearing for weeks and then coming back, the band members remember. It was lots of stress for them, was never easy. Jonny Dollar and Cameron and Neneh had to force them to concentrate and focus; their attention was otherwise often being lost. Because all three adored the young band's sound and noticed its newness.

Jonny Dollar progressively had a major role in the completion of the album, helping the band members overcome tensions notably. And with *Blue Lines*, a new way to make music was about to appear that would change popular music for the next decade, in Britain and beyond.

71   In a documentary produced by BBC Radio 6 Music, in 2004

Chapter 6
The Birth Of A New Form Of Band (1989-91)

"Suddenly, Massive Attack are happening," wrote Miranda Sawyer in Q magazine in March 1991. "That 'all-important' critical acclaim! Even seminal world rockers U2 want to meet them!"... From the caves of Bristol's underground and forbidden parties, the non-musicians emerged worldwide in only a few months...

From 1989, the work that Massive Attack's three core members started took a more definite shape, and it became clear for Cameron McVey and Jonny Dollar that an album was on its way, and not an ordinary album. Produced without a definite plan in mind, their art, which involves "copying and pasting" from an extraordinary playlist of references, seemed to work magically, just like 3D's art of collage at the time.

Meanwhile in Bristol, the street art movement was on the back burner because of increasing police surveillance. In March 1989, 72 young graffiti writers were arrested in Operation Anderson, after policemen found a contact book belonging to an artist with all his friends' phone numbers. Some of those arrested stopped writing graffiti; others carried on spraying, going further underground and found themselves in open conflict with the authorities. Others started spraying outside Bristol. London became a good place to hide and try new things.

3D found himself more deeply involved in music. His art remained at the core of the visual aspect of the collective, but for now, Massive Attack's priority was to produce their very own sound, beyond the DJ approach, a sound that could call itself a proper different and unique genre.

Very early on, Massive Attack sensed that the different approach they were looking for would be found in the vocal parts of the recordings.

One point seemed certain from the start, the band wouldn't have a lead singer. Collaborations were at the core of what they were creating, as DJs and as rappers, and they were looking for guest vocalists to complete their diverse identity in sound.

Find your own voice

Searching for a soul voice to add some softness to their mainly male influences, the idea of working with a female vocalist seemed obvious. The band wrote more songs with Shara Nelson, whose warm and powerful voice suited the slow tempo of their first compositions and brought a touch of melancholy, some contrast with the use of a beat box.

In 1990, Shara worked with Massive Attack while they were composing a track to be temporarily named 'Just a Matter of Time', a very slow and mellow hip-hop oriented track, featuring a few rapping vocals from 3D. They added a humming sound performed by Shara. The song finally wasn't included on *Blue Lines*, or on any other record, but it was used in a first promo video, produced independently and directed by Roger Pomphrey. Born in Bristol in 1954, guitarist for Eurythmics around 1980/82, Roger started working in films and music videos a few years later. For Massive Attack, he created a film in black and white shot in Bristol, mostly outdoors, taking viewers into the feel of the city, from the docks to the zoo, as well as into the band's mental universe, in a film full of humour.

The film starts with a close shot of an envelope dropping through a letterbox. Mushroom picks up the mail, which appears to be an invitation to a party. Inside the envelope is a card bearing the word "Massive" surmounted by a flame logo. He brings the card into an old-fashioned sitting room and hands it to an elderly woman whose head is shaking with spasms as she sits in an armchair… She doesn't seem to be able to understand the message.

Fade to black: a cupboard door gets open by the toweringly high Daddy G, picking a blouson and looking, with hesitation, for the perfect headgear for the day. Hat? Cap with his stage name on? Beanie hat? Yes, beanie with a 'G' it will be. Meanwhile, the screen is progressively showing shots from the football stadium, where a worker is repainting the field's white lines... Before he leaves his house, Daddy G picks up the phone to ring a friend who he calls 'Jack' (we'll soon discover the members of the crew all call each other 'Jack', including Shara), looking to find their mate Tricky, unsuccessfully.

The next scene is set in the stadium. A caretaker, cleaning the terraces, wakes up a crumpled, sleeping body; and 3D emerges from under a hat, holding a football programme. He avidly asks: "What's the score?" Only to be answered: "City beat 2-0 but the match finished two days ago"... And the film moves on indoors to Shara Nelson, singing in her bathroom, writing down some music notes on a sheet that she ends up drowning with her tap's water. Meanwhile, outdoors, 3D joins Mushroom, playing with an electric car, in front of his house, asking him if... he has seen Tricky. D then proposes going to the zoo – which leads to interesting close shots of the animals. But Mushroom, for some irrational reasons, seems to think that they don't have enough time. So they just go for a walk. The other side of town, Daddy G walks to the Montpelier Hotel. While wandering with 3D, Mushroom suddenly decides he wants to have a haircut... "Bristol is a city where we are easily distracted", the band members later regularly explained to the press. Here is it illustrated!

Meanwhile, Shara is heading to her kitchen, when the phone rings: Daddy G is calling, looking for... Tricky. For Mushroom, a large part of the afternoon is spent at the hairdresser with 3D, while Shara is getting ready to go out. All of them are reunited later around a friend's dinner table. Shara Nelson deeply sighs when 3D asks her... if she's seen Tricky. "No!" she replies, slightly annoyed. The film is often mentioned under the name "Where is Tricky?" in Bristol. The crowd starts drinking and chatting, while a tarantula is wandering around the candlesticks. And when the host proposes a toast, someone suddenly knocks on the door... It's easy to guess who is arriving late.

The generally relaxed atmosphere of the film is revealing of the daily life that the musicians led in Bristol, sending flyers, perfecting their look, wandering, watching football, composing music, also featuring visual representations of different parts of the city, from Montpelier to the Harbourside, and the... zoo. Bristol's underground universe is completely summarised in the film, showing the diversity of the group of friends, from different ages and backgrounds.

The video also reveals traits from the main characters' personalities: the elusive, solitary and incontrollable Tricky hardly gets to meet the cool and charismatic Daddy G; Mushroom is mostly silent, looking away in most circumstances; while 3D is voluble and fickle, most of the time hiding his feelings behind a forced serious gaze, then suddenly bubbly and jokingly warm. Surrounded at the dinner table by Shara, Grant, Willy Wee and Mushroom, he is the one standing out from the crowd, with his light eyes and skin tone, his angelic face most often artificially hardened by an unwillingness to smile.

Massive Attack paid a beautiful homage to Roger Pomphrey, after the announcement of his passing, early in 2014: "A lovely man and a brilliant filmmaker. He inspired us to treat each video opportunity as a movie making experience and paved the way for collaborations with other great directors[72]."

Musically, 'Just A Matter Of Time' – which will never be released – already sounds very different from the few Wild Bunch recordings produced in 1987 and 88: its style is definitely hip-hop but the rhythm is much slower, framed around a soft beatbox and a sweet looping melody, accompanied by Shara's humming voice for the first two thirds and ending in a slow rap performed by 3D. Some of its lyrics later reappeared partly in the track named 'Eurochild', on Massive Attack's second album.

Shara continued to work with the band for another year, composing a few melodies and writing lyrics. She is featured on their first album on 'Daydreaming', along with 3D and Tricky, 'Safe From Harm' and 'Unfinished Sympathy'.

'Daydreaming' was the first track finished for the album, followed by 'Safe From Harm'. The latter was originally developed by the three core band members, quite early on, based on a sample of the song 'Stratus', written by the Panamanian American jazzman and drummer Billy Cobham, for his album *Spectrum*, from 1973. The sample, suggested

---

72 In a text posted on the band's Facebook page notably

by Mushroom, is used as a rhythmic basis. A genius idea that brings a unique feel to the song. Other samples in 'Safe From Harm' include a percussions part from 'Good Old Music' by the band Funkadelic, elements from 'Chameleon' by Herbie Hancock, and a sentence from the lyrics of 'Looking Back' by American soul funk singer Johnny 'Guitar' Watson, written in 1961. The song's originality is taken to a higher level with the mix of rap and soul vocals. 'Unfinished Sympathy' took shape a few months later in 1990.

Massive Attack also had from the start its own voice in its main rapper and lyricist, 3D. In an article entitled "The Bristol Bunch", published in February 1991 in *The Face* magazine, John McCready underlined that what makes this music sound very different is "the polite West Country tones of 3D". D commented in the same article: "In a way I was just fired by the originality of the old-school rappers (…). The accent comes easy. I have to check myself sometimes before it gets too Bristolian and we end up sounding like the Wurzels." And the journalist concluded: "Hip hop heroes or Bristol's answer to Pink Floyd? Either way, Massive Attack are the sound of 1991."

Lyrically, 3D's plays on words fitted his reflexive social awareness. He mixed references to his Sony headphones and Studio One with mentions of his passions – from football to graffiti, quoting the Beatles, telling about the band's daily routines, as well as the urban environment they grew up in and the worries linked to the Thatcher government. Meanwhile, on top of hip-hop, the band were incorporating another major influence: reggae music.

Kingston Calling: Jamaican-Bristolian blending
Another featured voice on Massive Attack's first album came from Bristol too. Tricky was then collaborating with Nellee Hooper, Smith & Mighty, Mark Stewart and with 3D. He liked to follow his own path, though, never really joining any band completely, feeling different from the former members of the Wild Bunch, claiming his origins from Knowle West as a mark of identity. He often declared that "even Grant

would never come to Knowle West[73]." Tricky's incomparable voice owes a lot to his strong, popular and colloquial Bristolian accent, with a pinch of Jamaican tone.

Tricky wrote with D the raps featured in 'Daydreaming', using his talent in "storytelling" rap: *"Attitude is cool degrees below zero / Up against the wall behaving like De Niro / Tricky's performing taking his phono"*. He also mentions the social context a while later: *"Yes Tricky kid I check my situation / Maggie this Maggie that Maggie means inflation"*. And adds details on daily violence: *"Wise guys get protection when they carry a knife / They shouldn't have been born they're making me yawn"*, while 3D brings a more hopeful note: *"We're natives of the massive territory and we're proud / Get peaceful in the dance, no death or glory and the crowd / The problem ain't a different kind of skin, Tricks / I love my neighbour I don't wait for the Olympics"*.

Tricky and 3D also worked on lyrics for the songs 'Blue Lines' and 'Five Man Army', on which they're joined by Daddy G, Willy Wee and Horace Andy. The reggae singer, born Horace Hinds, in Kingston, Jamaica, on February 19, 1951, is the third main guest vocalist on the album. Grant considers Horace as a legend and knows by heart his first album, *Skylarking*, released in 1972, after a first confidential single in 1967, 'This is a Black Man's Country', recorded at the young age of 16.

Horace joined in 1970 the mythical Studio One, founded in 1962 by Clement Seymour Dodd, aka Coxsone, and nicknamed "the Jamaican Motown". Horace came to define the label's sound, alongside Bob Marley. In 1985, Horace started living between Jamaica and Ladbroke Grove, in London, where he got to meet Cameron McVey. His collaboration with Massive Attack brought to the band the reggae feel that they were looking for.

Massive Attack sent to Horace the basic demo of a song called 'One Love'. The elaboration of the final version of the track was key to the making of the album. The basics came from three main samples. One is from 'You Know, You Know' by the Mahavishnu Orchestra, a jazz-rock fusion band formed in New York City in 1971 by the British guitarist

---

73   In an interview with the author in Paris, in February 2015

John McLaughlin with Panamanian-American drummer Billy Cobham, Irish bassist Rick Laird, Czechoslovakian keyboardist Jan Hammer, and American violinist Jerry Goodman, later joined by Ralphe Armstrong on bass guitar. And two other short samples came from 'Ike's Mood I' by Isaac Hayes (from his ...*To Be Continued* album, released in 1970). Massive Attack added a slow beatbox effect and scratching sounds, but with the intention of keeping it simple.

Horace recorded the vocals partly in Kingston and Massive Attack mixed the track in Bristol. It sounded like a reggae song without a baseline, underlined Robert Del Naja, which is the opposite of what you normally associate reggae with. Therefore, 'One Love', more than a reinterpretation by the band of a reggae theme, became a 1990 Bristol song with a reggae inspiration.

In total, the band worked on *Blue Lines* for about eight months, with a break at the end of the year 1990 and the first of many career splits, this time taking the shape of a virtual *coup d'état* when Mushroom announced that he wanted Peter D. Rose, close to Rob Smith and Ray Mighty, to co-create the album with him. D and G left the studio in dismay. Luckily, they all later found a common ground and continued working on the album.

And these *Blue Lines* took shape

Spending more time in London with Cameron McVey, in 1990, Massive Attack received the interest of Circa Records when the label heard 'Daydreaming'. Its unusual tone, slow tempo and Bristol feel, with the two rapping voices and the soul singer, quickly convinced Circa of the band's novelty. A contract was signed to produce six albums and a compilation.

'Daydreaming' became Massive Attack's first single. It was released on October 15, 1990 – and entered the top 100 in the UK Singles Chart at number 81. The song includes a sample of the track 'Mambo' by French musician Wally Badarou, from his album *Echoes*, released in 1984. The Wild Bunch used to play the record regularly at their parties.

'Unfinished Sympathy' is one of the most emblematic songs on the *Blue Lines* album. Written throughout 1990, it became the second single, released on February 11, 1991. It was composed in different stages. Two samples are recognisable, one short percussive part taken from 'Parade Strut' (by the American jazzman J. J. Johnson), and a vocal extract from 'Planetary Citizen' by the Mahavishnu Orchestra, as the background vocals singing "hey hey hey hey". But this one was not credited as such on *Blue Lines*, and four years later, Ralphe Armstrong recognised it when he heard 'Unfinished Sympathy' in a commercial on television and complained. Massive Attack and Virgin Records, which bought Circa in 1992, faced a lawsuit. The disagreement lasted years and Armstrong finally got a settlement that brought him more than his song's original rights and more than all his collaborations with the Mahavishnu Orchestra... But the Massive Attack song has very little to do with the proper samples.

The vocals performed by Shara Nelson derived from a song she was writing in Bristol, at the Coach House Studio, while she was working with the band, a song named 'Kiss and Tell'. She wasn't sure what to do with it when Jonny Dollar heard her and encouraged her to develop it. "We were working on a track called 'It Will Rain', and bits of this other melody came into my mind," explained Shara Nelson in an interview[74]. "I couldn't shake it, so I took a break from recording, had a cup of tea, and stood in the corner and started singing it to myself to see if I could piece it together."

What she developed caught the interest of the rest of the band. Shara added the lyrics, including these beautiful, iconic words: *"You're the book that I have opened / And now I've got to know much more (...) Like a soul without a mind / In a body without a heart / I'm missing every part"*.

The song was however soon taken in another direction. It was an exercise in deconstruction, according to 3D. The song came with a traditional verse-chorus sequence, and D and Mush didn't like the pop nature of the chorus so D suggested removing it. This left a big void and they decided to fill the dead space with strings: That's how the song changed from a conventional pop song into something symphonic. Jonny Dollar contacted Wil Malone who scored it for an orchestra. The

74   In *Spin Magazine*, in June 1996

resulting beauty of the track is in Mushroom's break beat and scratch coexisting with the arrangement of the strings. It exaggerates Shara's vocal performance and gives to the simplicity of the words a classic feel.

The strings section was recorded at the Abbey Road studios, in London, and the song arranged at the Coach House Studio with all the band members, to adjust the mix between the symphonic parts, Shara's vocals and Mushroom's scratching. They had a philosophy about taking things out, according to them. They would write more than they wanted and remove parts, leaving the bare bones; that was the way they wanted to hear the music.

The title 'Unfinished Sympathy' was inspired by Austrian classical composer Franz Schubert's *Unfinished Symphony*, known as *Die Unvollendete* in German, originally his *Symphony Number 8*. Chosen firstly as a temporary fitting title, it eventually stuck.

Shara's voice depicts a lost love, but soon the song, with its powerful melancholic feel, talks to listeners about the stressful era, of a dramatic urban anxiety, that music enthusiasts and critics found as surprisingly intensely emotional, classy and unheard. The mix between the electronic music and the orchestral arrangements comes as a wake-up call. Critics also describe Shara's voice as unusual itself. Powerful and slightly broken, its sincerity is outstanding when Shara repeats *"Really hurt me baby, really cut me baby / How can you have a day without a night"*...

As *Blue Lines'* second single, 'Unfinished Sympathy' entered the top 20 of the UK Singles Chart, peaking at number 13, in mid-February 1991, and remained among the best sellers for nine weeks. It became a success in the rest of Europe as well, becaming number one in the Netherlands, reaching the top 10 in Switzerland and the top 20 in Germany. In 1993, the song was chosen to appear on the soundtrack to the American film *Sliver*, with Sharon Stone and William Baldwin, branded as an "erotic thriller".

Judged as modern as well as classical by the music reviewers, the song seduced all parts of the audience in Britain and was named Single Of The Week by *NME* and *Record Mirror*, and Single Of The Year in December 1991 by *The Face* magazine and *Melody Maker*, which also wrote that *Blue Lines* "will unquestionably stand as one of the greatest soul records of all time". BBC Radio 2 stated that "while this may be electronic music, it has just as much soul as anything to have ever come out of Detroit". The television channel MTV2 in the UK later placed it number one in a poll of the best songs ever. *NME* described "Shara's vocal tour- de-force" as offering "a heart bloodied by emotional loss and confusion[75]". In homage, American singer Tina Turner covered the song, in 1996, on her album *Wildest Dreams...*

Six week after the song's incredible success, *Blue Lines* was released in the UK on April 8, 1991. It comprises nine songs, in that order: 'Safe from Harm', 'One Love', 'Blue Lines', 'Be Thankful For What You've Got' (a cover of the song written by American musician William DeVaughn in 1972, featuring Tony Bryan), 'Five Man Army', 'Unfinished Sympathy', 'Daydreaming', 'Lately' (featuring Shara Nelson, which samples an instrumental segment of 'Mellow Mellow Right On', written by American soul singer Lowrell Simon in 1979) and a closing ninth one, 'Hymn of the Big Wheel', composed by 3D at Neneh Cherry's house, featuring Horace Andy.

But in the meantime, in January 1991, the Gulf War started with operation Desert Storm, launched by an international coalition led by the United States. The USA decided to attack Saddam Hussein's Iraq in order to try to "save" Kuwait following its invasion by Iraq. By the end of February, 28 countries had joined the coalition, sending on the ground in Kuwait 650,000 troops, half of them American.

In Britain, the phrase "massive attack on Iraq" became a favourite slogan in tabloids. So Massive Attack's label, Circa, insisted that the band turn their name into a simple "Massive". The band members were disturbed by this decision but felt they had no means to refuse. The general public hardly noticed and *Blue Lines* peaked at number 13 in the UK Albums Chart. 'Safe From Harm' was released as a third single on May 27, 1991, and 'Hymn of the Big Wheel' as a fourth on February 10, 1992, with 'Be Thankful For What You've Got' on the B-side.

The work on this album took over a year, involving many disputes and short separations, but also many more years of inspiration and

---

75 . In its edition published in April 1991

writing down ideas, from the Wild Bunch era to early 1991.

"The reason why the temple had to shatter": Abstract to concrete lyrics

With long raps intertwined with soul vocals, quotes from key songs' lyrics, allusions to social issues, references to clubbing nights, drug use and partying, sometimes naïve, sometimes ironic, mainly sincere, Massive Attack's lyrics resemble their authors. While the larger part of the writing is based on musicality and rhymes, the allusion to their social environment are clear.

The context they referenced is easy to get for the British audience, detailed and precise, incarnated in the Bristol daily environment, unlike most hip-hop of the late 1980s, which had until then mainly copied American rap.

Some other lines in a few songs sometimes become surprisingly poetical: in 'Unfinished Sympathy', Shara Nelson longs for *"the curiousness of your potential kiss"*. Shara's and Horace's vocals bring mentions of loss and of dreams of universal love... As soul music and reggae do. 3D's lyrics are conceived for multiple voices, like a dialogue in a film, he explained. His words are voluntarily cryptic. He advises Tricky to avoid overly explicit declarations. One does rap to confide, but saying too much destroys mystery, says D. He also likes allusions to cultural landmarks. In 'Blue Lines', he mentions the "hip data" and "antimatter" and Tricky talks about his "Tardis", probably thinking of the British TV series *Doctor Who*, in which appears a time machine named *'Time And Relative Dimension In Space'*, or TARDIS.

Indeed, the song 'Blue Lines' brings the listeners into a journey. Tricky first starts with a sort of philosophy of positive attitude (*"Can't be with the one you love then love the one you're with"*) then later introduces himself: *"Even if I told you, you still would not know me / Tricky never does, Adrian mostly gets lonely / How we live in this existence, just being / English upbringing, background Caribbean"*. And 3D describes a path: *"Yeah while I'm doing this I know / The place I really wanna go"*, then *"We cut the broken thread from flexibility / Mi chiamo 3D, Si sono Anglese... Ain't no sunshine in my life 'cause the way I deal is hazy"*. 'Ain't No Sunshine' being the title of a very popular soul song, written by Bill Withers in 1971, then made world famous by the Jackson 5 and Nancy Sinatra, among others.

The rest of the song's lyrics bring us back to Bristol, early 1990s, when the voice of Daddy G briefly intervenes asking: *"Are you predator or do you fear me?"* and 3D adds: *"Some go softly softly round the habitat / Ratchet in the right hand / They got no one to stab it at / Take a walk Billy, don't be a hero / Effort's on minimal though almost touch zero"*... The lyrics picture ambiguously some gangsters in the background, but affirm the night owls' hedonism as an act of positivity, preaching brotherhood around turntables and studios. According to 3D, the title was inspired by a dream Mushroom had about these ubiquitous blue lines that you couldn't escape from.

'Five Man Army' present the DJs and MCs of the collective more deeply. Daddy G starts by describing his walk around London's Paddington station (where the trains from Bristol arrive). Meeting with a girl, he summarises his way of life: *"We're house parties hip hop and smoking drugs"*. Tricky continues with his introduction: *"People call me Tricky for particular reason / I've got you see and I've got to let you know / See we're rockin' in your area rock beneath your balcony / My baby just cares for me well that's funny"*. This time quoting Nina Simone. Both joke about their dreams: *"Plan to go to America when I get a visa card"*, raps Daddy G, then Tricky replies: *"But getting' a visa card nowadays isn't hard"*...

3D's part is a declaration of love to his passions: the *Subbuteo* game, Studio One, his Sony Budokan headphones, lyrics, jam, nom de plume, pseudonym, dubplate, dub selection, etc. With beautiful rhymes like *"waxing lyrical"*, followed by *"satirical"*, *"spherical"*, *"circle"*, and *"miracle"*. Then Willy Wee intervenes: *"So whether you're black white or half-caste in your complexion"*... and 3D continues: *"Yes pull out your phono plug and tuck you in your phony / It's started by Marconi resumed by Sony / A summary by wireless history and only / The massive attack and only explosione"*... Mixing English and Italian words. Horace Andy closes the march with his own lyrics from his song 'Money Is The Roots Of All Evil', repeating *"Money money money / Root of all evil"*, calling for *"eternal love"* instead, *"away with you gangsters / We don't like it / Eternal love eternal love"*. The whole lot constructs both a musical curriculum vitae and statement of intent.

Drugs are mentioned as a primary source to escape a decadent world, without perspective for the youth, needing means to react against it. While Tricky talks in 'Blue Lines' about the "*Spliff in the ashtray*" and the red stripe beer, the expression "blue lines" is known to refer to Valium and other kind of pills. In 'Daydreaming', 3D simply claims: "*No drugs or pharmaceuticals for the body ain't suitable / Stick with liquid me and trick we've drop / A paper which you use my tongue to lick with*".

What also drives 3D's writing is obviously polysemy and ambiguity, to make his words sound more complex and his ideas more beautiful. He often writes down pages of notes before reducing them to his final lyrics. When he raps "*Blue lines are the reason why the temple had to shatter*", he sounds almost prophetic, the temple potentially evoking a building for payers or an outdated institution, and we are not sure if his prediction is indicating dangers or a promise of positive change. The whole text is following a metaphor on the idea of collapse, from the "shatter" to the "explosione", also simply referring to the band's name and to the Wild Bunch' years. Same with his cryptic "*son of many reasons searching for the daughter / Seeking knowledge, not acknowledging the jetset*".

Tricky uses fewer words, repetitions, and quotes from other songs, by Nina Simone (in 'Five Army Man') and the Beatles. And he will keep and reuse some of his texts in his first album, *Maxinquaye*. Other quotes from songs come out in 3D's lyrics, in 'Daydreaming': "*So you come on light my fire*', from the Doors, and "*Here comes the sun, little darlin', here comes the sun, it's alright*", from the Beatles' 'Here Comes The Sun', featured on *Abbey Road*. The lyrics from *Blue Lines*, just like the musical samples, create a sort of paper chase in music history.

The raps also describe the band's social background. Daddy G in 'Five Army Man' mentions the anti-racist ethos of the Bristol scene ("*So whether you're black white or half-caste in your complexion*"). 3D regularly calls on to fraternity, like in 'Daydreaming': "*Massive attack we keep it strong just like a vitamin / Going for the positive wiping out the negative songs / 'Cause brother it's relative*". Just like he did for Neneh Cherry's 'Manchild', and unlike most of this era's American and British rap. The Rastafarian ideology imported with the reggae culture might be the main source of inspiration for his positivity, where drug-infused dreams come along with universal values of love, to overcome a violent urban environment the young rappers grew up in.

Beyond provocation and humour, these lyrics reflect a sense of responsibility in such a world, and call for resistance in a pacifist mode, never resigned but refusing violence. Tricky in 'Daydreaming' mentions *"Maggie this Maggie that"* while the Prime Minister has been in power from 1979 to 1990; let's just say all his life so far. 3D adds: *"We're natives of the massive territory and we're proud / Get peaceful in the dance (...) The problem ain't a different kind of skin, Tricks / I love my neighbour and I don't wait for the Olympics".* 3D, who is colour-blind, also often refers to colours (*"I feel the colours fill my room beneath the patter of the rain (...) They wash away my shadow and don't even leave a spark upon my soul/ They leave the rainbows in the dark"*) and to the fact that he doesn't see skin colours. He claims his Italian origins and praises his Jamaican friends' roots. This is the kind of "attack" the band offer.

On that matter, one of the most abstract texts of the album comes with 'Hymn of the Big Wheel', referring to the environmental state of the planet. "It does build a bigger picture than the rest of the tracks on *Blue Lines*," 3D explained after the album came out[76], "because the rest are kind of unfocused – they just drift around and round in their own way, which is what we're into, rather than paint an obvious picture or leave a message. We're as worried about things like pollution as everyone else, it's just we don't want to write about it so obviously. We ain't got no solutions to the problems, we're just the same as everyone else living it. We're just pointing things out to ourselves, rather than to everyone else. It's just a story about a man talking to his son, talking about the future or what's gonna happen, what's it all about? Just questions. We don't offer alternatives."

The art of video
When, in 'Safe from Harm', Shara Nelson evokes the *"Midnight rockers / City slickers / Gunmen and maniacs"*, which can *"feature on the freakshow"*,

---

76   In the *NME* magazine, June 1991 edition

her voice is guiding the audience into a very cinematic experience already, depicting a nightly urban atmosphere. It is one of 3D's favourite types of lyrics. Encouraging a visual imagination, it will also inspire the filmmakers working with the band on their music videos. Massive Attack's members, as from the time of the Wild Bunch, grew up with a lot of cinematic references: from Sam Peckinpah to Martin Scorsese, Francis Ford Coppola and science fiction. Just like with *Just a Matter of Time*, they intend to display their visual signature.

Blue Lines came out at a time when music videos were running the game for musicians. Pop superstars such as Madonna and Michael Jackson dominated television screens, with film produced thanks to indecently high budgets. The music channel MTV, created in 1984 in the USA, and launched in 1987 in Europe, was counterbalancing the power of mainstream radio stations. In March 1990, Madonna came back with 'Vogue' and a short film directed by David Fincher. In November 1991, Michael Jackson released 'Black Or White', filmed by John Landis, who already directed his unforgettable 'Thriller' in 1983.

These directors had impeccable careers in films and ask for millions of dollars for a few minutes of their talent. Whirled into the world of fashion or technological prodigy, these videos also involve mastered choreography. Meaning, it's hard to compete. Interestingly enough, Massive Attack's 'Daydreaming' arrived in between and also involved beautiful visual references in black and white. It did it in a much more local, genuine and incarnated way, though, in a striking video that was much more DIY.

With a much smaller budget, the film created for 'Daydreaming' managed to surprise everyone. It was directed by British filmmaker Baillie Walsh, just as the two following Massive Attack films. Their passion for films is well known in Bristol, from 3D's painting glorifying Robert De Niro to their references to *Blade Runner* by Ridley Scoot.

The band worked with Baillie Walsh to bring a special, personal feel to the 'Daydreaming' promo film. The result is a five-minute black and white video, presenting all the band members, including their guests Shara, Tricky and Willy Wee. We can see them wandering into a living room, surrounded outdoors by a tropical, mysterious environment. It opens with a shot of a lizard in a bush beneath the window of a house. Sitting in the frame, Shara is literally daydreaming, cooling herself with a fan. At the table, a fortuneteller is looking at the cards she has picked out of her deck for Daddy G: "The tiger", she starts, "a very good card! It will bring you good fortune, good luck, good health and strength"... "Massive", replies the deep male voice, as the music starts.

At the other end of the table, Tricky and 3D observe insects through a microscope, doodle drawings, then struggle to cross the room because of the heat, to get to the 1950s-style refrigerator looking for fresh water, while Mushroom is isolated, observing his own jars of scorpions. The signs of the heat are visible on the rappers' foreheads and in Shara's slowness. Under the table, two babies of different background are playing. The camera moves from a corner to another, between the psychic now reading the cards for Willy Wee and Shara chanting her lovely chorus.

The film is wittingly playing with an amazing contrast of lights and shadows, in a flow of paradoxes, between the stereotypes of "blackness" and "whiteness". While the male characters look serious and even intimidating, Shara's grace is filmed with slow movements, as she stares outside or above, singing *I'm floating on air... when I'm daydreaming*. We seem far away from the Bristol's rainy English weather but the atmosphere perfectly suits its underground, slow and smoke-infused scene, with an inch of Rastafarian touch.

The video for 'Unfinished Sympathy', shot in 1991 on West Pico Boulevard, would mark the audience even more. This neighbourhood of the Californian metropolis is known for being a rough area, where different populations mix, from African-American, Hispanic, Korean and Jewish backgrounds. This inspiring boulevard was already mentioned in Charles Bukowski's poem named 'Hot' and was filmed by James Cameron for a critical scene in his *Terminator*. For the 'Unfinished Sympathy' video, Baillie Walsh filmed Shara Nelson as she wanders on the boulevard, in a five-minute-long sequence shot. She's followed in the background by the figures of the three main band members. Under the overly bright warm Californian light, they all linger along the shops and infamous housing, crossing path with the local crowd. The result brings an aesthetic short film, slow and thoughtful like the song.

Baillie Walsh also directed a film in black and white for 'Safe From Harm', shot in London, with Shara Nelson, 3D, Daddy G and Mushroom. They find themselves in an unwelcoming estate. When Shara tries to enter the lift, she is blocked by 3D, who seems to be occupied in a trade business with Mushroom. Climbing up the stairs, Shara is followed by D, murmuring his rap: *"I was looking back to see if you were looking back at me to see me looking back at you"*. While Mushroom is hiding behind superficial sunglasses, unnecessary in this nocturnal atmosphere, a mysterious man seems to be waiting on the last floor. And the story matches the song's lyrics.

Critics noted the difference between these films and regular pop bands' promo videos. The *Guardian* and *Observer*'s writer, Sean O'Hagan, praised the 'Unfinished Sympathy' video as a "benchmark in modern video direction, more a breathtaking short film than a mere pop promo[77]". In 1997, English alternative rock band the Verve made a kind of homage to the Massive Attack / Baillie Walsh film in the video for their song 'Bitter Sweet Symphony'. Theirs, shot in London, was directed by Walter Stern, who a year later would work with Massive Attack for one of *Mezzanine*'s videos.

Later in 1992, Massive Attack released a fourth video for 'Be Thankful For What You've Got', still directed by Baillie Walsh. The song appeared on the B-side of their single 'Hymn of the Big Wheel'. In this film, none of the band members are featured. Instead, is filmed a strip club. In the opening scene, through a woman's headphones comes out a self-referencing detail, as the dancer listens to 'Safe From Harm', singing along out loud, before she reaches the changing rooms. The rest of the film consists of one of the girls' strip show. 3D confessed that it remains one of his favourite, provocative and superbly filmed, away from conservative and sexist pop videos.

The band members wanted to minimise the use of their public image and chose carefully the few pictures they sent to the press. Their style was perfected with the work of designer Judy Blame and photographer

77   In an article published in the *Observer* on October 28, 2012, when the album was reissued

Jean-Baptiste Mondino, whom Neneh Cherry introduced them to. Blame's design work and visionary styling opened Robert's eyes to a new way of seeing the world. He didn't need to style manage them. They kept their natural tastes, from hip-hop references to male military punk-related clothing.

Jean-Baptiste Mondino shot the pictures for the album's back cover. Daddy G appears in the foreground wearing jeans and a blue sweatshirt, with Mushroom to his right, slouched in a couch wearing dark sunglasses, and 3D to his left, looking severe and enveloped in a large black raincoat. Other photo shoots took them to Bristol's train station, Temple Meads, and near the Ashton Gate stadium, where their favourite football club, Bristol City, plays, documenting the links between the band and their city.

Visuals: an extra dimension

These creative collaborations brought a touch of glamour to the band's image, but their core visual identity came from 3D. The same way he expressed the Wild Bunch's ethos on their early flyers and through graffiti, he intended to develop an artistic dimension for Massive Attack. Remembering Judy Blame and Anthony and Stephanie from *Michael Nash Associates* agency, Robert said: "I went into their studio and they had all these cameras and scanners, it was very exciting! And considering that the London fashion media and art scene can be quite arsey, they were the opposite, they were really friendly and inclusive. Me and Mushroom used to go to their studio regularly and just talk absolute rubbish to them for days on end. Judy Blame had a very strong visual identity and he really helped me to develop themes, from the sketchbook to the final product. I became totally hooked on the process[78]".

Blue Lines' front cover comes from a logo warning of flammable gas. The red diamond with a black flame is printed on cardboard, on which 3D added the band's name. It is for him a symbol of the changing and elusive nature of the band's music, also adding irony due to the nature

---

78   In an interview with the *Creative Review*, published on September 30, 2013

of the album's gentle sound. This visual identity is a reflection of the "DIY" ethos of the band too: it is handmade, created by cut and paste, inspired by punk music.

3D's main inspirations at the time were pharmaceuticals references, patterns used by Jean-Michel Basquiat, crosses resembling the Red Cross logo. He mixed his use of stencils and spray cans with paint, collage and drawing, then discarded a lot of his paintings and artworks before choosing the right ones.

The sleeve also parallels the musical process by sampling the Northern Irish band Stiff Little Fingers and the cover of their album *Inflammable Material*, released in 1979, which showed nine little grey flames on a black background, taking a public safety logo and modifying it to represent the band.

The flame logo is used in variations. On the LP, it is black and the diamond shape is red. On the 'Daydreaming' single, Judy Blame drew a wider fire of orange flames over a dark blue / violet background.

For 'Unfinished Sympathy', they shot a picture of a Claude (Willy Wee) Williams' open hand, with a plaster on a finger, covered by the band's name and a couple of tiny flames, references to the Gulf War through the Red Cross symbol on an oil-strained bandaged hand. "One of my favourite icons was the 'medical hand' – I had used it on various paintings including a series of monkey characters," explained Robert[79]. "The hand stencil got me thinking about the cover of 'Unfinished'. When we were shooting the video in LA, it was the build-up to the first Gulf War. We had major issues with the attack on Iraq personally and the press had begun to go loopy. I wanted to create an image using the hand but covered in oil as if in surrender with a bandage on it, mimicking one of the medical hazard symbols. It somehow suited the song."

For 'Safe From Harm', the flame logo appears once in black on a white male plug, with a small white "danger" triangle-shaped logo, and once in reverse, a white flame under a black danger logo. The whole name of the band, "Massive Attack", had by then reappeared on the single and the album. And for the 'Hymn of the Big Wheel' EP, a red

79   Ibid

flame appears on a white background, surrounded by two worms.

After experiencing their temporary change of name, D also became wary of the music industry's cynicism and of the political dimension present in every artistic endeavour. This tiny decision in the band's history would however come to stand out as an obligation for them to look more deeply at the relations between the United Kingdom and the Middle East…

Between explosions and implosions

"Despite their refusal to don pop's glamour wigs, Massive Attack are aware that too much shunning of the limelight could lead them back to the dole queues," commented Miranda Sawyer in Q magazine in March 1991. "It's a dilemma, really," added 3D in the interview section. "1991 is the only time in our careers that we've had the backing of a company like Circa, who've got the media potential as well as being small enough to avoid all the big-wig red tape. But if we don't have hits, we can't work with Circa any more. It's trying to get a balance, so that we can do our thing and get paid for it."

But by then, in 1991, with the success of *Blue Lines* and its four singles, the band members were enjoying their glory, joining Nellee Hooper and his many famous friends in London for fancy parties. It was a first for a Bristol band. Yet the three members of Massive Attack remained living in Bristol and quite enjoyed their anonymity. Mushroom, especially, was not so fond of crowds and media attention, while Grant was comfortable in any situation.

Blue Lines also drew an unexpected attention to Bristol. The album provided the first, truly viable British response to the American hip-hop culture, some critics wrote. "Instead of taking the easy option, Massive Attack have tried — and it shows", insisted John McCready in *The Face*, in an article entitled 'Hip hop heroes or Bristol's answer to Pink Floyd? Either way, Massive Attack are the sound of 1991'. "Their first big-label release, 'Daydreaming', burned a large hole in my consciousness, so much so that it made 1990's other releases seem like the work of artless amateurs," he added. "Massive Attack have a lot to say". Other compliments flew. "Massive Attack's debut LP, *Blue Lines*, is already a

British cult classic and the outstanding track 'Unfinished Sympathy' is destined to go down as one of the great songs of the decade (no less)," stated Jim Shelly, describing the band as "the ideal group".

"Bristol. Home of tit jokes," wrote the *NME* magazine in April 1991. "Back before Bristol was anything other than the place from which Johnny Morris presented *Animal Magic*, there was a posse called the Wild Bunch. They were into hip-hop, reggae, graffiti and all the paraphernalia that used to go with those musics like dancing on bits of your body that weren't designed for dancing on, such as your bollocks."

As soon as 'Daydreaming' came out, *i-D* magazine promised that "Massive Attack are among the rare ones who have the potential to become the heroes of the black music of the 90s". In *Mixmag*, Dom Philips later placed the album at the top of his list of the best *dance* albums of all time, writing: "*Blue Lines* wasn't a soul album. It wasn't a hip-hop album. It wasn't dub or trip hop or anything else, it was all of these and so much more and it melted its way across the musical consciousness of this nation like nothing before."

In 1997, *Blue Lines* was listed at number 21 in the "Music of the Millenium" poll for best albums of all times, organised by the *Guardian*, HMV stores, Classic FM, and Channel 4. In 2000, it was number nine on the list of the "100 best British albums" by *Q* magazine's readers. And in 2003, it appeared on *Rolling Stone* magazine's list of the "500 Best Albums of All Time", largely dominated by rock albums. The record also conquered the rest of Europe. And in 2012, when it was remastered and reissued, the musical press talked of a "masterpiece" and described its music as "both anxious and hedonistic, dancing and meditative, sensual and icy". Most writers saw, right away from 1991, that the sound of the album was the sound of the future. "This is a thinker's album," 3D explained to *The Face*. "You can rock to it, you can nod your head to it, and that's enough to stimulate the body."

But by mid-1991, once their success got more real, the band members were already questioning their own unity. They were aware of the clashes between their personalities. The album was made very spontaneously and they didn't have a plan for what would follow.

The band members had invested in a special new van in Bristol that was stolen and deliberately crashed into the window of an estate agency on Picton Street, in Montpelier... A sort of warning sign about the 90s bling. "It was a Shogun," said 3D to the *NME* in April 1991. "You know what happens when you get a record deal. You get carried away." And Daddy G confirmed: "You forget about your budget and do a Bros."

Massive Attack also had to evolve from their sound system expression to a more organic, stage-oriented expression in order to perform live a very awaited album. The band organised their first shows for the summer 1991, with a sound system on stage, and were invited on television. To interpret 'Safe From Harm', 3D and Shara Nelson were at ease, alternating vocals and rap. But for 'Unfinished Sympathy', the band would rather see Shara perform on her own, especially when the band were scheduled on the super popular show, *Top of the Pops*.

Their success reached Japan and the USA. But once in America, the sound system installation left the audience quite cold. The guys experienced even more serious tensions with the pressure of a tour. Dealing with a heavy year of promotion, the stress of responsibilities was adding to their burden. From 1992, Cameron McVey and Neneh Cherry were also busy working on her second album, leaving Massive Attack without a proper manager and no producer.

Meanwhile, in Bristol, lots of other bands wanted to follow *Blue Lines*' path. While Tricky already started working on his own, Shara Nelson thought of solo projects too. She came back in 1993 with a single, 'Down The Road', a hit in the chart, and a following album, *What Science Knows*. If local musicians voiced their fear for the band's future, *The Face* wrote that *Blue Lines* showed "Massive Attack needs nobody". They were expected to reproduce their feat with a second album. While imitators were trying to get in their way, ideas and new projects started to bloom in Massive Attack's mind... Their story was indeed only beginning.

Chapter 7
Times Of Reinventions (1991-97)

"Let's invent a group. Let's invent the ideal group," wrote the music critic Jim Shelley, in 1991, when *Blue Lines* came out. "Imagine that the Clash had stayed around to be influenced by 3rd Bass, the Young Disciples and Marshall Jefferson. Or Soul II Soul had been inspired as much by Public Image Limited's 'Metal Box' as Public Enemy. Or by the soundtrack to *Taxi Driver* as much as Pink Floyd's 'Wish You Were Here'. Imagine that De La Soul had been English punks, brought up on X-Ray Spex, the Specials, and Lee Perry. What if there was a band at the centre of a triangle whose cornerstones were Issac Hayes, the Slits and Marley Marl? Result in all cases: Massive Attack," Shelley concluded.

Blue Lines came as a perfect illustration of how Bristol runs at a different speed. Many artists from the city describe its slowness as one of the influences on their creativity. Bristol musicians are not concerned with commercial success only, and productivity is not a key value.

"It's like a town masquerading as a city," said Robert Del Naja, "and what it's always been good at is the underground scene, in both art and music. Bands would flourish locally before they reached a national level and because there was never a big media or music industry here, people were doing it for their own gratification. Creativity here never grew in a contrived way, people were just teaching themselves and beating off the competition to become a big fish in a small pond[80]."

In 1991, under the appearances of calm, a boiling artistic scene was about to burst. While Bristol plunged into this sea of creativity, Massive Attack had to face their own tensions and their first world tour.

While their producer Cameron McVey was busy working on other

---

80   In an interview with the *Daily Telegraph*, published on March 28, 2008

projects, Massive Attack had to get ready for their first tour dates, in England, in the summer of 1991. They still thought of themselves as a sound system and with turntables. Mushroom and Daddy G launched the tracks from DJ decks on vinyl, joined by 3D, Tricky, Tony Bryan and Horace Andy on vocals. When not performing, 3D and Tricky hung around with cans of beer or simply left the stage. But the scale of the concerts changed the feel of their events, unlike the ones they performed for years in smaller, indoor venues. The band members felt the audience was expecting more of a performance from them.

Stages and challenges

Later in the autumn 1991, they were booked with dates in America, where the audience was eager to see the creators of *Blue Lines*. Grant, Mushroom and 3D had to prepare themselves to leave Bristol for a while, for the first time since their strange experience in Japan with the Wild Bunch. Willing to remain faithful to their origins, they still presented themselves as a sound system, but the American audience didn't seem to be very receptive to their show with a bunch of MCs and DJs on such a slow-paced music.

The band played in Washington, Chicago, Los Angeles, New York, Boston, Minneapolis, and in Pontiac, Michigan, in October 1991, with their guest vocalists. But the audience was bemused by the slowness and lack of consistency between each song. One of the band's worst memories is their show in Minneapolis, in the famous club belonging to the singer Prince. "In the end they put the curtain down on us," 3D recalled, "bloody horrible[81]." In Europe, they were more comfortable in parties and clubs.

Even though this experience of touring America was one of the highlights of their career so far, back in Bristol, Robert and Mushroom started to think they should move on and go back to the studios. But one option was no longer on the table: working with Shara Nelson, who wanted to focus on her solo projects. Tricky was also working on his own material. Without Cameron McVey as a producer, the guys had to

---

81   In an interview with the magazine *Details*, in February 1995

learn to get organised on their own.

Mush by then had his own studio at home in Fishponds. 3D and Tricky were sharing the same house and composed with the members of the Startled Insects, Bob Locke and Tim Norfolk. Producing mainly soundtracks for films, Bob Locke and Tim Norfolk formed the band in Bristol in 1983, influenced by new wave.

3D was working on art projects as well. In 1992, he was contacted by the comic books writer and poet Malcolm Bennett. He wanted to create a new fanzine in Bristol, *Ultra!*, for football fans, with the visual artist Aidan Hughes, who had already launched the *Brute!* magazine. Robert would act as art director.

For a while, the band members all got distracted, lacking focus. "If we were based in London there would have been six months of bullshit, the release and then the kick in the teeth to follow. We would have turned into wankers after all the acclaim," said Grant to *Melody Maker* early 1992. "But they don't let you get big-headed here."

But soon the musicians were lacking money and orientation. Everybody thought they were really rich pop stars, because *Blue Lines* was so influential, confessed 3D. And it did really sell about 600,000 copies, but wasn't big in America.

They felt hassled by their record company, but had no intention of quickly producing *Blue Lines 2*. They had a lot of material and songs in the making, left over from the 1990 recordings, but they were not willing to rely on them. Yet staying in the studio together, without Shara, was not so easy.

Tricky and 3D continued recording at the Startled Insects' studio in Redland, Bristol. Their process was very social, with a lot of time spent in local pubs and clubs. Mushroom was more discreet and solitary; he was always a perfectionist and a bit wary of interferences in his musical plans.

The rest of the team often thought this type of research could end up becoming quite destructive. If D was sometimes accused of being quite wasteful, as he tried a lot of possibilities, a balance between him and Mushroom emerged from this chaotic energy. And this became the early identity of *Protection*, the band's second album.

They also looked to distance themselves from music genres. "Massive Attack are not a dance act. Let's make that clear," wrote the magazine *Melody Maker* in February 1992, when interviewing the band. "It's a recurring theme of our conversation; how can they re-educate the parts of the public who take it for granted that they are – because of their loose, anonymous structure – just another rap act or producers when, in fact, they are songsmiths, creators of moods and painters of pictures."

In the meantime, in 1992, the band released a new EP, 'Home of the Whale', the title track was recorded with Irish folk singer Caroline Lavelle, and in 1993, they produced a remix for the French alternative/ world music band Les Négresses Vertes, of their song 'Face à la mer'. This gives an idea of the numerous directions they were working in.

Between tension and protection

In 1993, between Bristol and London, Massive Attack finally began the proper recording of their second album, working with their old friend Nellee Hooper as a producer. The new project gathered a wide scope of new collaborators. Horace Andy was once again involved. But Massive Attack struggled to find a female voice that was inspiring and could help them renew themselves. They even placed an advert in the *NME* magazine, looking for someone sounding like Aretha Franklin or Tracy Chapman. 3D and Grant's dream was to record with a new Nina Simone...

Exploring many possibilities, they finally went in a completely different direction and contacted Tracey Thorn, from the English duo Everything But The Girl, formed in 1982. She started co-writing two tracks with them for the forthcoming album: one named 'Protection' (which contains a tiny beat sample from the song 'The Payback' by James Brown) – and 'Better Things'. The result sounded both new and enchanting. The general tone of the album took a new direction, still soulful, still hip-hop, but more electronic, unclassifiable.

More than for *Blue Lines*, the work of the band became fragmented. Mushroom wanted to keep the band's hip-hop feel while 3D experimented new production styles with Nellee Hooper or the Startled

Insects. D sampled their song named 'Cheetah', for a defining Massive Attack track, later-to-be-named 'Eurochild'. He worked further with the Insects on a few other tracks, one becoming 'Karmacoma', adding vocals recorded with Tricky.

Horace Andy was invited to sing his song 'Spying Glass' in a new Massive Attack version – which includes two samples, one from 'Chapter 3' by Jamaican singer Joe Gibbs, and one from the famous 'Shaft in Africa' soundtrack, from 1973, written by the American R&B musician Johnny Pate.

The band also wanted to include a collaboration with the female singer Nicolette. Born as Nicolette Suwoton in 1964 in Glasgow, from Nigerian parents, she released a first album, *Now Is Early*, in 1992, and was described by the press as a "Billie Holliday on acid". On *Protection*, she sang on the songs 'Three' and 'Sly' – which samples 'Africa Talks to You (The Asphalt Jungle)' by the psychedelic American band Sly and the Family Stone. 'Sly' was chosen as the first single from the album.

Massive Attack also worked in a different direction with the Scottish pianist Craig Armstrong. He played the parts on two instrumental pieces, 'Weather Storm' (which samples 'It's Time for Love' by the jazz group from Philadelphia, Pieces of a Dream) and 'Heat Miser' (co-produced with the English producer Marius de Vries). Later on stage, to interpret on 'Heat Miser', 3D would add some lyrics: *"Morning is blue / It's like my blood group too (...) Make a lot of trouble with you / It takes a lotta smoke"*.

Among a lot of other productions, these tracks started to make an album. The band also added a cover of 'Light My Fire' by the Doors, based on the soul version created by American singer Jackie Wilson. Theirs was recorded with Horace Andy.

The elaboration of the album began with the choice of the song 'Protection', one of the most seductive of the record, a perfect fit for the opening. The base of the song was produced with a beat created by Mushroom. "The hi-hat is a one-bar sampled loop," Mushroom explained in an interview[82], "then I programmed some James Brown snares and wah-wah over the top, then added some keyboards. The

82   With Dave Robinson for the magazine *Future Music*, in 1994

whole thing was programmed in my home studio. I just wrote it as a complete piece of music, without a song in mind."

Massive Attack sent the music to Tracey Thorn. "I was really surprised to be asked," Tracey told me in an interview[83]. "I'd loved *Blue Lines*, and especially Shara Nelson's vocals, and she seemed like a very hard act to follow. At that point no one could have predicted how much the band were going to progress musically, becoming much more eclectic and experimental – so although it seemed like a surprising choice when they asked me, I can see where they were going with it. It was very appealing to me to be able to work with them. It came at the stage when we as Everything But The Girl were having a resurgence of inspiration, and looking to try different things, so it was a great opportunity to experiment. We had the 'Missing' remix out there – then came *Protection* – and then we were working on our ninth album *Walking Wounded*. It all came out of the same moment of inspiration, and feeling creative again."

Tracey added the vocal melody and the lyrics."I recorded a demo vocal at home and sent it to them," Tracey continued, "so they could hear the song. And they loved it. I then got together with them – I think I may have gone to Bristol first. We then did some work in Nellee Hooper's studio in London. 3D and Nellee were the most forthcoming in terms of talking to me while I was doing the vocal. Mushroom seemed very reserved but he and Daddy G were definitely around as well. So it was a kind of big collaboration."

Their collaboration emphasised the role of the female presence on some of their songs, bringing a lot more softness and some femininity in the band's masculine world. The DJs liked to leave the singers some space to bring in their own universe. "I felt I was very much taking my inspiration from what Shara had already started," Tracey told me. "The lyrics to 'Unfinished Sympathy' and 'Safe From Harm' were incredible, and with her I thought the band already had a really strong female presence at the front of their music. So I just wanted to continue that really. It seemed like one of the best things about their identity as a band, and it's something they've always continued."

"You can't change the way she feels but you could put your arms around her," sings Tracey, adding later *"Could you forgive yourself if you left her just the way you found her?"* Tracey subtly reverses the stereotypical roles of a couple when she claims: *"You're a girl and I'm a boy"*... The lyrics give a modern and delicate feel to the love song, contrasting with the rap tracks on the rest of the album.

Tracey also co-wrote with the band and her partner Ben Watt the song 'Better Things', which became the sixth track on *Protection*. The music created by Massive Attack uses a sample from the unforgettable 'Never Can Say Goodbye', a beat and a bassline taken from the version produced by James Brown in 1972. *"And though you've found / You need more than me / Don't talk to me / About being free / That's freedom without love / And magic without love / Magic without love"*, invokes Tracey in a very feminist text.

She worked at the same time with the band again on a cover of 'The Hunter Gets Captured by the Game', written by Smokey Robinson in 1966 and popularised by the female Motown band the Marvelettes. Massive Attack's version was featured in 1995 on the soundtrack for the film *Batman Forever*, directed by Joel Schumacher and produced by Tim Burton.

But the production of the album was the most difficult stage. Nellee had just finished producing Björk's album *Debut*, released in July 1993, which was an enormous global success. He was introduced to Björk by another Bristolian, Dom T, aka Dominic Thrupp, a DJ active in the city in the mid 1980s who moved to London in 1990. Dom had met the Icelandic singer in Los Angeles, they fell in love and he introduced her to new trends in electronic music.

Nellee introduced Massive Attack to his programmer Marius De Vries who quickly became their new Jonny Dollar – a technical musician that could help them turn abstract ideas and samples into arrangements for songs. Nellee and Marius both worked with Massive Attack on the production of 'Sly', 'Three' 'Spying Glass' and 'Weather Storm', at Nellee's house in London. He was really into working with his mates from Bristol but Mushroom didn't really agree on how to work with him. When somebody's ideas get changed in the process, it's sometimes for the better and sometimes for the worst, thought the band members, looking back at this era. *Protection* could have been a very different sounding album, according to them. The tracks sounding like what they were originally are 'Better Things', 'Protection', 'Karmacoma' and 'Eurochild', probably the best-kept track for the Bristol era. The other tracks were more manipulated.

Nellee's influence certainly didn't totally please D and even less so Mushroom, who was looking for a more hip-hop sound, merged with a soul female presence. Mushroom also disliked Craig Armstrong's piano performance on 'Weather Storm' and wanted the looped sample of the track to be untouched, left to simply roll. At some point, the band even split again for about a month. Mushroom went back to his personal studio to work on his own demos and 3D spent a lot of time in London, trying to forget his own anguish about the separation, going out almost every night in London, most nights upstairs at Browns and back at Nellee's with Tricky, Michael Hutchence, Noel and Liam Gallagher, the Prodigy, Björk and Goldie.

However, soon, Nellee started working on the *Romeo + Juliet* soundtrack and was called by the pop superstar Madonna, who wanted him to work on her album *Bedtime Stories*, scheduled for October 1994. Nellee became more and more absent, while Massive Attack's second album was far from being ready. He would later apologise by introducing the band to Madonna for a future project...

Yet, by 1993, the setbacks and disputes forced the band to look for new and richer orientations for their album. This wouldn't happen without any pain, though.

'Karmacoma': Jamaica 'n' Roma

One of the defining moments of the album's composition came with a song that 3D and Tricky wrote. 'Karmacoma' became the album's second track and third single. Based on a rap between the two voices, an Indian rhythm and the sample from the Insects, 'Karmacoma' has a very oriental feel, coming from the use of other samples from Russian and various type of Asian music.

The chorus samples Alexander Borodin's opera, *Prince Igor*, specifically an extract from the 'Polovtsian Dances' in the second act. Another sample comes from a piece of Mongolian diphonic throat singing called a "Khoomei", of its harmonic part, used in 'Dream Time in Lake Jackson' by British acid house band the KLF on their album *Chill Out*. The rhythm of the 'Karmacoma' introduction comes from the beginning of an Indian song named 'Aaja Sajan Aaja', sung by Alka Yagnik and written for the Bollywood film *Khal Nayak*, in 1993. These Eastern inspirations would grow with Massive Attack's first visit to Istanbul in 1996 during a world tour... The song's bassline also samples a section of French singer Serge Gainsbourg's song 'Melody', from his concept album *Histoire de Melody Nelson*, released in 1971.

Already, 'Karmacoma' brought a new direction to the album, different from the songs written with Tracey Thorn. Intriguing and mysterious both in its sound and its lyrics, the track is a play on word on 3D and Tricky's origins, from Italy and Jamaica. And their cohabitation was more of a continuous effect of their personality clash than a smooth endeavour.

"*Are you sure you want to be with me? I've nothing to give*", both voices repeat alternatively. "*Walking through the suburbs though not exactly lovers / You're a couple, 'specially when your body's doubled / Duplicate, then you wait / For the next Kuwait*", says Tricky. With a direct reference to the recent Gulf War... 3D also appreciates the rich rhyme. And he continues: "*I see you digging a hole in your neighbourhood / You're crazy but you're lazy / I need to live and I need to / Your troubles must be seen to see through / Money like it's paper with faces I remember / I drink on a daily basis / Though it seldom cools my temper / It never cools my temper*".

Tricky later claimed that he wrote most of 'Karmacoma' and used some of the lyrics in his own track, 'Overcome', on his first album, *Maxinquaye*. "3D had a love/hate relationship with me," Tricky tells me when I meet with him in Paris, 21 years later[84]. Very close, the two friends also often ended up arguing for hours. As Grant doesn't really like writing lyrics, D, who enjoyed writing collectively, was enhanced

---

84   In an interview with the author at Le Bataclan, in Paris, in February 2015

by their collaboration. Tricky also felt a rivalry with Grant, who rarely took him seriously. So, quickly after the album release, Tricky decided that he and Massive Attack would go their separate ways. He wouldn't join the band on their tour. Grant later recognised that he often treated Tricky, ten years younger than him, as the baby in the group.

3D's lyrics became increasingly impacted by all the disputes and reflected feelings of insecurity and mistrust, both at a personal level and in a universal expression of this era as he perceived it.

Before he vanished from the band's close surrounding, Tricky appeared in Massive Attack's stunning video for 'Karmacoma'. Directed by Jonathan Glazer, it was a debut in music video for the director who would go on to make videos for Radiohead and feature films such as *Sexy Beast* and *Under the Skin*. It gathers an incredible series of cinematic references: from *Pulp Fiction* by Tarantino to *Barton Fink* by the Coen Brothers and *The Shining* by Stanley Kubrik. All the members of the band appear in the film, dressed in navy blue uniforms with the slogan "Tex Mex" on the chest, all apart from Mushroom, wearing a casual white t-shirt and a purple blouson, lying agonising on a couch, his hand on a bloody wound…

In the film, 3D and Tricky are rapping at the centre of chaotic scenes, with menacing expressions on their face. Meanwhile, in the different rooms of what appears to be a large hotel complex, many other scarier characters seem to find themselves in the midst of troubles: running away from the police after a robbery, avoiding a family member, setting a bed on fire or trying to write down indefinitely the word 'Karmacoma' on a typewriter with no letter 'K'… Filled with visual symbols, the film plays around a Kubrick-like atmosphere, where the main character, a runaway thief, is unable to recognise the door he is looking for, pointing his gun in the air in a deep sense of panic. With references to crimes, oil and mafia money, prostitution and illegal businesses, some parts of the video were censored in a few countries.

'Karmacoma' was released as a third single from the *Protection* album, on March 20, 1995, after 'Sly' and 'Protection'. Its sleeve featured a handmade drawing on cardboard, done by 3D, figuring a monster armed with a fork set on fire, ravaging a city and encaging two innocent characters, in a very "DIY" style.

The track definitely installed the rapping duet as one of Massive Attack's trademarks. It was remixed by a lot of the band's friends: by a newly formed local band Portishead (as 'Karmacoma - The Portishead Experience'); by the DJ duo U.N.K.L.E, formed in 1994 by James Lavelle and Tim Goldsworthy; and by the Italian collective Almamegretta. The latter version, renamed 'Napoli Trip', was the most different and was recorded in Naples, where, during one of his family trips, 3D met Almamegretta, a group of DJs with a ska/dub feel. This version was sung by D with Almamegretta's leader, Raiz, with extra lyrics in Neapolitan.

In September 1995, Massive Attack also recorded a new version of 'Karmacoma' named 'Fake The Aroma', as a duet between 3D and Daddy G, featuring Talvin Singh playing the tabla and enhanced with an electric guitar – which was included on *The Help Album*, produced for the charity War Child. This became the version the band performed on stage, as Tricky was not touring with them. In a few wonderful live recordings, they were also accompanied by Indian percussionists, who emphasised the song's intriguing Asian feel...

European children

3D and Tricky's second rap on *Protection*, 'Eurochild', came to define a part of Massive Attack's history, for two main reasons. It is a sort of social statement for England in the mid-nineties, that inspired the band's artwork and stage shows for the coming years. The track was also played a lot live and evolved musically, bending the collective's sound towards a more instrumental approach. 'Eurochild' became a regular on Massive Attack's set list by the end of 1994.

The lyrics refer to the state of the European Community, at a time when many countries were getting closed up, socially and politically, and less open to internal solidarity. They are written through the eyes of an observer bemused by the media's tales. *"Sitting in my day care, the art is dayglo painted (...) Glow from my TV set was blue like neon / Activated the remote I put the BBC on / I've seen this city somewhere / I'm looking out for no-one / Pallor in my eye it get blue like neon"*, starts 3D. He mentions the BBC and "the neon" as he did in Massive Attack's early, unreleased song,

'Just A Matter Of Time', in 1990, and also voices the defining phrase *"no go zone"*, often used by politicians to describe poor areas, stating *"no go zone I go through"*, underlining where he comes from.

Tricky continues: *"Hell is 'round the corner where I shelter / Isms and schisms we're living on a skelter / If you believe I'll deceive then common sense says shall you receive / Let me take you down the corridors of my life"*. A sentence he uses just a while later comes from the song 'Blank Expression', by the Specials, one of his all-time favourite bands: *"I walk in a bar and immediately I sense danger / You look at me girl as if I was some kind of a / A total stranger"*.

As the chorus is instrumental, Tricky repeats in between the last verses, as a motto: *"Take a second of me"*. The rest of the song describes a worrying evolution of our society, increasingly marred with fear. 3D's most famous line probably remains: *"I function better with the sun in my eyes"*, adding a slight of hope. It was written as a strange imaginary paranoid version of Europe.

Inspired by all the themes of the song, 3D created a series of artwork, representing a distorted European blue and golden flag and symbols of consumerism, including a fork and a knife, around an abstract central character. This figure appears at the centre of the album cover, and later in the band's stage shows.

At the time when the lyrics and artwork were created, the Maastricht Treaty had been signed amidst disagreements between the European states, defining trade rules more than political principles, after months of disputes between Brussels' technocrats and the British government. For years, the UK had been following the threat stated by Margaret Thatcher, "I want my money back!" Up until John Major's government. In 1994, the British Prime Minister was still fighting his corner to oppose the European institutions' will to move towards a more federal union. A political view, which is far from representing Bristol's inclusive and open-minded culture, as the song reminds us.

'Eurochild' was soon chosen to be featured on the compilation album *The Beautiful Game*, created for the 1996 Euro football competition. Massive Attack worked on a remix version renamed 'Euro Zero Zero' and 3D even travelled to Naples in order to record the sound of the crowd in the San Paolo stadium with a binaural microphone to include it in the remix. D worked on this version with the band's new stage guitarist, Angelo Bruschini, from the Bristol band the Blue Airplanes, to add a stronger guitar part that gives a more "grunge" feel to the song, according to them.

On this version, the vocals are now performed by 3D and Daddy G, instead of Tricky, with a new bridge sung by Horace Andy (*"Can't be nothing wrong / Inside of me"*). The band really liked to perform this version on stage, which appeared to be very powerful. From 1995 to 1999, it evolved along their different tours, opening an experimentation field for their live shows. 'Euro Zero Zero' was also used as a B-side on one of their future singles, two years later ('Teardrop'), and appeared on the band's *Singles Collection* in 1999.

The live reinterpretations changed the way the band composed. For the first time since the birth of the Massive Attack, their artistic desires for their studio recording evolved with the experience of the live shows. D wanted to rethink their performances but also their way of composing. And he started to experiment new unreleased songs on stage before finalising their recording.

For the *Protection Tour*, D also wanted to increase the visual dimension of the band's shows. He worked on a Massive Attack live warehouse party and built the giant 'Eurochild' figure that was kept for the band's tour, with Marc Picken who was working for *i-D* magazine. Asked by the band members, Marc became Massive Attack's manager at that time and remains so today. In the meantime, around the summer 1994, Massive Attack's second album was almost ready and a release was scheduled for September 26.

From the sound of Bristol to the Bristol Sound: *Dummy*

Meanwhile, in Bristol, while Massive Attack were taking their time to work on this second album, the success of their first record had a profound effect on many musicians, among them notably was Geoff Barrow, who was working as a tape operator/tea boy at the Coach Studio when *Blue Lines* was recorded. There, Geoff befriended the band members as well as Tricky, their then producer Cameron McVey,

Neneh Cherry and a local jazz musician, Adrian Utley, born in 1957 in Northampton.

Geoff started making a name for himself as a remixer, working with Primal Scream, Paul Weller and Depeche Mode. In 1991, he composed a rap track with Tricky, 'Nothing's Clear', for the charity compilation album, *The Hard Sell*. And in 1992, he worked with Cameron McVey and Neneh Cherry on the singer's second album, *Homebrew*, released in October.

From 1993, Geoff also launched his own project with Adrian Utley, a band named Portishead.They were joined by a female singer, Beth Gibbons, born in 1965 in Exeter, in Devon. The name of the band comes from the town in which Geoffrey Paul Barrow, born in 1971, grew up in, in Somerset. "I was working on another project when we met," remembers Adrian Utley when we meet. "Geoff was mainly interested in sampling techniques. I didn't know anything about hip-hop music at the time. I had discovered the first albums by Public Enemy and was fascinated by them, though in the blues/jazz scene, no one knew about them. And I understood quickly that Geoff was really knowledgeable on how to produce this kind of music[85]."

Throughout 1993, Portishead developed their first album. They also produced a first promo video directed by Alexander Hemming, entitled *To Kill A Dead Man*, a film inspired by crime movies, which reflects the band's cinematic feel. "We wrote the film ourselves with our sound engineer Dave McDonald, and a music to illustrate it," adds Adrian, "working in an independent spirit[86]." The band was soon signed by Go! Beat Records, receiving only a small advance, which enabled them to work without any pressure from the label.

Thanks to the energetic personality of Geoff, young and self-taught, Portishead developed an innovative sound, based on sampling, with the classic feel of Adrian's jazz touch and the amazing voice of Beth Gibbons. Shy and frail, the singer literally radiates once in front of a microphone. The band worked with Dave McDonald as a producer and drummer. Portishead released a first single, 'Numb', on June 6, 1994.

85   In an interview with the author in Bristol in September 2015
86   Ibid

Their first album *Dummy*, recorded at the Coach House Studio and the State of the Art studios, in Bristol, was out on August 22.

The popular success was immediate and the critics followed. The *NME* described it as "without question, a sublime debut album. But so very, very sad". The record reached number two in the UK Albums Chart; three of its singles peaked at number 13, including 'Glory Box', the band's third single released in early January 1995. And *Dummy* was certified gold by 1997, selling more than two million copies in Europe; 825,000 in the UK alone.

The album was quickly compared with *Blue Lines* by the media, underlining its slow tempo, cinematic influences and avant-garde atmosphere. After the slowness and soul feel of *Blue Lines*, *Dummy* surely came to define the sound from Bristol as melancholic. The press started talking about a Bristol Sound, as if *Dummy* came to confirm the outburst of *Blue Lines*, which surprised the music world. Portishead was consequently willing to distance themselves from these attempts at labelling them. This didn't prevent music journalist Andy Pemberton to pen the term 'trip-hop' in the magazine *Mixmag*, to define a new music genre, the sound of Massive Attack and Portishead influencing dozens of other bands everywhere in the UK and beyond.

The term is however mostly disliked by both bands. Adrian Utley often claims that Portishead have nothing to do with Massive Attack. And Grant Marshall hates to hear his music compared to that of his fellow Bristol bands. But the social links between the two bands are undeniable. They emerged from the same circles of influences and the same venues in Bristol. Geoff Barrow was definitely inspired by the Wild Bunch performances, from their renowned party for the Arnolfini's *Graffiti Art* exhibition, around 3D and his graffiti artist friends, in 1985. The hip-hop and sampling effects are at the core of the composition of *Dummy*. And the first people Geoff came to see with his early tapes were the guys from Massive Attack.

Geoff Barrow, who used to work at the Coach House studio, played his first demos to Massive Attack, which became the first Portishead record. And Cameron – who was still managing Massive at the time – became Portishead's manager.

Geoff remained thankful to the band for their help. "Neneh, Cameron and Massive Attack helped us so much at our beginnings," Geoff Barrow later explained to the media[87]. "They invested money and made things easy for us. I don't know where we would be today without Massive Attack."

For Adrian Utley, *Dummy* and Portishead's sound mainly came about through the encounter of his musical world and Geoff's influences. "Geoff had started writing 'Sour Times' when we met, and I composed the guitar part for it," he explains to me[88]. 'Sour Time' became Portishead's second single in early August. "I wanted to bring a direct, instrumental dimension into his experimentations. Geoff also had the track named 'It Could Be Sweet' and we created the rest of the album together with Beth. If Geoff had kept on working with Massive Attack, his sound would have been completely different." And surely, the release of *Dummy* opened a new chapter in Bristol's cultural history.

No Protection: between fragility and creativity

After selecting the definite track list with Mushroom, the whole team of Massive Attack entered the Olympic Studios in South London, with Nellee, Marius, the mixing engineer Mark Stent, known as 'Spike', and Marc Picken.

While contemplating *Dummy*'s success that they partly helped foster, Massive Attack released their second album, *Protection*, on September 26, 1994. They finalised the record in the middle of internal tensions. The pressure between the band members was sometimes so high that they could not stand it. "We had a lot of arguments," later explained Grant Marshall[89]. "Have you noticed how both sides of the album are symmetrical? Five tracks on each: one with Tracey, a rap, one with Nicolette, a soundtracky one, and one with Horace."

Despite the tensions, *Protection* received critical acclaim. *Dazed & Confused* wrote that there were "no doubts on that score: *Protection* is a work of genius". The album peaked at number 4 in the UK Chart

---

87   In an interview with BBC Radio 6 Music, featured in a 2004 radio documentary about Bristol
88   In an interview with the author in Bristol in September 2015
89   In an interview with the magazine *Dazed and Confused* in 1994

and later entered the list of the '50 coolest albums of all time' by the American *Rolling Stone* magazine, which wrote that it "delivers brilliant body music that doesn't neglect the brain". In 1995, *Protection* received a Brit Award in the 'Best Dance Act' category.

"It's a masterful return: an immense mix of urban real and heady surreal, lined with an unexpected dose of analogue electronics and the kind of spacious sonic views that only Massive can manipulate," *DJ Magazine* wrote in September. "It's more laid-back than their *Blue Lines* debut, but shows no signs of the much talked about 'difficult second album' syndrome."

The first single, 'Sly', was released on October 17, 1994 and reached number 24 in the UK Chart. It was accompanied by a video directed by French American filmmaker Stéphane Sednaoui, shot in Manhattan, in New York. Sednaoui had previously worked with Björk, Madonna and Red Hot Chili Peppers. The short film shows the band members and their featured singer Nicolette in different environments, some very urban, other more bucolic. 3D is lost in a crowd of busy businessmen on Wall Street while Daddy G is filmed daydreaming in a field, surrounded by Indian dancers and Buddhist monks. Mushroom appears surreptitiously between psychedelic dance scenes and Nicolette is featured in most of the different settings, singing in a Chinese costume... The result is very colourful and fashionable but the band never fully liked it. 3D finds it "complicated".

For their second single's promo video, the band worked with the French director Michel Gondry, who demonstrated the whole project to them in a pub, in the form of a scale-model to be looked at from above, to be filmed on a crane in one take.

It features a seven-minute long sequence where the camera moves from a room of a Parisian building to another. In each room appears a member of the band in a different domestic situation: Daddy G is coming home with his little daughter; Tracey Thorn is singing in her kitchen; a teenage boy is watching TV on a couch; 3D is fixing a television set's electronic system; Mushroom is playing with toy cars; a mother is struggling to feed her little girl; etc. The whole life of the building is depicted in a mesmerising filming technique, in which most scenes are shot with the band members lying on the floor or against a wall to make the camera movements function…

The song 'Protection' was released as a single on January 9, 1995, and the short film became one of the band's favourite, also winning "Best Video" at the MTV Europe Music Awards. A success that came to reward a bold piece of music. "It's very unconventional in structure," thinks Tracey Thorn. "But the length, and repetitive figures that swirl through it, make it quite hypnotic I think, which is where its power lies. And the contrast between the hard edges of the backing track – all space and angles – with my lyrics and warm vocals – I think that's what made it a success, the tension and the contrast[90]."

Ten weeks later, the album's third single, 'Karmacoma', was released on March 20, and reached number 28 in the Chart. Its hand-made cover art was part of a series 3D created for the album and its singles. He produced many other paintings and drawings around that time, representing the climate of tension the band is evolving in, and more generally the capitalistic context, featuring skeletons and ghostlike figures, forks and knives representing consumerism. These paintings were entitled *Hungry Ghost, Happy Eater* or *Naked Lunch*. A series was named *Insect President*. Two other patterns were used in regular posters: one of a new version of the hand with plasters on a finger and a cross in the palm – a symbol of the idea of protection – and the *Eurochild* figure, thought as an antifascist statement.

He often reused his paintings scanned in the negative, inversing the colours, where the characters appear almost as X-rays, with their ribs and teeth exposed. The piece entitled *In Europe* represents a male figure, head down without face features but with apparent teeth and rib bones, surmounted by a ring of blue pentagrams. Some of his paintings were also portrait of friends, including Neneh Cherry and Tricky. Others represented monstrous characters, like the one used for the 'Karmacoma' single, featuring a robot surrounded by flames.

3D also created in 1994 sleeves for the label Mo'Wax, for their records *Headz* (Volumes 1, 2A and 2B). The label was founded in 1992 by James

---

90   In an interview with the author in October 2018 in London

Lavelle and Tim Goldsworthy in London, gathering productions from various DJs and hip-hop crews including DJ Shadow, James Lavelle's own electronic duo U.N.K.L.E, DJ Krush and Attica Blues.

New inspirations also arose in 3D's painting around 1994, like in his *In Baghdad* artwork, obviously influenced by the political development in the Middle East. It features a human figure in despair, surmounted by two dark airplanes, flying in an orange sky and over a red sun. Another of these paintings shows a mother and her child trying to flee an attack; it will be used on *The Help Album*, released in 1995, by the War Child charity, in aid efforts for war-stricken areas. "A series of images reflecting a hedonistic period filled with dread and inter-band tension," said 3D[91].

D felt that it was important to feed his creativity with all possible means. After the album release, he was spending a lot of time in London with Nellee, partying, drinking, thus looking for answers to his anxiety. Partying and drugs became a form of compensation for him.

In 1994, the band also contacted the DJ Mad Professor, born Neil Fraser in Guyana in 1955, to remix a track in a dub version and soon decided to get the entire album remixed. Named *No Protection*, it was released in February 1995, with a special cover created by Scottish artist Stephen Bliss, representing the band members fighting alien monsters, as requested by Robert Del Naja. The record was unanimously celebrated as one of the most interesting albums of the dub music's revival era, in the mid 1990s.

"Massive Attack's management and label got in touch with me about remixing a song from their (then) new album," Neil Frasor told me in a short interview[92]. "I had first heard from them in 1993… The song I was asked to remix was 'Sly'. The remix entered the top ten, they were quite pleased and offered me another song to remix. Then another, then along the way… it transferred into an album."

And Massive Attack later invited Mad Professor to join them on their tour. The band still presented themselves as a sound system, but 3D worked to enrich the stage with visual effects, including some of his

91   In an interview with *Dazed and Confused*, in November 2013
92   In November 2018, from Australia

art and some visual light effects. Describing their next concerts to the press, 3D revealed in October 1994: "We prefer the term 'installations'. It's going to be a sound system again, like in the Wild Bunch. I don't know whether Tricky is going to be 'installed' or not, ha! ha! We don't like pressuring him into doing things[93]." They started the rehearsals in London and scheduled dates in the UK and the US.

Mushroom was particularly satisfied with the turntable installation. Grant even told *The Face* magazine mid-1994: " It'd be wrong for us to play as a band. That's not what we're about. We're studio-based." But the band soon had to slightly change their stage shows, to introduce more energy, with more lights, and more instruments. Angelo Bruschini and his guitar became a pillar in the interpretation of songs like 'Eurochild'. The reversed title of the remixed album, *No Protection*, therefore sounded like a prediction: the band needed to change to evolve and thrive, getting out of their Bristolian comfort zone.

Where the Bristol scene evolved

Until then and since the mid 1980s, Britain had associated the Bristol sound with sound systems, but Portishead came to offer a more traditional form of band. Their second single 'Sour Times' was a huge success in the US and their third, 'Glory Box', reached number 13 in the UK Singles Chart, in early 1995. Then, another album from Bristol came out: Tricky's first record *Maxinquaye*, released in February 1995. The name of the record is inspired by the name of Tricky's mother, as well as much of the lyrics.

After releasing independently a first track named 'Aftermath', featuring female vocalist Martina Topley-Bird, in local record stores in September 1993, Tricky got a record deal. Martina had met Tricky around 1992, at 17 years old, while she was still studying at Clifton College. At the time, the rapper was mainly living with Mark Stewart in Bristol. Tricky ran into her, singing, in his street.

Born on May 7, 1975 in London, Martina is the daughter of Martin Geoffrey, who passed away before her birth, and Charlotte Topley –

---

93   In an interview with *Select Magazine*

who moved to Bristol and remarried to Drayton Bird. Martina always loved music and grew up taking piano and violin lessons, also singing in a children's choir. Via her extended family, she had been introduced to many artistic and musical influences, from the Beatles to the Specials. "I remember hearing their song 'Rudy' in my estate and the Beatles' 'I Wanna Hold Your Hand' in my nursery or in the place my mum took me to get my ears pierced!" Martinal told me in an interview[94]. Her piano teacher introduced her to jazz by from 14 years old, asking her to sing in his little school jazz band.

Getting closer to Tricky, a few years later, Martina and him later kick-started their musical collaboration then a love story. "The first track I sang with Tricky was called 'Shoebox' and he told me that Neneh Cherry and Cameron McVey liked it and were thinking of using it for Neneh's album," Martina added. "About five weeks later, I sang the song 'Aftermath', in the same studio in Bristol. One of my best friends had just left Bristol and there was a weird melancholy in the air for me..."

Tricky played the first demo of 'Aftermath' to 3D, who immediately loved Martina's voice, but Massive Attack didn't pay much more attention to the track at that time. This led Tricky to finally work with Island Records, a parent label of Fourth & Broadway. "I got to work with Chris Blackwell and Island Records," retells Tricky[95]. "And from the start, they let me do what I wanted, it was never a business."

Tricky asked British producer Mark Saunders to co-produce *Maxinquaye*, impressed by his previous work with the Cure. The album was recorded the first half of 1994 at Tricky's new home studio in Kilburn, London, set up by Island Records, with further recording at the Loveshack and Eastcote studios in Notting Hill. Martina is the lead singer on 'Overcome', 'Ponderosa', 'Black Steel', 'Abbaon Fat Track' and 'Feed Me'; and other featured vocalists include Mark Stewart and Alison Goldfrapp (on the track 'Pumkin'). "I definitely knew that what we were doing was different and new," Martina told me. "And due to my involvement in the record, I did feel quite of sense of owernership. I already wanted to explore my own ideas but I wasn't there yet at the

---

94   In November 2018
95   In an interview with the author in Paris in February 2015

time." Martina would later release her first solo album, *Quitoxic*, in 1998, and a second opus, *The Blue God*, in 2008.

Tricky raps on the tracks 'Suffocated Love', 'Strugglin' and 'Hell Is Around The Corner'. He also sampled the unforgettable 'Bad' by Michael Jackson on 'Brand New You're Retro' and covered Public Enemy's song 'Black Steel In The Hour Of Chaos', from their album *It Takes A Nation of Millions To Hold Us Back*, renamed 'Black Steel'. 3D actually came up with the suggestion to cover 'Black Steel' when Tricky and him were working on a rap version of Prince's 'When Doves Cry'.

'Aftermath' was re-released as a proper single on January 24, 1994 and entered the UK Singles Chart at number 69, followed by 'Ponderosa' in April 1994 and 'Overcome' in January 1995. *Maxinquaye* was released a month later on February 20, 1995 in the UK, and mid April in the US. It soon reached number three on the UK Albums Chart, selling over 100,000 copies in a few months, more than 500,000 copies to this day.

Dark, mysterious, ambitious, audacious, the qualifications abounded in the press, in a critically acclaimed reception. Jon Pareles, critic at the *New York Times*, hailed a "first album-length masterpiece". Tricky heavily promoted the album and started a tour with Martina, who was soon pregnant with their daughter, Mazy.

Lovers of the Bristol sound also recognised in *Maxinquaye* many references that Tricky shared with Massive Attack and Portishead. 'Overcome' uses some of the lyrics that Tricky wrote for 'Karmacoma': *"You sure you want to be with me? I've nothing to give..."* sings Martina in the fist verse. And later: *"Walking through the suburbs / No, not exactly lovers / You're a couple, oh, 'specially when your bodies double / Duplicate and then you wait / For the next Kuwait / Karmacoma, Karmacoma / Jamaican an' Roma".* In 'Suffocate Love', Tricky uses a phrase from 'Eurochild': *"Take a second of me".* And 'Hell Around The Corner' uses a sample base as from 'Ike's Rap 2', by Isaac Hayes, just like Portishead's 'Glory Box'.

Soon, Tricky worked with Neneh Cherry and Björk. After ending his relationship with Martina, he was even involved with Björk, but their love affair soon turned sour. He later recognised that sampling her music was like a way to transcend the moments when he was not good enough to her on the personal level...

Enhanced by his success in America, Tricky moved to Greenwich Village, in New York, in 1996. He later lived in Los Angeles, London again, Paris, and in Berlin from 2015.

Meanwhile, in 1995, Massive Attack were invited to play their first show at the prestigious Glastonbury Festival, in June. A defining rendezvous for British music, the festival was celebrating its 25th anniversary that year. PJ Harvey, Pulp, Blur, Oasis, Sinéad O'Connor and Jeff Buckley were also programmed. Massive Attack performed in the Dance Tent, a brand-new festival venue that they suggested for the summer, declining to play any of the other stages, determined to use a sound system set up. Mushroom was starring at the centre of the stage behind his decks, with an Afro hairdo that suited him like no other. They were joined by Horace Andy and Deborah Miller, interpreting the female vocal parts. The event was a huge success.

Portishead were also added in the Glastonbury programme closer to the date but declined the offer to perform on the main stage and played in the smaller tent for acoustic sets, with bass player Jim Barr and drummer Rob Merrill, and, despite a few technical problems, attracted a huge audience.

In July 1995, Bristol already seemed at the centre of the English music scene when, on top, *Dummy* received the *Mercury Prize* for Best Album – beating Blur, Oasis, Suede, Pulp, and two musicians from West England: PJ Harvey and Bristol's very own Tricky. The Mercury Prize was created in 1992 and has since become defining for the British music industry.

1996 saw this surge of creativity increase even further: Geoff Barrow worked on remixing tracks of bands from all over the country, from Primal Scream to Depeche Mode, and Massive Attack was awarded in February with a Brit Awards, for the Best *Dance Act*, beating Tricky and M People. 3D only briefly commented on stage with this short remark: "It's ironic as none of us can dance"... The 'Protection' video directed by Michel Gondry was also nominated for *Best Promo Video*.

When in March, Massive Attack was invited to perform live on Channel Four in the famous show the White Room; they appeared transformed. The performance relied increasingly on instruments, especially a drummer, a bass player, a keyboardist and a guitarist – Mushroom still standing at his deck at the centre of the stage. They interpreted 'Karmacoma' in a slow, vibrant, electric, more punkish version, followed by 'Eurochild', in the 'Euro Euro Zero' format, joined by Horace Andy dressed in oversized dark clothes just like 3D, adding no introductive nor conclusive word to their flawless performance. The band, more comfortable on stage than ever, was warmly applauded. In other television performances, they interpreted 'Karmacoma' with a delightful set of Indian percussionists.

In September, Massive Attack also launched their own label: Melankolic Records, with the slogan "Glad to be sad"... Distributed by Virgin/EMI Music, it signed a number of friends such as Lewis Parker, Horace Andy, Craig Armstrong, and later Alpha, Sunna and Day One, allowing them to make their albums without interference.

Trip-hop era? And so much more

From 1995, the music press increasingly defined the "trip-hop" genre as pioneered by the three major Bristol bands. The phrase was used for the first time in June 1994 by Andy Pemberton, a journalist for Mixmag, while talking about Mo' Wax Records, very much inspired by Massive Attack. With this term, Pemberton underlined the hip-hop elements in this music and emphasised the references to smoking weed. He also compared Massive Attack's work to the trippy Pink Floyd.

The tag soon became synonymous with "Bristol sound" or "slow tempo". 1995 seeing Massive, Tricky and Portishead taking centre stage in the UK with three defining albums that quickly influenced other bands, a shift was undeniably taking place in British music.

In Bristol many soundsytems had emerged in the meantime such as Roots Spot Crew, Kama Dread, Addis, Henry & Louis, Armagideon. From 1990, Jack Lundie & Andy Scholes started publishing their own production under the name of Henry & Louis and launched the Two Kings label. Their first release was the EP *How Can A Man*, mixed at Smith & Mighty's studio, on Ashley Road, in St Pauls, with vocals by Andy Scholes, heavily influenced by reggae.

But Tricky absolutely hated the term and looked at how to distance himself as much as possible from Bristol, while Geoff Barrow was dreaming of sounding different, working with Tim Saul, rapper Mau and their band Earthling on their first album, *Radar*. Grant Marshall stated as often as could be that he felt his band were ahead of these changes. He and Andrew Vowles both resented the followers and the whole idea of a common genre.

"We used to hate that terminology so bad," Daddy G later explained. "You know, as far we were concerned, Massive Attack music was unique, so to put it in a box was to pigeonhole it and to say, 'Right, we know where you guys are coming from.' And we didn't know where we were coming from half the time, you know what I mean? It was a resistance, but then slowly but surely you come and realize that people need some direction, and some pointers as to where to go for this music. We made this slow, ambient music that was meant for the head, not for the feet, you know, to dance to. There was nothing like it. There was nothing slow or intelligent[96]."

In its list of the '100 Best Albums Of All Times', *Rolling Stone* magazine wrote in 2011: "The Nineties were the all-time high-water mark of silly genre names, and trip-hop may be the silliest of all. But Massive Attack really did invent a whole new style, manipulating hip-hop's boom and reggae's throb into their own slow-motion funk noir, inspiring Bristol, England, neighbours such as Tricky and Portishead to explore cinematic dance grooves heavy on the atmospherics. Their influence has spread to all corners of pop and rock, not to mention upscale shoe stores and cafes everywhere." *Protection* is listed at the 51st position in these rankings, *Dummy* at the 47th and *Maxinquaye* at the 70th.

For *DJ Magazine*, there was no doubt *Protection* largely standed out: "Back in 1991, there were two albums that mattered loads to loads of people; reflecting and magnifying the uniquely British hybrid of international cultures that exist in and around the club scene. *Blue Lines*, of course, and Primal Scream's *Screamadelica*. Fast forward to 1994 and so far there's only one album that matters in so much as it breaks rigid genre moulds. Primal Scream are off on a sad trip of their own and

---

96   In an interview with *Hour* magazine, in Canada, published in September 2006

Protection is out in front. Crossing boundaries with ease[97]."

But the Bristol scene also embodied at this time a vibrant group, an 'out of the box' creativity, away from the mainstream lines of so-called 'Britpop'. And a few bands felt even more grateful for that sense of independence. "I'd attended the Brits in 1995, too, and wrote later in *Bedsit Disco Queen* about how proud I was to be sitting with Massive Attack," Tracey Thorn later explained[98]. "*Protection* was up for a couple of awards, and though it was the height of the Britpop Oasis v Blur battle, I felt that ours was the table to be on, with Massive and Tricky and Björk. The rock kids seemed to be trapped in a dreary rehash of the past, still repetitively harking back to the yawn-inducing Sixties, while we were with a group of people who were looking forwards[99]."

Raising the point of putting the bands in different categories, Tracey added: "By 1996, the two strands of the music scene were in direct competition. Our song 'Missing' was up for Best Single and 'Protection' the single for Best Video. Massive Attack won Best British Dance Act, while *Batman Forever*, featuring Massive and me singing a Smokey Robinson cover, won Best Soundtrack. But Oasis won Best Album and Video and Group, beating Blur and Pulp and Radiohead in those categories, and when Massive went up to collect their award, 3D made a sardonic comment, saying, 'It's quite ironic, 'cos none of us can dance.' It was a joke but he wasn't laughing, and I think he was making a point. He might have said, especially given the most recent album that they'd made: 'Why are we in a different category from Blur and Radiohead? Why is *Protection* a 'dance' album? What is 'dance' code for?' It was a classic piece of Othering. The implication of the awards, and of Blair's speech, was that the white boys with guitars were the Norm, and deviations from that were the Other, and certainly not the main story[100]."

Singularity and innovation became increasingly more important for all three bands from Bristol. With his two following records, *Nearly God* and *Pre-Millenium Tension*, both to be released in 1996, Tricky wanted

---

97   Article published on September 1, 1994
98   In her column published twice a month in the *New Statesman*, on May 2, 2017
99   In her book, *Bedsit Disco Queen*, Virago, 2013
100   In the *New Statesman*, published on May 2, 2017

to sound more punk. Portishead were taking their time... And Massive Attack started working on a third album. In the meantime, the band were contacted to work on a compilation project dedicated to the great Motown soul singer, Marvin Gaye.

Born in Washington DC in 1939, Marvin Gaye was assassinated in Los Angeles in 1984 and is remembered as a legend of songwriting. Entitled *Inner City Blues: The Music Of Marvin Gaye*, scheduled for October 1995, the double album also included collaborations from his own daughter, Nona Gaye, Bono and Lisa Stansfield. Massive Attack's contribution was produced by Nellee Hooper, who put the band in contact with Madonna, as promised in 1993. They chose to cover 'I Want You' but Mushroom wanted nothing to do with Madonna at that time... So Grant and Robert worked on the backing track with the Insects in Clifton. Craig Armstrong wrote the scores for strings. And Robert travelled to New York with Nellee to record her voice.

"It was quite freaky for me because I'm just a Bristol boy," 3D said later[101]. "She was singing in my ear as we were playing the music down, giving me her version of it. I wasn't taking any notice at all really. I was just thinking about how mad it is. She is such an icon it takes you a while to adjust. When she was in the vocal room, it was amazing. We did a few takes just to cover it, but she sung it so well we could have done it in one take. It was that beautiful." The song was also featured on Madonna's compilation album, *Something To Remember*, in November 1995.

And in May 1995, Massive Attack's *Protection Tour* started with Horace Andy, Angelo Bruschini on the guitar, Winston Blissett on the bass, and many DJs including Nick Warren, who was also from Bristol and launched his own collective with Jody Wisternoff, Way Out West, and Henry & Louis in England, France and Germany. Mad Professor later followed as the opening act.

Massive Attack opened their show with an instrumental version of 'Protection', followed by 'Safe From Harm', 'Karmacoma', 'One Love', 'Daydreaming', 'Spying Glass', 'Eurochild', 'Hymn of the Big Wheel' and 'Five Man Army', with Willy Wee also on the mic. They closed it

101 In a television interview in 1998

with a version of 'Heat Miser' including a rap by 3D and 'Unfinished Sympathy', sung by Deborah Miller with a small orchestra.

"While two inflatable 'Eurochild blobs' holding cutlery float above the stage and people think of Pink Floyd and flying pigs," wrote Craig McLean in *The Face* magazine, "and as 1,500 Italians crowd the staggered concrete steps of a club in Milan called Rolling Stone, gazing at the flickering TV screens and the curtains of camouflage netting, a figure steps forward through the gloom to stand behind two decks. A record in each hand, Mushroom raises his arms in the air in gladiatorial triumph. Lights flash, smoke billows and the crowd roars. Massive Attack are in the house." The music critic could not hold his astonishment when the show moved on: "Mushroom is joined by 3D, Daddy G, Horace Andy and - gulp - a band. You know, guitars and stuff. Live instruments. It's all a bit - to be read with a pejorative sneer - rock. It will sound fantastic," further described McLean, after their show in Italy.

In the interview with the journalist, 3D explained: "Going out live, we just thought, well, that's not really how we set out. We didn't plan to be a live band. We knew that we were a sound system and we could fucking do it that way... What we've done over the year is basically discover ourselves[102]..."

The first part of the tour was followed by a second leg in the summer 1996 and the band were chosen to be the first act opening for one of the greatest living legends in British music: David Bowie. They travelled to Israel with him for a show scheduled in Tel Aviv on July 3. Massive Attack's part opened with 'Hymn of the Big Wheel', followed by an incredibly energetic interpretation of 'Light My Fire' with Horace Andy. 3D then entered the stage for 'Heat Miser' and 'Euro Zero Zero', dressed in a long sleeve black shirt, despite the severe heat, his hair dyed in blue. The band left acclaimed. In an interview with the national radio, the host described them as the "most important group of the 1990s", which 3D tried to understate as "press stuff", announcing they were working on their third album.

Indeed, D was thinking a lot about the band's future and wanted to

---

102 Interview with Craig McLean in *The Face* magazine, in November 1995

move on, renew their music, and constantly evolve. While they were booked for more dates early 1997, he started composing on tour, with Angelo. He was disappointed by Tricky's departure just as Mushroom was disappointed by their work with Nellee, so their studio work obviously had to mutate. Mushroom still thought of their collective as a hip-hop-based sound system, nourished by outer influences. But the recent stage performances of the band showed that the live instruments had brought of lot of energy to their sound. With Grant not so keen to re-enter the studios, the trio was at a crossroad, looking to redefine their functioning as well as their sound.

In 1997, Massive, Portishead as well as Tricky were searching for renewed types of expression when a new trend exploded in Bristol: *New Forms* by the drum & bass band Roni Size and Reprazent came out in June and hit number 8 in the UK Albums Chart in July, selling more than 325,000 records. The act was formed by Ryan Owen Granville Williams, aka Roni Size, born in Bristol on October 29, 1969 and raised in St Andrews in a Jamaican family. He regularly worked with DJ Die, DJ Suv, Krust, vocalist Onallee, and with Clive Deamer and Rob Merrill on drums. Highlighting the success of the whole drum and bass genre, *New Forms* won the Mercury Prize for Best Album in late August, beating off the Chemical Brothers' *Dig Your Own Hole*, Primal Scream's *Vanishing Point*, the Prodigy's *The Fat of the Land* and Radiohead's *OK Computer*, among others. But Bristol hadn't even said its last word yet.

Banksy's Massive take on Bristol

From the second half of the 1990s, while 3D abandoned Bristol's walls for a worldwide music glory, the world of graffiti artists was deeply evolving. And from 1992, Banksy's name started to appear on certain walls, hardly noticed at the beginning. In his rare interviews, the now legendary street artist seldom forgets to mention how much he owes to 3D, as an inspiration, and to John Nation and his *Barton Hill Youth Club*.

In a 2006 interview with the magazine *Swindle*, Banksy said: "I came from a relatively small city in southern England. When I was about ten years old, a kid called 3D was painting the streets hard. I think he'd been to New York and was the first to bring spray painting back to Bristol.

I grew up seeing spray paint on the streets way before I ever saw it in a magazine or on a computer. 3D quit painting and formed the band Massive Attack, which may have been good for him but was a big loss for the city. Graffiti was the thing we all loved at school. We did it on the bus on the way home from school. Everyone was doing it."

From these days, Banksy worked totally anonymously. And no one in Bristol would reveal his identity. A few of his fellow Bristolians know his real identity, and 3D and Inkie are among his small circle of confidants. By the time Banksy was making a name for himself, 3D had become quite disappointed with the graffiti scene and preferred to work on canvas and to save his creations for other forms of expression.

In the *Daily Telegraph* in 2008, Robert Del Naja publically described Banksy as "iconic, mad and creative" and as "a friend"[103]. But of course he won't say much more. Who knows if I've even really met him? he pondered mischievously when discussing his art in his studio mid 2015, a few weeks before the opening of Banksy's *Dismaland* theme park. Banksy's anonymity is a part of Bristol's culture and treasure.

According to other sources close to the artists, and to a few articles from the *Guardian*, Banksy could have been born in Yate, in Gloucestershire, near Bristol, in 1973 or 74, which he himself never confirmed. On the website of his former manager, Steve Lazarides, he is said to have been born in 1974 in Bristol. From 2008, British tabloids stated that his real name was Robin Gunningham, born in Bristol in a middle-class family, but as Banksy could stay in his own style: What do they know? The rumour spread when his so-called former schoolmates confirmed this identity and described him "an early very talented drawer".

On his own website, Banksy wrote temporally in 2008: "I am unable to comment on who may or may not be Banksy, but anyone described as being 'good at drawing' doesn't sound like Banksy to me." From 2006, his was regularly referred to as Robert Banks. In diverse articles and books written about him, he is named Robin Banks or Robin Gunningham. He published a book in 2001, entitled *Banging Your Head*

---

103 In an interview published on March 28, 2008

Against A Brick Wall[104], signed as Robin Banksy, but adding no further details on his identity. Of course. In Bristol, most people who pretend to have met him do call him 'Robin' most of the time.

As the press became increasingly obsessed with unmasking his identity, other rumours appeared. Among his admirers and Massive Attack's fans, some like to spread from the end of the 1990s the rumour that he is indeed... Robert Del Naja. Or at least that Massive Attack and Banksy are a "super collective crew". An appealing theory because Banksy's art became more prevalent as Del Naja abandoned his outdoor work. Yet their career took them in different locations and on diverse artistic paths. Both artists deny the claims.

Let's go back to facts. Banksy's first graffiti were identified by Bristol police around 1990/91, when he was spraying with DryBreadZ, or DBZ crew, along with artists known as Kato, Lokey and Tes. They all emerged out of the *Barton Hill Youth Club*, led by John Nation, a social activity leader with a keen interest in graffiti. Banksy first worked freehand with spray cans but soon started using stencils, as 3D did from as early as 1984. The stencil technique became Banksy's trademark in the early 2000s.

In his book, *Wall And Piece*, published in 2005 by Random House, Banksy recalled his own beginnings: "When I was 18, I spent one night trying to paint 'LATE AGAIN' in big silver bubble letters on the side of a passenger train. British Transport Police showed up and I got ripped to shreds running away through a thorny bush. The rest of my mates made it to the car and disappeared so I spent over an hour hidden under a dumper truck with engine oil leaking all over me. As I lay there listening to the cops on the tracks, I realised I had to cut my painting time in half or give up altogether. I was staring straight up at the stencilled plate on the bottom of a fuel tank when I realised I could just copy that style and make each letter 3ft high. I got home at last and crawled into bed next to my girlfriend. I told her I'd had an epiphany that night and she told me to stop taking that drug 'cos it's bad for your heart."

Banksy's work became better known from 1996. But his anonymity remained. "This came as Steve Lazarides' genius strategy," claims Inkie[105]. "Steve found the right marketing tools for Banksy and we were all amazed and overrun by the scale of all this. Once his anonymous ethos got spread in the press, it wasn't possible to go backwards on his identity. But the myth according to which he's a collective is not real. He is one man, not a collective, and he's a very talented artist. 3D and I know him and are proud of him."

Banksy was by the late 1990s about to make his mark and to impose his art nationally and eventually worldly. The press even tends to forget he is from Bristol, spotting his artwork in London, New York, Los Angeles, Melbourne, Timbuktu and Gaza. But he regularly visits Bristol and he and 3D remain linked. In 1997, he was actually seen at the Christchurch Studio, where D was working with Neil Davidge and Angelo Bruschini on a few new songs in between live shows.

As Massive Attack did before him, Banksy's revolutionary art and unorthodox spirit soon epitomised Bristol. For Inkie, he embodies the need to impose his mark on society and not in the society. And for both Massive and Banksy, the year 1998 was a pivotal time in this achievement.

---

105 In an interview with the author in Bristol in June 2015

Chapter 8
Black Blossoms, Melancholy And
Metamorphosis (1997-98)

In the mid 1990s, British culture and politics were thriving like they had not been since the Swinging Sixties. On May 1, 1997, the United Kingdom underwent a huge political turning point when, after the long Tory domination in Parliament, New Labour led by Tony Blair won the general election, with their most comfortable majority since 1935. Mr Blair became Prime Minister and in July the new Chancellor, Gordon Brown, set the budget with a new vision. He planned to increase spending on education and healthcare by £3 million, and to help single mothers and unemployed youth.

Moreover, the government negotiated a renewal of the ceasefire in Northern Ireland in August, a historic deal that would lead to the Good Friday Agreement in 1998. The only cloud in Britain's sky in 1997 seemed to be the tragic death of Princess Diana in Paris on August 31.

Culturally, the country was also at a high, notably when collector Charles Saatchi opened the *Sensation* exhibition, with artworks by the Young British Artists, at the Royal Academy of Art, in London. The show ran from September to December and received stunning reviews all around the world. One of the most noticed pieces was *The Physical Impossibility of Death in the Mind of Someone Living*, created by Damien Hirst, an artist born in 1965 in Bristol...

Mezzanine's Genesis

Since the end of 1996, Massive Attack had been working on a new album with the working title *Damaged Goods*. The band actually tried to remix Gang Of Four's track of the same name into a rap version. After their successful tour dates and a winter break, they returned to Christchurch

Studios, in Clifton early in 1997. But the making of this third album wasn't easy, to say the least. A rumour first announced a release for the summer 1997, but it was postponed to the end of the year, because of internal conflicts, said the media. The band scheduled new live dates instead.

The main issue was that the three members had a different view of what their new record should be. Mushroom was mostly satisfied by *Protection* and by the show centred on the decks with live scratching effects. His inspirations still came from hip-hop influences. But for 3D, the last gigs had shown that the band had to evolve to surprise and open new paths, and that they could. In the same way he had stopped painting graffiti half a decade earlier, when he felt it was becoming mainstream, he thought that what the press had baptised "trip-hop" had been a thousand times copied and therefore worn out.

At this time, the band started working permanently with Neil Davidge as a producer. Neil studied graphic design and started painting before becoming a musician. Like 3D, he had an aesthetic approach to music, which enabled him to communicate better with him, through visual and verbal means of expression, working on his coming experimentations, and he could help D in expressing them to the rest of the band.

Born in 1962 in Bristol, Neil knew Nellee Hooper and Mushroom from school. He met with Massive Attack through Craig Armstrong, when the latter was recording *Protection*'s piano parts, and Neil worked with them on finishing their cover of 'The Hunter Gets Captured By The Game'. His first musical references went from jazz to the Beatles and soul music, including Marvin Gaye, Stevie Wonder and Nina Simone. And, like Grant and D, he became passionate about post-punk in the late 1970s, going to see the Pop Group's gigs and hanging out at Revolver Records.

Neil and D started recording improvised guitar parts with Angelo Bruschini. Some of their jam sessions could last for hours, then Robert and Neil looked for their dream sound, sampling bits of them. Robert also sampled extracts from his favourite new wave albums, from Gang of Four, Public Image Ltd, Stiff Little Fingers, Wire and even some tracks from the Pop Group. He wanted to go back to the source of his first musical influences, which inspired him as a teenager, energetic and supercharged. But at first, he didn't know how to get this method to work.

For Mushroom though, this type of sound only reminded him of narrow cultural references, very English and too dominant. He didn't attend the *Rock Against Racism* concerts like D and Grant did. He was more into looking for an R&B groove for the album.

These differences in tastes resulted in a tense atmosphere in the studio. Soon the band were scattered and each of the three members worked in shifts in the studio, on one specific idea at a time, taking the lead for just a short period on a track, having no right to make any final decision without the consent of his two counterparts. A democratic rule at the core of their communal attitude. But tensions arose consequently in 3D's lyrics, which were filled with negativity. His work evolved better when granted the pace it needed. To him, it had bothing to do with a search of perfection but more with looking for the muse, finding a sense of belonging in what one's creates.

The choice of a new team

The band's team had become quite different from the one involved on their second album. Key members in 1997 were 3D, Neil Davidge and Angelo Bruschini. Neil had become a real right arm for the band, orchestrating the recordings, almost a fourth member. Unlike Cameron and Nellee, he was very often present in the studio, and very patient. 3D completely trusted him. The band also worked with the instrumentalists Jon Harris, Bob Locke, Winston Blissett (on bass guitars) and Andy Gangadeen (on drums and percussion).

D wrote raps to share with Grant and worked on a couple of other tracks for Horace Andy. Regarding a new female voice, Grant and Robert looked to the former singer of the Cocteau Twins, Elizabeth Fraser, whose unique soprano voice, refined and extremely emotional, fascinated them. Born in 1963 in Grangemouth, in Scotland, between Glasgow and Edinburgh, Elizabeth started singing and writing for the Cocteau Twins at the age of 17, in 1980, and worked with legendary musicians including Peter Gabriel and Jeff Buckley. The Cocteau

Twins' last album, *Milk & Kisses*, was released in March 1996 and the trio disbanded soon after, partly because of the meltdown of Liz's relationship with the band's guitarist, Robin Guthrie, her then partner.

Massive Attack had already tried to contact her in 1994 but Elizabeth was notoriously secretive and reclusive; she didn't reply. In the meantime, she started a relationship with the drummer of Spiritualized, Damon Reece, and they settled in Bristol, attracted by the lively music scene. Soon, Damon left Spiritualized with the band's bass player Sean Cook, despite the success of the third album, *Ladies And Gentlemen We Are Floating In Space* (released on June 16, 1997), and they both started to work in Bristol with the musicians from the Insects. Massive Attack could then contact Elizabeth through their common friends in the Insects.

3D also worked with a singer from Sheffield named Sarah Jay, whom he met via the band's manager, Marc Picken. While on tour, D composed a couple of songs, including a track called 'Wire', with the voice of Thom Yorke in mind. Robert sent him the track, the Radiohead singer was very interested in the collaboration and wrote something new for it. But Robert remembers the project "being scuppered by time". 'Wire' was tried live by Massive Attack with Sarah Jay as a vocalist, interpreting it at some of their shows from the spring 1997. Sarah later voiced a different version of it in the studio in Bristol, but the song was never finalised and not selected for their third album. 'Wire' finally appeared in an instrumental version named 'End Titles' on the soundtrack of Michael Winterbottom's film, *Welcome To Sarajevo*, released in November 1997.

Despite these major steps forwards in the recordings, the atmosphere remained tense between the band members. Mushroom was uncomfortable with these new directions. Like the working title of the album, *Damaged Goods*, Massive Attack's music seemed to resemble an ever-deconstructing project. Each member disappeared from the studio when upset by the others' choices, sometime for days, and hours of recorded improvisations remained unused.

Back on tour mid 1997, Massive Attack performed in Dublin with Radiohead, on June 21, before an important gig in Glastonbury on June 27, then travelled to Istanbul and to Central Europe. Back in

England, they played in more summer festivals. During the tour, 3D kept on writing, especially lyrics, which displayed an increasing feeling of isolation and panic. When back in the studio, he felt oppressed and struggled to express his ideas.

"Quite often he wouldn't actually be able to verbalise what he wanted," explained Neil Davidge in an interview[106]. "It was a matter of trying to get inside his head and understand him as a person – all the things that are going on in his personal life, everything." Despite his communication issues, D had a vision and direction in mind for this album. With Angelo, he was the mastermind of their new single, 'Risingson', that the band played on stage during the summer before its release in July 1997.

"D can be very conceptual and very visual," Neil tells me years later when we meet in Stokes Croft. "I tend to like to capture quickly the feeling when recording while working with him often implies working hours, days, on a track, then changing the whole of it, only to realise we've turned it into crap. You have to accept defeat when trying so hard on things[107]." Neil reckons he witnessed a lot of fighting between the band's members, especially between 3D and Mushroom. "I saw the three of them arguing for days, falling out. Then I would remain in the studio with D and receive a call from Mushroom asking me to tell D to leave so that he could do his part. In that sense, I found the collective work difficult, because I care about all of them equally. And keeping on working meant living up with this pressure[108]…"

With his soft nature, Neil quickly became a go-between in the band: "D has always been very good at being himself and completely honest in complex situations. He also looks at things in a perspective of global issues. We had a lot of arguments in those decades of working together, but I love the way his mind works. He could be pulling me apart then I'd listen to what he'd done and went 'wow, this is amazing, how do you do that?' I think our relationship became central for the band at some point and for many years. Now I'm thinking, actually, it may also partly

---

106   With *Q Magazine*, published in January 1999
107   In an interview with the author in Bristol in March 2015
108   Ibid

be why Mushroom left the band, because he could not relate to D the way that I could[109]."

At this stage, Neil realised that the key to the album, soon to become *Mezzanine*, was inside of 3D's mind. They yet had to make it come alive in the studio.

Bristol Sound, next level

With its busy music scene, Bristol had been radiating far from its own borders since 1996. When Tricky released his second album, *Nearly God*, in February, he explained to the press that the title was inspired by a German journalist, who asked him, after the success of *Maxinquaye*, what it felt "to be a god… or almost a god". After working with Björk and Neneh Cherry, after covering Siouxsie and the Banshees and collaborating with one of his all time heroes, Terry Hall from the Specials, Tricky started composing with Damon Albarn from Blur. But he didn't get along very well with the king of Brit Pop… The collaboration soon turned sour. Yet Tricky's success was undeniable and gained him the attention of superstars up to American artists, including Prince. He was aware though that he needed to push himself higher to evolve, without waiting, and produced a third album with Martina, *Pre-Millenium Tension*, that he considered more risky and experimental. He was also playing around his own image, stating he was still hard to understand and mysterious, and released in 1997 a single entitled purposely 'Tricky Kid'.

Soon after, Portishead announced the release of their second album, simply named *Portishead*, for September 30, 1997. The record reached number two in the UK Albums Chart, number three in France and 21 in the USA. The first single, 'All Mine', released three weeks earlier, reached number 8 in the UK Singles Chart, the highest ranking for a track from Bristol so far. The reviewers were mesmerised, underlining how the band managed to use hip-hop in a way that was absolutely not segmenting and could therefore reach a wide audience. This can also be interpreted as a strictly musical use of hip-hop, which does not include

109 In an interview with the author in Bristol in March 2015

the social background it emerged from, nor any underlying political or cultural value, as African-American hip-hop does. Sociologically, this attitude clearly differentiates Portishead from Tricky or Massive Attack.

Around that time, Massive Attack were also working on their own label, Melankolic, claiming their so-called "dark" side with their slogan, 'Glad to be sad', and producing a Horace Andy album. The label was meant to enhance their own attitude, erring on the dark side, privileging soulful, slow and elegiac sounds. For Robert Del Naja, this went deep to his early tastes as a child, when the most melancholic songs of an album always captured his heart, from the Beatles' 'I Want You (She's So Heavy)' to Roxy Music's 'In Every Dream Home A Heartache'. To him, this kind of songs offered some sort of tragic moments from which we emerge illuminated.

The label's goal was also to help local talents to develop. "It's a family thing and it's all fucking good," 3D explained. "Everything is about being hopeful and promising. No one's got in each other's way. Everyone is being helpful and supportive[110]."

Melankolic thus produced a first album from a Bristol band named Alpha. Formed by Andy 'Spaceland' Jenks and Corin Dingley with singers Helen White, Martin Barnard and Wendy Stubbs, they released *ComeFromHeaven* in September 1997. "We wanted to create an electronic music influenced by reggae and hip-hop sounds", explains Andy years later when I meet with him in the Christchurch Studios. "Bristol has a wonderful and integrated music community, where many musicians were fed by St Pauls parties in the 1980s", he adds. "Corin and I met with the Insects who had worked with Massive Attack. The Insects gave our first demos to 3D. And what we wanted to do with Alpha was to get the best of the encounter between sampling and emotional vocals[111]."

With their label, Massive Attack also produced the Londoner Lewis Parker, who released *Masquarades & Silhouettes* in October 1997, hard-rock band Sunna and Day One, encouraging them all to find independence and creativity.

110 In an interview with *Inner Views* published in 1998, in an article named 'Friendly Fire'
111 In an interview with the author in Bristol in April 2015

In the meantime, while their third album kept being postponed, the band had surprised everyone when announcing the coming release of a new single, 'Risingson', for July, which entered the UK Singles Chart at number 11. 3D had been composing while on tour for many months, mainly with their guitarist Angelo Bruschini. This new track revealed how much their sound had evolved with their recent touring.

In England, the news came out just as the influence of Massive Attack's electronic and hip-hop touch began to appear very evidently in British bands' new releases. Bands like Radiohead and Blur evolved towards electronic music. Mid-June, Spiritualized had released their acclaimed third album, *Ladies and Gentlemen We Are Floating in Space*, praised for its "vast array of musical influences". Radiohead's third album, *OK Computer*, out in May 1997, showed complex, atmospheric and less rock-and-roll arrangements. The second single released in August was 'Karma Police', a title reminding of Massive Attack's emblematic 'Karmacoma'. The band from Oxford often recognised how much they love Massive Attack.

The two bands had actually met on tour in America in 1995, on a long bus journey along the West Coast from Canada to San Francisco. They all had a day off at Ashland, Oregon, and when Radiohead's bus broke down, Massive Attack offered them a lift. They came backstage after a couple of their shows; Radiohead came to one of Massive's. And they bonded. They remained in touch, Radiohead listening carefully to Massive Attack's sound evolution on stage in 1996/97. Thom Yorke even sent the demo of *OK Computer* to 3D on cassette before its release, to check what he thought of it... Something made with magic, D felt.

Meanwhile, Blur's leader, Damon Albarn, was preparing a new project, an alternative hip-hop/rock/electro collective to be named Gorillaz, with the comic book artist Jamie Hewlett. They shared the same house for a while in London mid 1997. The band was officially formed in 1998. The members of Blur and Massive Attack had met at the Glastonbury Festival in 1995 and regularly crossed paths since then in London. Damon had befriended 3D and soon came up with his own pseudonym for Gorillaz as 2D.

Damon was fascinated by Massive Attack's multicultural expression, and shared their passion for reggae and hip-hop music. While the music press underlined how unique Massive Attack's diversity is, Damon felt stuck under the 'Brit Pop' label. "I remember being on tour and listening to their first album, *Blue Lines*, and being really jealous of their freedom, not to be tied to a band structure. It was a model for the future," he later confirmed in an interview with the *Guardian*[112]. The journalist described how Gorillaz was "initially inspired by the collective approach of Bristolian pioneers Massive Attack," to get away from what Damon called "the weight of being in a rock group," looking for a much looser role.

Massive Attack's visual creativity also influenced the British music world. *OK Computer*'s artwork was much deeper than the one on Radiohead's previous album, *The Bends*. Both covers were created by the English artist Dan Rickwood, known as Stanley Donwood and The Chocolate Factory, who met Thom Yorke at university. They had been increasingly looking for a more audacious visual presentation for the band. With Gorillaz, Damon went even further as the band members presented themselves as a collective of virtual animated characters, created by Jamie Hewlett: 2D, aka Damon Albarn; Murdoc Niccals (Morgan Nicholls in real life, and bass player); Noodle (bass, guitar and keyboard) and Russels Hobbs (real name Remi Kabala, drummer of Nigerian descent). They were joined by featured artists and vocalists.

When these musicians opened themselves to hip-hop influences, electronic experimentations and a deeper visual aesthetic, Robert Del Naja was inspired by the idea of sampling songs from his earliest tastes, including post-punk guitar riffs and new wave rhythms. But from the year 1996, he felt he would have to convince the rest of the band to go along and to prove to them that it was time to metamorphose.

'Risingson' and 'Superpredator': birth of a new sound

Because a few songs were ready and the album was not, Massive Attack, pressured by Virgin, agreed to release an EP. It was announced for July 7, 1997. The album was postponed to the end of the year and at this

---

112 Published on April 27, 2014

stage, the working title *Damaged Goods* was abandoned. The band had a lot of material but none of the members saw it as a whole album yet. They already knew the deadline would be hard to respect.

The new release on July 7 was an extended play with the main song, 'Risingson', and on the B-side a new instrumental track named 'Superpredators', completed by a couple of remixes. 'Superpredators' featured a sample from the song 'Metal Postcard', by Siouxsie and the Banshees. 'Risingson' contains a vocal sample from the Velvet Underground's 'I Found A Reason' and a discreet musical sample from the song 'Practice Makes Perfect' by the band Wire, appeared on their 1978 release *Chairs Missing*, a sample not credited officially by Massive Attack. These choices gave a definite tone. And the band was quite nervous ahead of the reactions.

'Risingson' started off with quite a funky beat, which came from Mushroom. 3D added the guitars over it with Neil and then played the second bassline on the keyboard. It created this track that changes halfway through; the guitars completely changed the feel of the beat. When D sampled the Velvet Underground, that took the track in completely different psychedelic direction. The layered melodies came out. But this marvel of assembled sounds and ideas only puzzled Mushroom.

Lyrically, D wanted it to be a duo and asked G to listen to it, but it wasn't easy. Luckily, 'Risingson' finally became one of Grant's favourite tracks of that era. "The way we approached the vocals on that track and the fact that it was a totally different way of doing things than we usually do," says Grant; "with the whole thing with the chorus to chorus that we got on it. Quite an unorthodox way of approaching a rap track[113]." The song perfectly reflects the changes in progress in the band's sound.

When the EP reached number 11 of the UK Singles Chart, it came as a relief for the band. The music press described it as sublime and unexpected, noting its feelings of doubts, what they saw as "darkness" and a new direction for the band's music, which they used to qualify as "dance for the brain".

113 In the *Mezzanine* promo interview with the label, in March 1998

The slow melody of 'Risingson', melancholic and menacing, is allied to lyrics describing cryptically a dysfunctional relationship, begun in a *"club maze"* to culminate in this statement: *"Now you're lost and you're lethal"*, in a series of references to sadness, tears and danger. *"I sink myself in hair upon my lover / It's how you go down to men's room sink / Sad we talk how madmen think / I sink myself in hair upon my lover / I don't know her from another miss / I don't know you from another / See me run now you're gone, dream on"*. The song's lyrics also display in other moments feelings of fragility and an elegiac sense of abandonment, about the loss of something that has been left behind...

Daddy G's deep and sombre voice adds to the grim atmosphere when he follows: *"Why you want to take me to this party and breathe / I'm dying to leave / Every time we grind we know we severed lines / Where have all those flowers gone / Long time passing / Why you keep me testing, keep me tasking / You keep on asking"*. These last words are quoting the American folk-style song written in 1955 by Pete Seeger, 'Where Have All The Flowers Gone?'. Backing vocals complete the menacing feel of the music, repeating 3D's words *"Dream on"*... The song has since become a classic of the band, a pillar in every one of their shows.

'Risingson' was a sort of statement of intent for the band, because of their absence of three years, after *Protection*. A statement of intent on what was going to happen next. And their 1997 summer tour allowed them to experiment with what their new show would be, in a transition period between *Protection* and *Mezzanine*.

The single was released with a promo video directed by Walter Stern, who emphasised the track's paranoid and nightmarish universe. Walter Stern had picked up on the kind of press and stories that were going around the record.

It shows the band members in a house that is attacked from the outside by a team of workers armed with hammers and chainsaws. While 3D gets more alarmed by the danger than the others and runs from the ground to the first floor, Daddy G remains emotionless and Mushroom gets busy on his record player or in the kitchen, preparing a sandwich, absorbed in the deep observation of tiny details such as the jars' vibrations on the shelves... When a final assault occurs, chainsaws destroying doors and windows, 3D is walking in circles in the living room and Daddy G simply leaves the house, by the main entrance.

The video plays with connotations already explored in the films produced for 'Safe From Harm' and 'Karmacoma' and imposes even more the complex image of the band. The vocal and visual tightening of the band, around the three core members only, is very outstanding, as the track has no featured vocalist. It revealed a band at the height of their creativity. And the song acted as a teaser for the rest of the album, while the audience waited for its completion.

Meanwhile, the band continued their summer tour, with a show including many new tracks: 3D and Daddy G duetted a proto-version of a song named 'Mezzanine'. And after their interpretation of 'Karmacoma', Sarah Jay entered the stage to sing a new track entitled 'Dissolved Girl', that she wrote with 3D and Angelo. And, some nights, she pursued with 'Wire'. The show closed with 'Risingson' and of course 'Unfinished Sympathy', with Deborah Miller on vocals. Winston's bass patterns, added to the strong drum effects and Angelo's guitar riffs, halfway into some key songs, worked miraculously well on stage. The guitars were really dominant on the new songs, 'Mezzanine', 'Dissolved Girl', 'Wire' and 'Risingson'.

Grant appeared more and more relaxed, wearing light colours, singing a hand in his pocket. 3D, always dressed in black, brought in the tension and the layers of mystery with his murmured voice, while Mushroom was still handling the samples, live from his decks, appearing moody though. When Sarah Jay or Deborah Miller joined them for 'Dissolved Girl', 'Wire' then 'Unfinished Sympathy', they were introduced by D, whose presence became catalytic on the stage. The set was mostly plunged in the dark, illuminated from the background with hypnotic blue spotlights.

From 'Angel' to 'Teardrop': on the *Mezzanine*

3D and Mushroom still worked on 'Angel' together, a track given to sing to Horace Andy. Mushroom put the original keyboards into it, which the band distorted with amps that inspired D to add the guitar progressions. Even though Mushroom didn't like the guitar part on

'Angel', it was a collaborative moment. And they ended up writing the final version of the song in one day because D tried to get Horace to sing some of the words from 'Straight to Hell' by the Clash but he hated the work because it had the word 'hell' in it.

These lyrics were abandoned. A new sample was added later, from the bridge part of 'Last Bongo in Belgium' by the American rock band The Incredible Bongo Band, founded in 1972 by Michael Viner. G suggested Horace should sing a version of 'You Are My Angel', one of the old songs ; 3D and Mushroom rewrote a few lines and that spontaneously changed the track.

The lyrics announce a love song: *"You are my angel / Come from way above / To bring me love"*, but with the tension in the music, the feeling of the vocal interpretation gets increasingly polarising: *"Her eyes / She's on the dark side"*, Horace continues, *"Neutralise / Every man in sight"*, like a clash between the desire for tenderness and the impossibility to give in to it and trust.

'Angel' was finalised in London's Olympic Studio with Horace, D, Mushroom, Grant and Mark 'Spike' Stent, the band's mixer for the album. It was one of the few last occasions when they were all in a room together that year. "D and Horace went next door," said Neil Davidge, "we were kind of throwing vocal ideas around, I was in the studio with Spike and we were messing around with the track, chopping things together. Then Horace put the vocal down and it was like 'Wow, shit, that is magic'[114]". With guitarist Angelo Bruschini, they got to "this sort of club-dark-ambient-romantic-soul, with these really heavy guitars and drums pounding in," Neil added.

'Angel' showed the progression that the album has gone through creatively – from samples to programming and live jamming. In the studio, to get more comfortable, everyone discusses details of their everyday life, to ease the conflicts, losing time but appeasing the tensions. The song became Mushroom's favourite so far and everyone agreed it would make a perfect opening for the record.

An obvious single, 'Angel' was released on July 13, 1998 in the UK as

114 In an interview with *Fact Mag*, published on December 28, 2013

the third single from the album, *Mezzanine*, featuring a remix by Blur. It reached number 30 in the Singles Chart. A video was produced by Walter Stern but finally not released that year. The band really liked it but judged it too estranged from the song's atmosphere. The film shows Daddy G getting out of a parking lot at night, soon followed by Horace Andy, 3D and Mushroom... then a huge crowd of men running after him, in a scary dark urban environment. It later appeared on the band's selection of short films released on DVD in 2001.

The song, with its own cinematic feel, soon attracted filmmakers. Among many others, it was featured in the 1999 film π (*Pi*) by Darren Aronofsky and appeared on its soundtrack album. The following year, it was chosen by Guy Ritchie for his new film, *Snatch*, with Benicio del Toro and Brad Pitt. In 2005, it was featured in David Benioff's psychological thriller, *Stay*. It was also used in many television series.

Before releasing 'Angel', Massive Attack chose 'Teardrop' as a second single. Written soon after 'Angel', this sublime ballad was one of their last compositions together. It also increased the divisions between the band's members in new ways. Paradoxically, sonically, it became the most serene and comforting moment on the tortured album.

The first notes of 'Teardrop' emerged in April 1997. Neil was working in the studio when Mushroom arrived and liked a tune that Neil started playing on a harpsichord. Mushroom wanted to work further on a demo using the tune with Neil. They recorded instrument parts, worked on it on their computer and Mushroom added a beat that he liked, following the hip-hop feel of some of the songs on *Protection*. The result was temporarily named 'No Don't'. Mushroom would like a soul singer to interpret it.

Neil and D worked separately to further develop the backing track and, after consulting Grant, they decided to send it to Elizabeth. She worked on the demo and started writing lyrics. She soon worked on a vocal melody that would become 'Teardrop'. D and Grant had long wanted to give such a track to Elizabeth Fraser and while she was working on it, they announced to Mushroom that they had contacted her.

But sadly Mushroom hated the result at first. He said he didn't want to work on the track anymore and removed his beats. Neil called D with a rescue plan and they made a collage using the song, drums and percussion from another track they had been writing, that was influenced by Talk Talk's *Spirit of Eden* – D had been listening to it on repeat. They changed the rhythm and added percussions, then developed the song with their studio engineer at the time, Dave Jenkins who played the piano parts. They lastly added Mellotron choir parts to give it melodrama.

The final composition sounded like a slow ballad, with a rhythm recreating the sound of a heart beating, reinforced by the piano and keyboard parts. It incorporated a sample from 'Sometimes I Cry' by American jazzman Les McCann, from his album *Layers*, released in 1973, not credited. 3D, Neil and Grant were delighted by the result.

Then, while Liz was writing the lyrics for the song, she was informed of the death of her close friend Jeff Buckley, on May 29... He drowned himself in the Mississippi river at just 29 years old. After her break-up with the Cocteau Twins' leader, Robin Guthrie, and before her encounter with Damon Reece, Liz and Jeff had been really close and even worked together, notably on the unreleased song, 'All Flowers In Town Bend Towards The Sun', known to their fans through demos.

"That was so weird," she told the *Guardian* in November 2009. "I'd got letters out and I was thinking about him. That song's kind of about him – that's how it feels to me anyway." Her minimal lyrics for 'Teardrop' were very much influenced by her deep sorrow. Robert Del Naja was also a deep admirer of the singer whom he met briefly in 1995, at a hotel in Bayswater, in London.

"*Black flowers blossom / Fearless on my breath / Teardrop on the fire*", she sings, adding "*Water is my eye (...) You stumble in the dark*," wrote Liz. "I just got so depleted and exhausted by everything," she later told the *Guardian*[115]. "I was in a horrible place. I had always thought of myself as a sanguine person, quite light and airy. But for a long while, no one could have possibly made me laugh or smile. It was awful." Her emotional fragility irrigated the song, inspired by a deep feeling of melancholy.

115 In an interview published on June 24, 2012

But in the meantime, in June, the band received a phone call and were told that someone had sent the 'No Don't' demo to... Madonna. And her management wanted Massive Attack to know that she would be delighted to work with them again, still loving their collaboration on Marvin Gaye's cover, 'I Want You'. As 'Teardrop' was almost ready, the band had to decline and politely apologise to the American pop star. Mushroom wanted to work with Madonna, though he had refused to have anything to do with her in 1995, when Massive Attack worked on the tribute to Marvin Gaye.

Interviewed when the single was out, Robert Del Naja expressed his disappointment in an understatement: "Me and G were obviously really unhappy about the situation. It was at a point where, after a lot of meandering, the album was finally starting to develop. There were seven or eight tracks happening which were really sounding like they made a lot of sense[116]."

The trust between 3D and Mushroom was definitely damaged by this episode, and their differences, which until then had nourished the band's creativity, henceforth only produced acrimony. They decided to work completely separately.

'Teardrop' became *Mezzanine*'s third track and second single, released on April 27, 1998, a week after the album, out on April 20. The track reached number 10 in the Singles Chart after the record entered the UK Albums Chart at number one.

Walter Stern directed a third video for the band and surprised everyone with a film centred on an animated foetus, miming the song's lyrics from inside a uterus. When it was made, Liz Fraser was coincidently pregnant. Everyone in the band saw it as an optimistic celebration of life. Robert Del Naja still displays the animated baby in his studio in Bristol among his affectionate personal souvenirs...

The film won a prize at the MTV Europe Awards, in October 1998, in Milan, Italy, where the group once more proved their rebel attitude as they discovered that the trophy was handed over by the Duchess of York, Sarah Ferguson. When she mispronounced the band's name,

---

116 In an article published in Q magazine, in January 1999, entitled "Are We A Fucking Punk Band Now?"

Mushroom and 3D got even angrier and refused to shake her aristocratic hand, D taking the microphone only to state: "What a joke, fuck you very much!" Before thanking warmly Walter Stern.

Just like 'Angel', 'Teardrop' appeared in many films and series, including *Prison Break, Charmed* and the more recent *House*. It was also chosen by Sam Mendes to be the central song featured in his film *American Beauty* but the band finally turned down the offer.

'Out of body experience'

With 'Angel', 'Risingson', and 'Teardrop', the album had its three first tracks and three decisive songs. The band had a lot of material for the rest of the album, including 'Wire', 'Superpredators', 'Mezzanine' and 'Dissolved Girl', but struggled to make choices. And the studio work became even more fractured after their mid-1997 tour dates.

3D finalised the track 'Dissolved Girl', played on stage in 1997, with Sarah Jay. The song was soon chosen to be featured in the soundtrack *The Matrix*, by the Wachowski brothers, due out in March 1999. It was played in the scene where Neo, asleep with his headphones, is called by his computer to wake up from the lies of this world and to follow the white rabbit... The Wachowski brothers selected the song specifically for that moment.

D also worked on the final version of 'Mezzanine' and on the track 'Group Four' with Liz, as well as a song called 'Inertia Creeps'. Like almost the entire album, the track 'Mezzanine' was reinvented many times before finding its final form, tested through different versions on stage. Its lyrics, written by 3D for Grant and himself, seem to refer to an unstable love story: "*I could be yours / We can unwind / All these have flaws*", D repeats... But they mainly leave space to the imagination of the listeners, cryptic as ever, as this suggestion does: "*Why don't you close your eyes and reinvent me*".

And the track finally gave a name to the album. Designating a floor between two floors, the word carries a metaphor of hybridisation. The album was becoming a halfway between the band's roots in hip-hop and reggae sounds and their older influences, from Robert's tastes mainly, which seemed to come back to his memory like an old dream demanding reinterpretation.

Even once achieved, D still felt that the album hadn't found its ground in between two trends. "We didn't want it to be too perfect," he told journalists after the release. He described his choice for the word "mezzanine" as a feeling characterising a moment once remembered the next morning: "It's that particular point of the day when the night-before feeling turns into the morning-after feeling, and you're up and you're with someone and it's just you two against the world. That idea reflects me, my kind of lifestyle[117]." Asked about it by the *Mixmag* magazine in February, Grant Marshall replied: "The mezzanine? I think D spends half his life there. I don't think he knows whether he's coming or going..."

In between concerts, 3D was working further on 'Inertia Creeps'. The rhythm was inspired by the band's recent trip to Istanbul, in July 1997 for a concert, where they bought some Turkish music on cassettes. The city made a big impression on them and, back in Bristol, D and Mush worked on sampling the music to put a track together. Mushroom had a drum and horn loop on a cassette that started the track. D recorded vocals and Neil arranged them. Working further on the track, they added another sample to it, taken from the very first seconds of the song 'ROckWrok', written in 1977 by the post-punk band Ultravox, which gave a different feel.

"All their acknowledged samples – including the joy-buzzer synths from Ultravox's 'ROckWrok' ('Inertia Creeps'), the opulent ache of Isaac Hayes' celestial-soul take on 'Our Day Will Come' ('Exchange'), Robert Smith's nervous 'tick tick tick' from the Cure's '10:15 Saturday Night', and the most concrete-crumbling throwdown of the Led Zep 'Levee' break ever deployed (the latter two on 'Man Next Door') – were sourced from 1968 and 1978," underlined *Pitchfork* in January 2017, in a piece on the unforgettable-ness of the album, "well-travelled crate-digging territory. But what they build from that is its own beast."

3D wrote the lyrics for 'Inertia Creeps', inspired by the ending of a personal relationship. They seem to describe a parenthesis between a

117 In *Mixmag*, in an interview published in February 1998

dream and a nightmare, burdened by a worrying atmosphere. The music seems to come from the East, and the lyrics from the west, around the notions of domestic bliss and relationship's failure...

"Can't endure then you can't inhale / Clearly / Out of body experience interferes / And dreams of flying I fit nearly / Surrounds me though I get lonely / Slowly". His writing often emerged out of pages of lists and notes made at night, after parties or during the insomnia that follows. The main character in the song is expressing his will to mourn an unhealthy relationship he should have left long ago, evoking *"Two undernourished egos four rotating hips"*, describing switching rooms, loneliness and broken homes (*"Room shifting is endearing / Between us is our kitchen / Would you found my irritant's itching / Been here before / Been here forever"*). The vocalist tries to implore (*"Hold on to me tightly I'm a sliding scale"*), recognising the whole situation is lacking a real meaning: *"It can be sweet though incomplete though"*, longing for some more profound bond (*"Awake I lie in the morning's blue / Room is still my antenna in you"*), mixing references to sex and separation (*"She comes / She comes / I want to x you / She comes / I want to x you / She comes"*).

"It's about being in a situation but knowing you should be out of it, but you're too fucking lazy or weak to leave," explained Robert when the song was released as a single. "And you're dishonest to yourself and dishonest to the other person. You're betraying them everyday and the whole scene feels like it's closing in on you. The idea is a combination of movements propelling yourself forward and pulling yourself back at the same time[118]."

The song's lyrics exhale a sense of catharsis, which enables the character to overcome his personal anguish, especially through the frenzied Middle-eastern feel of the music, sensual and intoxicating, which transforms the human dark sensations into a sonic light. These extreme emotions create a hybrid song, musically out of any categories, inspired both by new Turkish discoveries and old memories from the punk culture, interiorised since childhood. 3D combined the urgency of the Turkish rhythm and the text that deals with inertia and stagnation.

---

118 In an interview with *Inner Views*, published in 1998

He also found that it suited the whole atmosphere of the album's recording, moving a step backwards after each two steps forwards.

'Inertia Creeps' is one of the most powerful songs on the album and soon became an unmissable moment in every Massive Attack show, with 'Risingson'. The journalist John Bush of *All Music* described the song as the highlight of *Mezzanine*: "With eerie atmospherics, fuzz-tone guitars, and a wealth of effects, the song could well be the best production from the best team of producers the electronic world had ever seen." It was released on an EP on September 21, 1998, including five remixes and another new song, 'Reflection', composed by 3D and Neil Davidge around the same time.

The promo video for 'Inertia Creeps' was directed by The Wiz – a nickname used by a British director. It shows 3D sitting alone on the floor of an empty room watching a video, then switches to another room to let us see what is in that film: a scene where D's girlfriend is caught flirting with Mushroom and Grant. The film in the film is reflected in D's blue-green iris, mixing these images of betrayal with a trait of fragility, a vulnerability characterising both the trust one puts in love and the person trusting...

Supplement of soul

Back in the studio, with 'Inertia Creeps' added to 'Angel', 'Risingson' and 'Teardrop', the band had already defined half of their coming album. It built up twenty minutes of a crescendo, melting a new wave sound with dub, electro, hip-hop and a touch of Eastern influences of an incredible strength. To move on with the rest of the album, they decamped to Cornwall in shifts, Grant and then D with Angelo.

One day, as D and Angelo were relaxing, walking on a beach near Padstow, they were stranded in a cave by the rising tide. "I thought, this is what life comes down to: one silly mistake in a cave, miles away from your comforts and your home," later said 3D. "There's a warm studio round the corner, everyone sitting in front of the Pro-Tools with tea and coffee — and here we are arsing about in a cave[119]..." The journey

---

119 In an interview with *Mojo* magazine, published in July 1998

came across as a metaphor for the general artistic contradictions of the album...

Despite the general confusion, D worked on the song 'Group Four' in Cornwall. It ended up being the last track of the album. Its format is even longer that the other five-minute songs, "like a dub track," specifies D, but with sounds of saturated guitars. He reworked the song in Bristol with Liz Fraser, as a duet. This resulted in the merge of two different songs, like in some of the Beatles' best compositions.

In his part, 3D tells the story of a man who works at night as a guard, and therefore manages to escape the responsibilities he cannot deal with (*"I see to bolts / Put keys to locks / No boat are rocked / I'm free to roam / On dummy screens / And magazines"*). Liz adds a completely different element, bringing a dream state and feeling of peace (*"Closed eyed sky wide open / Unlimited girl unlimited sigh / Elsewhere / Indefinitely / Far away / Magnifies and deepens / Ready to sing / My sixth sense peacefully placed on my breath / And listening"*).

They wrote lines for different characters from a story. D wrote about the abstraction in the background, and the girl, who talks so beautifully about feelings, is like a sudden character coming in to tell her story. That gives the time, the place and then the person involved. It can be very cinematic and give a sense of storytelling with layers. It shows what happens when there is a good energy between the band and the people they work with.

But D needed to convince himself first that all these experiments were going in the right direction. He felt lots of doubts and sometimes feared to lose the thread he was trying to follow. The tensions and arguments that occurred in Bristol still haunted him in Cornwall.

Grant started working on 'Black Milk' in Cornwall and finished the track with Mushroom, Neil and Liz Fraser, who is the lead singer on it. 3D was working in Christchurch Studio on another song at that time. The song has a stronger soulful dimension, infused with dub and a touch of hip-hop. *"You're not my eater / I'm not your food / Love you for God / Love you for the Mother,"* sings Liz. *"Eat me In the space / Within my heart / Love you for God / Love you for the Mother"*. "This is an excursion in Liz's own language, which I'm a big fan of," 3D later said in an interview with *Vox* magazine, in May 1998, obviously liking the result. "We usually jam and come up with random stuff, which we then re-record. It's quite exploratory."

Grant used a sample of the track called 'Tribute', by Manfred Mann's Earth Band, from 1972, without getting clearance for it. Grant and Neil thought that the sample would not be noticeable... But a German fan of Manfred Mann later reported it to him towards the end of 1998. And the band claimed damages of £100,000 from the Bristolians. At some point, they even tried to interrupt the album's sales. Massive Attack had to settle amicably out of court with Manfred Mann. The deal wasn't disclosed... and 'Black Milk' was later remixed by 3D without the sample into a more punkish version named 'Black Melt'.

The band also worked more with Horace Andy in Bristol, on two tracks: a cover of the ska song 'I've Got to Get Away', written by John Holt and The Paragons in 1968, which became 'Man Next Door'; and on 'Exchange', a lighter dub reggae experimentation. 'Man Next Door' also includes a very noticeable sounding drum break, similar to Led Zeppelin's 'When the Levee Breaks', previously sampled by the Beastie Boys on their first album *Licensed to Ill*, release in 1986.

'Exchange' appears twice on *Mezzanine*, in the middle of the album as an instrumental transition, and in the end, in a closing track, after 'Group Four', with added lyrics sung by Horace (*"You see a man's face / You will never see his heart / You see a man's face / But you will never know his thoughts"*).

The band members were still working on other demos when this selection of tracks were chosen to start mixing the album, at the end of November 1997, in London's Olympic Studio. The song 'Mezzanine' in its last version as well as 'Dissolved Girl' were definitely selected. Massive Attack negotiated with Circa a few more weeks to work on the album, promising to end the last arrangements by Christmas.

Meanwhile, late in 1997, with the success of the 'Risingson' EP, and despite the unbearable atmosphere in the studio, 3D was passionate by the band's live performances. A few dates remained memorable to him: On June 21, when Massive Attack was on stage ahead of Radiohead in Dublin, and their show in Glastonbury a week later. Recorded in

Oxfordshire and in Bath, near Bristol, *OK Computer* had been released on June 16, peaking at number one in the Albums Chart and critically acclaimed, and Radiohead's aura was at its height.

Increased live experience and Radiohead's proposal

Radiohead had asked Massive Attack to come and support them in Dublin. The concert was acclaimed by the press. This common experience on stage was important for both bands. For 3D, *OK Computer* was a game changer for almost everyone in British music; it literally influenced everyone, he thinks. Radiohead were also in awe of Massive Attack's work. Even before the release of their own second album, *The Bends*, they had been impressed by the sound of *Protection*, as their guitarist Ed O'Brien, admitted on BBC Radio 6 Music in October 2016. Around the mid-1990s, Radiohead wanted to move into a more experimental direction, and according to Ed, they "knew we had to get our stuff together," he told BBC 6. "And, so, who do we look towards? The coolest band at the time – and they're still very cool – were Massive Attack, as far as we were concerned."

Later in the year 1997, Radiohead secretely asked Massive Attack if they would consider remixing entirely *OK Computer*. In December on MTV, Ed O'Brien said the bold idea already kept them dreaming about the intriguing sonic possibilities: "A lot of people say why are you getting the whole album remixed? It's like, well, I think musically it could be really interesting and it's a lot of stuff. I think there are similarities between, yunno', attitudes between what Massive Attack and what we do. So we come from very different fields, but it'll be very cool to see what happens[120]."

But with their own recording for *Mezzanine*, Massive Attack had to make a choice... Radiohead's bass player, Colin Greenwood, explained: "Massive Attack. Well they're really nice people and we really like where they come from, which is Bristol, not like London. It's West Country, left of centre, like being from Oxford. And the same goes for Portishead. Massive Attack got really excited, and they really want to remix the

120 On December 23, 1997

record, and they really wanted to do it over a short period of time. They wanted to go into a studio and just do it over a week or whatever. But we kind of said no, because we were really busy and we wanted to hang out with them. We're such huge Massive Attack fans, and they're really slow workers, so we really wanted them to finish their album first. They're on tour in March and their record should be coming out early springtime, so we really can't wait[121]."

For 3D, it was a very tempting proposal but the timing was not right. From that time, Radiohead's influence on British music became undeniable. But less people know how much Massive Attack influenced Radiohead, making them look into more electronic sounds.

By the end of 1997, Massive Attack went back to their studio to finish their third album, and Robert and Thom remained linked, eyeing on other possibilities for collaboration, despite their aborted trial on 'Wire'. Robert admired Radiohead's capacity to take risks and it motivated him into his own new sonic research. With *Mezzanine*, Massive Attack looked to prove their need to free themselves from labels or comparisons.

But the artistic divides between 3D and Mushroom were deepening. The encounter of their differences proved that their alchemy could do marvels, notably on two tracks composed a few months earlier, 'Angel' and 'Inertia Creeps'. The conflict-driven but fertile approach between the two enabled them to reach a musical hybridisation, and, through it, a real sonic metamorphosis.

While the band were still perfecting the record for a couple of months, the label finally decided it had to be released. "They said 'enough's enough. You've got to put the record out now'," explained Mushroom. "It just got done, really. We just write the music and choose the tracks and certain tracks made it through and some didn't[122]."

And *Mezzanine* was finally scheduled to be released in April 1998.

After doubts, catharsis and acclamations

Although the significance of this choice was not understood at the time, the album was first released online on April 13 via *RealAudio*, a streaming

121 In the same interview on MTV, on December 23, 1997
122 In the band's interview with *Inner Views*, published in 1998

system on the internet. The BBC's technology section wrote: "Massive Attack, the band that has been called 'so hip it hurts', is pioneering again. But this time, it is not a new sound. It is a new way to sell its music". The internet made the news of the release even louder. The record was then released in CD and vinyl in the UK on April 20 and went straight to number one in the Albums Chart, selling more copies in a week than *Protection* did in a year. Grant and 3D had expressed the feeling that their two previous albums had arrived too soon for their audience and were anxious to see the reception of *Mezzanine*. They were overwhelmed by an acclaim.

"The guitars have spilled over from their live shows," Alexis Petridis wrote in *Mixmag*, in February 1998. "The grinding loops are 3D and Grant's new wave influences, samples pinched from arty punks like Wire and Bristol's own Pop Group. But there's something darker at the heart of 'Mezzanine' than just playing with sound. For the first time, Massive Attack sound menacing."

"'Passion's overrated anyway' mourns Sara Jay on 'Dissolved Girl'. Whatever Massive Attack have found as a replacement, it works with frightening potency on *Mezzanine*," Andy Crysell wrote in *Vox* magazine in May 1998.

In January 2017, *Pitchfork*, looking back at the album's influence, was still mesmerised by its uniqueness: "It's hard not to feel the album's legacy resonating elsewhere – and not just in 'Teardrop' becoming the cue for millions of TV viewers to brace themselves for Hugh Laurie's cranky-genius-doctor schtick. Graft its tense feelings of nervy isolation and late-night melancholy onto two-step, and you're partway to the blueprint for Plastician and Burial. You can hear flashes of that mournful romantic alienation in James Blake, the graceful, bass-riddled emotional abrasion in FKA twigs, the all-absorbing post-genre rock/soul ambitions in Young Fathers or Algiers. *Mezzanine* stands as an album built around echoes of the '70s, wrestled through the immediacy of its creators' tumultuous late '90s, and fearless enough that it still sounds like it belongs in whatever timeframe you're playing it."

The band programmed a tour starting from April 15 until December 18. A second leg added 25 more dates mid 1999.

Mezzanine soon won a Q Award for Best Album and was nominated at the Mercury Prize. The day before the Mercury ceremony, in August 1998, Massive Attack were in Montreal, in Canada, and their performance of 'Inertia Creeps' was filmed to be broadcast on British television. 3D dedicated the song to the previous winner from their hometown, Portishead and Roni Size and Reprazent, praising their authenticity and direct communication, independent from media. When the prize finally went to Gomez's album *Bring It On*, the press was evoking "one of the worst decisions in the award's history[123]".

Some critics described their singles as too long and unsuitable for radio... But the band members were proud to overstep the music radios' diktats. The audience and most of the critics praised the album and its "out of time" sound.

In Bristol also, *Mezzanine* shook the ground. It was generally judged as a middle way reconciling all the city's musical influences. "This album is more Bristolian than any other," Mark Stewart tells me 17 years later[124]. For Sean Cook, former bass player of Spiritualized soon to work with 3D, "with *Mezzanine*, many things merged, some different sounds, at the perfect time to be understood. Here in Bristol, you hear a bit of 'D, he can't play an instrument'. But it's just not about that. That's not what music is about. If it becomes a competition of who can play the guitar the best, Steve Vai would be the most popular guy on the planet, and it would be fucking awful. It has nothing to do with that. It's about what you're saying and the creative manner in which you say it. And that's what D is very good at. And he still has the means, he still keeps carrying on[125]."

The album was also very much acclaimed in France and in America, where music journalists praised the "end of century" feel of *Mezzanine*, describing both its excitement and anguish, with evocation of an urban solitude, meditation, claustrophia and lyricism. They commented on the references to darkness as well as the "humanistic project" of the band, as a French critic wrote. This darkness seemed truer than any

---

123 In the *Daily Telegraph* in January 2010, among others
124 In a phone interview with the author from London, in June 2015
125 In an interview with the author in Bristol, in April 2015

uplifting pop music, for the band, and could inspire a real form of hope.

Indeed, the references to darkness and blackness are omnipresent in the lyrics, from 'Black Milk' to the *"Black flowers blossom"* and *"Stumble in the dark"* of 'Teardrop'. Even 'Angel' mentions "the dark side". These are accompanied by words describing loneliness and isolation, especially in 'Risingson', 'Man Next Door', 'Teardrop', 'Inertia Creeps' and 'Dissolved Girl'. Many elements also describe a threat: *"Now you're lost and you're lethal"*, sings D in 'Risingson'; *"They come to move your soul"*, adds Grant. Same in 'Man Next Door' (*"I've got to get away from here / This is not a place for me to stay / I've got to take my family / We'll find a quiet place"*).

On the other hand, seven songs out of nine are calling for love: 'Angel' (*"Come from way above / To bring me love"*), 'Risingson', 'Teardrop' (*"Love, love is a verb / Love is a doing word"*), 'Inertia Creeps', 'Dissolved Girl', 'Black Milk', and 'Exchange'. Unlike the deeply anguished *OK Computer*, by Radiohead, Massive Attack's *Mezzanine* manages to reconcile anguish and exaltation, bringing a feeling of release and relief – the edgy 'Risingson' and 'Mezzanine' contrasting with the softer 'Teardrop' and 'Black Milk'; 'Inertia Creeps' and 'Angel' navigating between all trends.

The artwork created for the album also reflects this idea of hybridisation. Disturbed at the idea that his role in the band had increased so much, D was not willing to use one of his paintings for the sleeve. He worked with the fashion photographer Nick Knight and the designer Tom Hingston on a series of photographs in black and white. "I had been obsessing about spiders and the patterns on their backs," said Robert Del Naja to the organisers of the National Album Day's exhibition in 2018, this eventually led to the beetle image." They worked from a photograph created by Nick – who had taken shots of insects for the Museum of Natural History – and manipulated it into a new image, mixing pictures of a shiny black beetle and metallic objects, so well intertwined that it is impossible to distinguish the insect and the machinery.

This choice emphasises the transition the band was in and the mutation this third album represented. The sleeve displays a mutant animal, between a beast and a machine, just like the album, or the band, maybe even the artist himself, after a chaotic year of composition and internal musical transformation.

"I wanted to take a more aggressive approach to music, to go back to the punk approach to making music, instead of looking at American hip-hop, old soul and jazz," Robert confessed in the interview completing of his art book, published in 2015. "And I wanted to do the same with the sleeve, to almost go back to a black and white fucked up aesthetic but with brand new materials, which is what we did. There's also a bit of JG Ballard to it, sexual dark undertones, which was definitely in the record – this repression, sexuality, passive-aggressive."

This is probably what then separated the most 3D's approach to music from Mushroom's. The latter didn't see music as an effort and didn't value touring much either. Whereas, for 3D, to create meant to evolve, sometimes painfully, and to look ahead. "I think if you want to do something different, you have to take yourself out of a comfortable area and feel exposed," Robert explained in the press in 1998. "You comfort yourself in your joys. I'd rather use hobbies to comfort myself. I don't consider music a hobby[126]." D takes art and music seriously, even if it has to take him on tortuous paths, just like the cave in Cornwall where he got frightened, a few months earlier.

And obviously, the anguish at the core of the album also reflected the political and general context of 1997/98. When *Mezzanine* was composed, Robert was preoccupied by the tensions between the US and Iraq, while a new "massive attack" on the Gulf was prepared. In September 1996, the American administration had launched the *Desert Strike* operation to target air defence in southern Iraq, in response to the Iraqi offensive in the Kurdish Civil War. The crisis erupted as the United Nations' weapons inspection process in Iraq neared its seventh year. Then in November 1997, a new crisis erupted when Baghdad expelled the UN inspectors, sent to monitor the country's armament arsenal.

In February 1998, when Massive Attack started to promote *Mezzanine*, the news commented daily on a potential invasion. The tension was at its highest from December 16, 1998, when the United States and the United Kingdom started bombing Iraq, in code-named *Operation Desert*

---

126 In the article named 'Friendly Fire', by Anil Prasad, in *Inner Views*, in 1998

Fox, allegedly to respond to dangerous military behaviours. Just like in 1991, the band saw their name, "massive attack", headline again the international politics pages of the newspapers. Instead of evoking an explosion of creativity, it was used as an understatement for "war".

Since Circa had decided to shorten the band's name in 1991 because of the first Gulf War, 3D had been particularly sensitive to the parallel between the band's history and the wider and much grimmer international context, especially when it came to the relations between the West and the Middle East. The history of Britain, from the history of Bristol in particular to the wider colonial spectrum, haunted Robert's artistic explorations. His paintings continuously depicted images including references to imperialism and war, at a time where the British art market was filled with non-politicised artists.

Four to five years later, this situation of extreme tension led to the second war in Iraq. Looking at history repeating itself, Robert Del Naja was appalled. The band's recent trips to Israel in 1996 and Turkey in 1997 left a deep mark on the musician, who could not stand that conflicts with the East had to prevail. And the introduction of Eastern influences in his music came to reflect his worries about the geopolitical context – as much as his paintings had until then.

Mutant, genius, and at their highest, Massive Attack were never going to sound and appear again as we knew them. The band had proven that they had no cultural or sonic limitations, and the punk roots of their early influences were from then on fully part of their own history. Hungry for evolution and new waves, at the end of 1998, the musicians were about to hit even bigger tides and swells.

Chapter 9
Beyond Bristol's Walls (1998-2001)

With the success of *Mezzanine* in 1998, the influence of Massive Attack on British culture became bigger than ever. When asked if the band opened doors in the *West Country* and Bristol, 3D humbly answered: "I don't feel that we're responsible for that, but we're not gonna deny that we did open the window and a few doors in Bristol. We're all different in our own way – the only thing that really associates all the different artists in Bristol is the fact that we all take our time when we work on musical projects[127]."

Mezzanine proved that the band were not only an electronic or hip-hop act, and that electronic music and hip-hop could master an instrumental approach to music and reach the top of the charts as well as the general audience's heart. Many musicians and critics had thought the band would simply not recover from their creative and personal differences. Instead, their conflicts have nourished their work and forced them to push themselves higher. This third album was considered their best and the band had never been more radiant on stage. Freedom and slowness seemed key to their creativity.

Massive Attack were also proving how much each of their albums took their sound to a new level and *Mezzanine* offered a futuristic and revolutionary record, fed with sounds from the band's oldest tastes. The press was unanimous; the BBC stated that the band had reinvented itself ahead of the new millennium.

Massive live revolution

Early 1998, in the tense political context, the band were rehearsing for a

127 In an interview with *Dance Music* magazine, published on March 26, 1998

large set of tour dates, with Angelo Bruschini, Winston Blissett, Michael Timothy, Deborah Miller, Horace Andy, and on certain dates Liz Fraser. 3D planned a new form of shows, more dynamic, more centred on live instruments, with more interaction between the band members. The role of Angelo's guitar, used very differently than in a rock band, became key to the general energy. At this stage, D didn't think of the band as a sound system anymore, despite Mushroom's will to remain the same as they used to be. During the rehearsals, 3D also emphasised the role of the drums.

The *Mezzanine Tour* started in April 1998 and included 123 dates, before a second leg in 1999, mainly in Europe and North America. Three shows were also scheduled in Australia in June and in South Africa in October, before dates in Brazil. Over the years, the band's members had observed their audience and tried to learn how to react to them and to win them over. The new post-punk energy of the band was very apparent from the first shows.

The typical set list varied but most nights opened with 'Heat Miser' and 'Superpredators' followed by the new album's tracks, 'Angel', 'Risingson' and 'Man Next Door', with Horace Andy. The stage remained mainly plunged in the dark but was illuminated from the background with powerful blue and white lightening effects. Grant was also more present, as his vocal parts had increased. He was regularly appearing at the front of the stage, 3D at his right, while Mushroom remained in the middle part or at the far left, between the vocalists and the instrumentalists, at his decks.

A few tracks were entirely reworked, including 'Daydreaming', sung by 3D and Daddy G with Deborah Miller, emphasising the rap parts and the percussions with an added guitar part. It was generally followed by 'Teardrop', interpreted by Liz Fraser or Deborah Miller. Liz was notably present for the band's memorable show in London's Royal Albert Hall in July 1998. Soon after, she left the tour, as her pregnancy had progressed.

The second part of the show featured 'Karmacoma', 'Hymn of the Big Wheel', 'Eurochild' and 'Spying Glass', followed by the new track, 'Mezzanine'. Then the band offered a trio of songs from *Blue Lines*: 'One Love', 'Safe From Harm', and 'Unfinished Sympathy', before closing the show with 'Inertia Creeps' and the grandiose live version of 'Group Four'.

The band's live transformation was generally acclaimed. In Bristol, where the musicians' community often felt that Portishead had the better stage presence, many were amazed. Arriving in the US, interviewed by *Rolling Stone*, 3D promised: "Wait til you see our show, it rocks. We've even surprised ourselves with how the crowd reacts[128]." During the European leg of the tour, the magazine *Electronic Sound* described the show as "a moving experience", the journalist writing: "'Teardrop' actually makes my eyes well up and the guitar onslaught at the end of 'Group 4' is powerful enough to slice the top off a mountain. There's no slack, no half-assed moments of doodling. Pure gold from start to finish."

In Canada in September, the French language magazine *Voir* stated that the only possible comparison was with Radiohead. In France, journalists noted that even a bad night of the band was a great show, underlining nonetheless the distance between 3D and Mushroom, now rarely on stage together.

For Mushroom, the life on tour was getting every month more painful, though. He was on stage for about twenty minutes in total but struggled to enjoy himself. 3D was on the contrary more often on the mic, his voice more assured. Appearing self-controlled, often smoking, gazing afar and eternally dressed in black, his passion and intensity were strongly visible and his pleasure communicative. At 33 years old, looking much younger, he appeared deep and distant while on stage, but once at the aftershow he became again the boyish and joyful party animal his friends had always known.

Breaking ranks

The massive praise *Mezzanine* received went beyond the year of its release and beyond Britain's headlines. In France, in January 1999, Massive Attack were named "Best Band of 1998" by the weekly music magazine *Les Inrockuptibles*. In the US, *Stylus Magazine* wrote that

---

128 In an interview printed in an article published on June 1, 1998

Massive Attack combined "rock, hip-hop, dub", proving they were an "undeniably great band". Lots of their recent tracks inspired filmmakers but also other musicians.

Mezzanine's legacy was directly visible in Bristol, obviously. And Massive Attack's record label, Melankolic was booming, producing Alpha's second album, *The Impossible Thrill*. Alpha were also touring with Massive Attack that year. "It was a dream come true," says Andy Jenks about working with Melankolic, "an opportunity that only this label could give us. For me, the Bristol sound means above all not a sound but a family, friends connected and helping each other[129]."

The label received demos from all over Europe, including one from the French electronic duo Air – soon to embody the movement baptised "French Touch". Melankolic didn't sign them in the end. Grant would say as an excuse that they were busy producing local friends... They produced the Bristol hard rock band Sunna; Neil Davidge really admired them and even tried to convince Massive Attack to work with them on stage. Their first album, *One Minute Silence*, was scheduled for 2000; Alpha's second album for March 2001. Grant singularly sang on one of their tracks, 'Wishes'.

This encouraged many musicians in Bristol, one of the most successful of them being the alternative rock band Kosheen. Their first album, *Resist*, was released in 2001; four others would follow. And, all over Britain, many imitators arose.

Bristol's previous generation of musicians was on the contrary looking for inspiration from afar... Tricky made his debut in cinema working on *Le Cinquième Elément* (*Fifth Element*), by Luc Besson, released in 1997. The following year, he was back with a new album, *Angels with Dirty Faces*, recorded with Martina Topley-Bird and offering a track featuring PJ Harvey (on the gorgeous 'Broken Home'). A singer most of the Bristol scene deeply admire. "I would work with her as soon as possible," Tricky tells me, very enthusiastically. "She's one of the greatest artists I've met. She completely transformed music. Everyone should have at least her first album. She is as talented as Kate Bush or

---

129 In an interview with the author in Bristol, at the Christchurch Studios, in April 2015

Jimi Hendrix[130]."

In August 1999, Tricky released *Juxtapose*, produced for the first time without Martina, who started working solo. He adopted an even more hip-hop approach, also working with the American rock heroes from Red Hot Chili Peppers. Tricky was by far the busiest of Bristol's musicians, always in a hurry to produce. He was also constantly touring.

Later in 1999, Tricky launched a very unseen and exciting project: *Product of the Environment*, with the keyboardist Gareth Bowen. They recorded voices from inmates, retelling their life stories from their prison cells, to be featured as the only lyrics and vocals of the album. The album was released in September 1999. Tricky was really proud of his encounters with them, whom he described as "real gangsters", including Mad Frankie Fraser, Charlie Richardson and Dave Courtney. Some of the interviews were apparently reported to the London police... And Tricky prefered leaving the country for the album's release.

In the meantime, Portishead had recorded a live album in New York, at the Roseland Ballroom, in July 1997, released in November 1998. They worked with the city's 35-musician philharmonic orchestra. *Roseland NYC Live* conquered the American audience and a DVD was soon published with the whole concert and additional videos. The band toured in the US, Europe, Australia and New Zealand.

Meanwhile, for Massive Attack, while on the intense *Mezzanine Tour*, the band members knew that it was time to distance themselves from their accomplishments and to explore new territories, with their show, but also in their musical research.

Last goodbyes

While on tour, if 3D hoped that his differences of tastes with Mushroom could be washed away by the excitement of the stage, the latter felt more and more isolated. Being vegetarian, not drinking alcohol, he didn't enjoy the hedonistic atmosphere of the road, where numerous guests were joining the afterparties in a flow of alcohol. But his main grievance was related to the band's musical evolution that he didn't agree with.

---

130 In an interview with the author in Paris in September 2017

So during the tour, the band members were from then talking to the press separately. As long as they didn't talk about music, they managed to get along, as old friends do. But they could not foresee returning to the studio together. "There are tensions," explained Mushroom at the beginning of the tour[131], "but these things happen in long relationships. It's just the way things have gone, really. It creates something; you can hear it in the music. It's where we're all coming from musically that causes the clash. We used to accept it, but now it's just worn a little thin."

A few weeks later, Daddy G said bluntly to French media that the recording had left him traumatised, talking of a hellish atmosphere in the studio and of a stress that made him loose his hair... But he reckoned that comfort would kill their project and that they needed doubts to avoid settling down. "I don't want to become Oasis," he insisted[132].

Luckily, the tour itself was successful. When Neil Davidge joined the band for a few shows in Europe, he came to think the tensions were behind them, that 3D and Mushroom had now faced their disagreement and would come back in the studio together. In May, while in Canada, Mushroom asked the *Toronto Sun*'s journalist: "Are you a fan of Pink Floyd? What happened to us is like what happened to Pink Floyd. I guess it happens to all the bands with strong creative will, strong personalities, big battles[133]."

But in July, in Ireland, Mushroom confessed that he struggled to recognise himself in the new album: "I don't tolerate this new direction, there are a lot of problems, a lot of bad stuff going down about this album, a lot of arguments – but that's the creative process. Arguments may be good creatively but it's not good for a band in so many other ways. And then you go on the road[134]..."

When asked in Germany, "Are you at your happiest when you're on a stage?" 3D replied: "There are moments during songs when I'm totally away with it. Last night, I really enjoyed doing 'Mezzanine', it was really intense, it was really loud on stage and loud out front, the bass was rocking, I could hear myself on the mic for a change, and I really got into

131 In an interview with the magazine *Electronic Sound*, in 1998
132 In an interview published in *Les Inrockuptibles*, in France, in April 1998
133 In an interview published on May 9, 1998
134 In an interview published in the Irish magazine Muse, in July 1998

it. But as soon as the song ends, I start feeling uncomfortable. It's just between songs, I start thinking, 'What the fuck am I doing here?'[135]…"

Between the shows, D was already looking for new ideas for a potential album. Like in 1996, he started writing new lyrics on the road. During a short pause from the tour in the summer, he got back to Bristol and recorded a new track with Neil, named 'Reflection', that he described as a "little sister" to 'Inertia Creeps', only a bit more abrupt, obviously influenced by post-punk. It was added to the show's set list and released on the 'Inertia Creeps' EP in September.

While back home, 3D also opened his collaborations with other bands. He worked with Neil on a remix for the Manic Street Preachers's song 'If You Tolerate This Then Your Children Will Be Next', which was released on a second version of the single, on its B-side. The song was talking about the Spanish civil war and recalled the Welsh fighters who battled against General Franco with the Spanish Republican groups. The single was number one in the Chart in late August 1998. And a Manic Street Preachers remix of 'Inertia Creeps' appeared on Massive Attack's EP a month later.

D was also collaborating with the duo U.N.K.L.E, James Lavelle and Tim Goldworthy. He had created since 1994 a couple of their most memorable album covers, for their label Mo'Wax, for *Headz I* and *II*. But in 1998, he collaborated with them musically too, remixing their song 'Rabbit In Your Headlight', voiced by Thom Yorke, from the duo's first album, *Psyence Fiction*, released in late August. The record also used samples from 'Unfinished Sympathy' and 'Teardrop'. It reached number 4 in the UK Albums Chart.

In this period of transition, Massive Attack also released a singles collection, *Singles 90/98*, in December 1998. The box set comprised their eleven singles from 'Daydreaming' to 'Inertia Creeps', including many remixes and a few diverse versions and rare tracks like 'Any Love', 'Euro Zero Zero', 'Superpredators' and 'Reflection', on eleven CDs, containing 63 tracks. 3D created with Tom Hingston a special design and an ultramodern packaging, sensitive to human touch and heat, the

---

135 In the interview with the American magazine *Electronic Sound*, published in 1998

box' colour varying in different tones of grey when held. The box set included new sleeves for each single vinyl. It came with a booklet and a poster, displaying 3D's artwork for the band.

However, just when this release was announced, in November 1998, while the band was in Copenhagen, a note published by the news agency Ceefax was wrongly quoted in Britain by *the Sun*, which announced "strong indication of a potential separation" of the band. Massive Attack had to publish a press release to deny. Mushroom had even said to Ceefax that he was thinking of re-entering the studio as soon as early 1999, Daddy G adding he could imagine working in the style of the Beatles' sessions for the *White Album*, famously known for their separate recordings.

Mid-November 1998, the tour culminated in Bristol's *Anson Rooms*, in Clifton, in a triumphal homecoming show, with Horace Andy, Angelo Bruschini and Liz Fraser. Visibly moved, Robert Del Naja declared, before launching a blistering version of 'Mezzanine': "It makes us really proud to be playing in front of you tonight". The crowd didn't know it yet, but it was Mushroom's last concert with the band.

The following year, Andrew 'Mushroom' Vowles left the band. He was only 31 years old and at the height of his success. However, the official announcement was not made until almost a year later in September 1999. In the meantime, the band explained his absence in the summer 1999 shows saying he was unwilling to tour any more.

Robert thinks that their *entente cordiale* has been wrecked by non-stop discussions on accounts, management, touring and copyrights. It became evident, with time, that the maze of *Mezzanine's* recordings had estranged the two opposite personalities of the band, evolving into two irreconcilable minds.

Once gone, Mushroom would not contact his former band mates again in years. 3D has missed the passion they put in Massive Attack ever since. Mushroom's departure left D and G face to face. They would have to redefine their relationship, looking, each on his side, for new fuel for their creativity. And the *Mezzanine* Tour went on until the end of 1999.

Extra collaborations, new directions

Back in Bristol, Massive Attack were then a duo... for a while. 3D went back to the studios but Grant was mostly absent. Looking for new diversionary projects, D said yes to many film soundtracks. One of his productions appeared in an unexpected context: 'Inflight Data', a song that he had worked on with his friend Liam Howlett from the Prodigy, was chosen to be featured in the first porn film supposed to be set in space... *The Uranus Experiment* was directed by John Millerman. For D and Liam, both laughing at an easy provocation, the experience was too fun to be dismissed. And the song became one of the fans' favourites, as it is one of their rarest tracks. D also wrote the song 'Doldrums' for Horace Andy's second album, *Living In The Flood*, released in October 1999 on Melakolic Records.

Around the same time, 3D was contacted by a young female singer from North London, starting to make a name for herself: Amy Winehouse. She came to Christchurch Studios and worked with Alex Swift, a young programmer who settled in Bristol in 1985, working with Peter Gabriel and from 1999 with Neil Davidge. Amy was looking for a label and working on songs for her first album, but she was worried about sounding too "world music" if she worked with the Bristol crew. But in 2000 she was still looking for her own style. Her first album, *Frank*, was finally signed by Island Records and released on October 20, 2003.

Called by friends in London, 3D worked on other projects with Damon Albarn and David Bowie. Spending a lot of time with Damon in London, they composed a song named 'One Day At A Time', in his 13 Studio, for the soundtrack of the film *Ordinary Decent Criminal*, with Kevin Spacey, directed by Thaddeus O'Sullivan. The film was released in March 2000.

When 3D and Damon met in London's club Browns, in the mid 1990s, Damon was trying to work with Tricky on his *Nearly God* album but their cohabitation soon became too chaotic. With 3D, Damon started a productive collaboration from that point. They both seemed to learn from the experience, as they worked very differently. "We tend to disagree a lot in the studio," said Damon Albarn[136], describing their habits. "Damon tried to do happy things and I find it depressing," added 3D jokingly[137]. Soon after, Gorillaz's first album, *Gorillaz*, was released in late March 2001, with many featured vocalists, influenced by Massive Attack. Damon even chose "2D" as a pseudonym...

During the summer 2000, 3D was called by one of his idols, David Bowie, to work on a cover for another soundtrack. The chosen song was 'Nature Boy', written by American jazzman Eden Ahbez and popularised by James Brown and Nat King Cole, among others. The film, *Moulin Rouge*, was directed by Baz Luhrmann. It was shown at the Cannes Festival, in May 2001, and released worldwide in June. On MTV, David Bowie described his collaboration with 3D as stimulating, praising him for fabricating "a fascinating track!"

Busy as ever, freed from the heavy promotion he had to go through for *Mezzanine*, 3D also worked with the Scottish band Primal Scream, remixing their song 'Exterminator', and with the Prodigy again, composing the track 'No Souvenirs' for the film *The Beach*, adapted from the book by Alex Garland and directed by Danny Boyle. D's close friend Robert Carlyle starred in the film, and both D and the Prodigy were very committed to the project. They spent the whole summer recording and mixing, then remixing, at the expense of Richard Russel of XL records. Yet, when Pete Tong eventually became the music supervisor, the boys backed away from the project for creative reasons.

The song 'No Souvenirs' is very electronic, very guitar-centric, very produced and very sombre. D described his influences at that time as a halfway between Pink Floyd and the Beach Boys. For a while, Liam Howlett thought about including it on the Prodigy's next album, but it finally remained unreleased.

D also started painting again intensely around that time. And, looking back at the evolution of his art, he published in July 2000 a first art book: named *Fitting In*, it gathered artworks from the past ten years and a few new paintings. It was only distributed in a very limited edition of 150 copies, the profits being sent to the Red Cross.

136 In an interview with the *Independent on Sunday*, published on February 9, 2003
137 Ibid

Convolutions and explorations

From the summer 2000, 3D wanted to work on a new Massive Attack album, though. He travelled to the Ridge Farm Studio, in Sussex, with Neil Davidge and a few musicians, mainly the instrumentalists from the band Lupine Howl – guitarist Mike Mooney, bass player Sean Cook and drummer Damon Reece. They all used to be in the Spiritualized before the band's split. Damon had by then become Massive Attack's most permanent stage drummer. They recorded more than eighty hours of material in a few weeks and 3D worked further on it in Bristol, sampling the instrumental parts, looking for inspiration, and worked on about thirty tracks, but 3D never really decided how to finish them. He liked the way they sounded live but couldn't arrange them in an album format.

The result was finally mostly abandoned. "Some of the work has been used on some stuff, on some soundtracks," says Sean Cook when I meet with him in Bristol 15 years later. "I was paid handsomely. Then they own what you do. I was always pretty well looked after with MA. I know the situation and freely run into it[138]."

The record company was a bit puzzled by the method, and kept on dreaming of a *Mezzanine II*. But nothing seemed less stimulating for Robert Del Naja. He wanted to renew his sound more than ever. He received many propositions for other collaborations and Virgin tried to convince him to work on his own...

"Through my experience of MA, D is the driving force," adds Sean Cook, "and the one with the talent. I also have a lot of respect for D because he hasn't moved to London; he could have easily done that and I bet everyone, the record company and all, asked him to[139]." But Robert felt he still had more freedom in Bristol; he dared to take his time and to allow himself to feel when he was ready to reinvent himself.

So he officially decided to abandon his exploration started with Lupine Howl, despite the pressure. Two tracks survived the lot, the first being 'Nature of Threat', sung by 3D, broadcast from Massive Attack's website in August 2000. It came online a week before a long webcast

138 Interview with the author in Bristol, in April 2015
139 Ibid

interview on Virtue TV. It was also used in an instrumental version by British artist Marc Quinn in one of his installations, named *Life Support*, later that year, in December, in London. "We wrote this for a movie last year but we're now adapting it for the artist, Marc Quinn," 3D told the *NME* magazine[140]. "It's not intended to be an LP track at the moment, it's more of a sketch." The song 'Aftersun', interpreted by Scottish singer Dot Allison, also emerged in 2001 and used in a soundtrack for a film, but never formally released.

Mid 2001, Massive Attack's next project seemed blurred but the band's success was still very significant in England. More than ever, 3D was looking into ways to renew his creativity and explore new territories. This was when he received a call from an old friend who was preparing a very unusual kind of exhibition for the next Christmas: a show named *Santa's Ghetto* and orchestrated with a group of artist friends by the one and only now world-famous but still anonymous Banksy.

Street art's new explosion

In one of his rare interviews, when asked if he had been inspired by French stencil artist Blek Le Rat, Banksy declared: "I copied 3D from Massive Attack, he actually can draw."

Asked about Banksy's influence on his work, Robert Del Naja replied: "James Lavelle and Banksy seemed determined that I should not remain in my happy self-induced delusion of rock stardom. Along with the ever-supportive Steve Lazarides. I'd get the call once or twice a year, so I'd get my shit together and knock something up. The *Santa's Ghetto* shows and PoW (Pictures On Walls) gave me a chance to try one-off pictures which seemed to be topical, depending on where they put it – Jerusalem or London[141]."

Between 1998 and 2000, Banksy's art took a different echo in Britain and beyond. He started travelling in Europe and in the United States. In the book *Seven Years With Banksy*[142], his so-called friend Robert Clarke

140 In November 2000
141 In Robert's interview for his art book, *3D and The Art Of Massive Attack*, published in 2015
142 Published in 2012, by Michael O'Mara Books Ltd

described how they had met in New York in 1994 and said Banksy very often mentioned 'Delge', aka 3D, complaining about the fact that his early pieces had been defaced in their hometown. Clarke also described that when Banksy was back in Bristol in 1998, he attended some of Massive Attack's recording sessions for *Mezzanine*.

Banksy became an unmissable phenomenon around the summer 1998. He painted a lot in Bristol and created a large piece for the Glastonbury Festival, in June, in collaboration with Inkie. The piece, painted over three days outside the festival's Dance Tent, measures 2.4m (7.8ft) by 9.9m (32ft). Known as *Silent Majority*, the artwork was painted on the side of a truck belonging to friends. It was signed by Banksy (with his usual stencil signature) and Inkie (free-handed), with the mention "Love". It depicts DJs, festival goers and clubbers dressed in military suits, with this message as a caption: "It's better not to rely too much on silent majorities… For silence is a fragile thing… One loud noise and it's gone". The quote comes from the graphic novel *V For Vendetta* by Alan Moore and David Lloyd, published in series between 1982 and 90, which describes a dictatorial state with fighting terrorism as only ideology. Quotes soon became an important part of Banksy's work.

The owner of the truck said to different local media: "We have known Banksy for more than 12 years. He heard that we were travelling down to Glastonbury and asked if we would give over the sides of the truck as a workspace. He wanted a large white canvas (…). The significance of *Silent Majority* is that it depicts this era and was painted whilst the free party movement was in its prime… *Silent Majority* depicts the last rave and hip-hop scene of the time."

The following summer, Banksy painted on the other side of the truck at Glastonbury again. The artwork was later authenticated by Banksy's own certification services, Pest Control. And in 2008, the owner finally sold it in order to buy a new home, with Banksy's permission. It was put on sale again a few years later and fetched £445,792 at an auction in Paris in 2015.

In July 1998, Banksy came to spray at St Pauls' Carnival, just like 3D did more than a decade earlier. And in August, with Inkie, he organised an exhibition named *Walls on Fire*, along Bristol's Harbourside. The event was scheduled over a long weekend and attracted street artists from all over the country as well as the Bristolian Nick Walker. And a few months later, in 1999, as he planned to leave Bristol for London, Banksy painted a large mural on the side of the Hamilton House, in Stokes Croft, known as *Mild Mild West*. It displays a figure of a big Teddy Bear throwing a petrol bomb, facing three over-protected policemen. The title says it all...

By that time, Banksy had become friends with a photographer from Bristol too, named Steve Lazarides. Born in 1969, Steve grew up in an estate in Yate, near Bristol, and his family moved into town when he was about 15 years old. "I remember seeing 3D's paintings on walls by then, all over the city, and being fascinated," Steve tells me. "Some days I would spend hours on buses just to chase his graffiti! He was way ahead of his time and has kept on being so, moving on with new technology, etc. He is very respected in the art scene. He was there way before everyone else. I have vivid memories of his stencils at the Montpelier Hotel, from as early as 1987. I used to hang out there myself; they had a lot of character, they were not only graffiti, and he inspired us all[143]." Steve at that time wasn't in his circle but befriended Inkie, who is the same age.

Working with Banksy, Steve soon wanted to open a gallery – "though I had never been in a gallery at that time apart from the Bristol Museum!" insists Steve[144]. But he became one of Banksy's key helpers. They both decided to move to London by the end of 1999. Inkie followed them soon afterwards. And Steve started selling reproduction of Banksy's artworks on prints, to help their ventures. By 2000, Banksy was said to be living in Hackney, in East London, in our days a real temple for graffiti, later to be defined as "street art"... "Street art at that time gave a voice to those who didn't have any," adds Steve; "they could finally make their opinion heard. And for us who grew up under the Thatcher years, it meant a lot[145]."

---

143 In an interview with the author from London in January 2017
144 Ibid
145 Ibid

Banksy's murals abounded in East London in 2000 and 2001. In February 2000, he came back to Bristol for a first exhibition, at the Severnshed floating restaurant. At the same time, he drew a first artwork for an album cover, for Hombre Records, the label of his friend from Bristol, Jamie Eastman, founded in 1997. According to some newspapers' later investigations, Jamie was probably his flatmate in Hackney at that time.

In 2001, Banksy organised with Steve his second exhibition, in London this time, in the Rivington Tunnel, in Shoreditch, where he painted on twelve walls of the underground passage. A few months later his first Santa's Ghetto was launched, just before Christmas, in central London, where he invited artist friends, including 3D.

From there was launched the print company *Pictures On Walls*, or PoW, with artworks from Banksy and from 3D, later followed by Mode 2, French artist Space Invader, Cyclops, Modern Toss, Paul Insect, David Shirley, and the Italian genius Blu. PoW soon came to be a reference for British street art. A new generation of artists was following Banksy's steps, like Cheba, born in 1983.

Bristol remained a place for emulation and stimulation more than competition. The artists know and help each other. But from 2001, Banksy reached a new level. "Between 2000 and 2002, things really changed for Banksy and Steve," summarises Inkie, "I had to work on top of doing art, but I remained in close contact with them, and Banksy never stopped painting! He was always at it. And Steve really understood how to deal with the marketing aspect[146]."

Inkie was himself inspired by his childhood memory of a schoolteacher, Mrs Sciavo, a Native American with long black hair, and produced profiles of a dark-haired woman all over South England and soon beyond. One is displayed in the underpass of Temple Meads' train station. Inkie soon curated an annual event in Bristol to gather street artists, called See No Evil, with Mode 2 involved. "And all our connections, even with the artists from New York, come back to the years that we all spent following 3D everywhere in Bristol, from the

146 In an interview with the author in Bristol, in June 2015

Special K Café to the Dug Out!" Inkie laughs[147].

In 2003, Banksy was noticed nationwide when organising his *Turf War* exhibition, in Hackney, in July. Meanwhile, he reproduced Santa's Ghetto, near the very commercial Carnaby Street, with false shops mocking the capitalistic Christmas habits of Londoners with silly drawings and strong statements. He also worked with new artists, from the video maker and plastic artist Chris Cunningham to Gorillaz' Jamie Hewlett.

A few months later, Banksy created the cover art for Blur's new album, *Think Tank*, representing two characters in diving suits and helmets, trying to hug and kiss... He repeated *Santa's Ghetto* in 2004 in Soho and in 2006 on Oxford Street, before going in 2007 to... Bethlehem, in the West Bank. He had in mind to show that art could raise awareness on what was happening in the world. From 2005, he painted murals in Jerusalem too, on the world's most famous wall, known as the "separation barrier".

Massively political

From 2001, for obvious reasons (and we will get back to them), Banksy and 3D's artwork evolved and deepened. Something shifted in their relations to world issues and they both wanted to go a step further, to directly deal with the current political changes and to express their values more openly.

While Daddy G was often travelling to perform his own DJ sets, 3D was working on his own, on a remix for American rock band the Dandy Warhols, of their song 'Godless', released in July 2001, discussing atheism and consumerism in our current society.

In his daily life, 3D was more concerned by politics than music at that time. He was worrying about the local political changes, the lack of representation of Bristol's diversity for instance, but also about our society's financial and production-driven excesses, and above all about the general war-going international context.

In February 2001, the US and the UK launched new strikes over

147 Ibid

Iraq, with the official justification of dismantling Saddam Hussein's military arsenal. But civilians were the first victims and the strikes were condemned by many Arab countries, as well as the United Nations. In the United States, a large part of the newly elected George W. Bush administration was in favour of a full intervention on the ground to get rid of the Iraqi leader. And they wanted British support. When, in the June 2001 general election, Tony Blair's New Labour obtained a large majority, many expect him to stand against a war in Iraq. Meanwhile, in England, the summer was marked by riots, in Brixton, South London, when a young black man Derek Bennett, was killed by a policeman.

During that summer, 3D coincidently was working with U.N.K.L.E and the video artist Shynola on a film for the band's single named 'Eye For An Eye'. The song was released a year later on the duo's second album, *Never Never Land*. Shynola, who worked with animation, had recently came to fame with his video for Radiohead's 'Pyramid Song', from their new album, *Amnesiac*. Shynola and 3D's film was shown at the Edinburgh Festival in August 2001. It shows a world made of little characters inspired by 3D's *Insect President* series, created for Massive Attack's *Protection Tour*.

The film starts like a fairy tale, with these characters living in a luxurious paradise, surrounded by butterflies and delicious fruits. But soon a floating ship arrives accompanied by airplanes, which liberate menacing and violent creatures, infecting the friendly indigenous people... The villagers become monsters too, and plant the invaders' flag everywhere on their own land, while fighting destroys the fields. The space ship soon departs for new conquests, leaving the land wrecked and hellish.

Interviewed at the Edinburgh Festival, 3D described the film as "anti-war" and his original characters as "anti-global, anti-corporate, anti-oppression and anti-imperialism", relevant for the message of the song.

Then, less than a month later, on September 11, 2001, New York's Twin Towers at the World Trade Centre were attacked by two airplanes, hi-jacked by the Islamic and terrorist organisation named Al Qaeda. The US initially blamed Saddam Hussein, who denied any implication, later accusing terrorists based in Pakistan, at the border with Afghanistan. The Afghan war was launched in a few days.

In November, 3D and Damon Albarn organised two concerts to raise funds for relief in Afghanistan, for December, one in London and Bristol. The night at the Bristol Academy, on December 15, featured Gorillaz and live DJ slots by U.N.K.L.E, Massive Attack, Geoff Barrow from Portishead, Asian Dub Foundation, Richard Fearless from Death In Vegas and Howie B. The proceeds from the two events went to the Red Cross and the Muslim Red Crescent, to help those whose lives had been devastated by recent military strikes. D and Damon also joined the Campaign for Nuclear Disarmament.

The anti-war message that had been evident in 3D's art since 1993 was cynically underlined in U.N.K.L.E's prophetic title – 'Eye For An Eye', referring to a text in the *Exodus* chapter of the *Old Testament* on human and divine revenge. This remained what was at the core of 3D's thoughts and creations late 2001, but his pacifism was more than ever challenged by a changing world.

Chapter 10
Depths And Heights (2001-2004)

In 2001, while Banksy was shaking the art world with a twist of political wit, his musician friends from Bristol got inspired by a very different theme: vulnerability.

In the summer, Tricky released a sixth album named *Blowback*, judged as much softer than his previous ones. One of the highlights of the record is the track 'Evolution Revolution Love' (*"Now that I understand this right / Let me take it to the mic / This revolution has just begun"*). His trio with the American soul singer Stephanie McKay and the Canadian singer Alanis Morissette, 'Excess', opens the album (with his now famous line *"I'm Jamaican on your radio station / Got a curse in / Could be worse in"* and the chorus *"I believe in people lying / I believe in people dying / I believe in people trying / I believe in people crying / I believe in people balking / I believe in people talking / I believe in people breathing / I believe in people being"*).

And Tricky immediately started working on his next album, *Vulnerable*, to be released in 2003. He described it as his most honest and most open record. Then, for the first time since 1994, he remained silent for five years, until the release of *Knowle West Boy*, and was still living abroad.

Unlike Tricky, Portishead and Massive Attack remained at home, in Bristol. While Portishead was inactive, their lead singer Beth Gibbons released an album in 2002, with the musician Rustin Man, known in real life as Paul Webb. He was the former bass player in the band Talk Talk. *Out Of Season* entered the Top 50 of Albums Chart in many countries, reaching number 28 in the UK, 19 in France. It displays a very soft and tender folk/electronic music, especially in its single, 'Tom The Model', and in the track 'Mysteries' (which was chosen a few years later by the French filmmaker Cédric Klapisch for the soundtrack of his film, *The Russian Dolls*).

As for Massive Attack, 2001 was a time of introspection, after ten years of a flawless career. With Mushroom's departure and the abandonment of the project started with Lupine Howl, the formation would never be the same again. *Mezzanine* was regularly described as their masterpiece, but, though he was the main brain behind its genesis, Robert Del Naja was not interested in reproducing the formula; he was looking to distance himself as much as possible from its creative process in order to produce a more personal record. Yet, unfortunately for the artist who really cared to work in a team and believed collaborations are the secret to great work, he would have to achieve his goal much on his own.

Deadlocks and redemption

The two remaining members of Massive Attack had just spent a year splitting up officially with Mushroom and arranging their paperwork when, at 41, Grant Marshall told Robert Del Naja that he wanted a break. He was exhausted by the long period of touring that followed the release of *Mezzanine*, disillusioned with the exhausting work 3D had put into place in the studio and he was about to become a father. His first daughter, Ava, was soon born.

"D and I weren't getting on that well, musically or personally," Grant explained a couple of years later. "So I just decided to walk out. I never really had it in my mind that I would leave the band for good, but it's really hard working with D sometimes. He's so headstrong and has to have things his own way. That can build confrontation. He likes to have total control of everything he does[148]." Grant started working on his own project, a compilation album praising his music tastes as a DJ.

For Robert, it was a difficult timing. Their label as well as their fans were expecting a fourth Massive Attack album with impatience. He could not foresee if Grant would actually come back, and himself, at 36, considered that music was at the core meaning of his life. From

---

148 In an interview with *World Magazine*, published in October 2003

then, 3D was working only with Neil Davidge, his producer and sound engineer and the only person he could completely rely on. At the end of the summer 2001, they decided to start again from scratch, from early 2002, to work on codename "LP4" project. D was looking for some soul singers, contacting different people including the unique Nina Simone, tracking her to the south of France... and Aaron Neville. None of these plans came to fruition.

But then suddenly the context became even grimmer. "What really kick-started the making of *100th Window* to me was September 11 and the terrorist attack on the Twin Towers in New York," Neil Davidge told me. "I remember being in the studio and getting a phone call from our manager saying: 'put the TV on'... We felt as if we were watching a science-fiction movie. The feelings that followed pioneered that album. We also all had been through some kind of crisis; we felt pretty isolated, extremely isolated indeed, individually as politically[149]." And Neil can still hear it when he listens to the record.

From then on, the artist whose artwork was already haunted by images of war and frightened, fragile, human beings was facing a project that would only echo further his demons. D's lyrics were increasingly dealing with a feeling of desolation, loneliness and unfathomable quests, describing an anguishing world, where individuals were belittled by giant organisations and systems, vulnerable to violence. "I'm naturally quite a dark character inside and it was a dark time: post September 11 and the Iraq War," described Robert Del Naja a few years later. "It was symptomatic of the isolation, of having to do it alone. It was painful but everyone was demanding a Massive Attack record. I'm pleased by the way it turned out but I couldn't make a record like that again[150]."

A total of 67 British citizens were killed in the New York attacks, the country was the most affected after the US and the Prime Minister Tony Blair decided to get involved in the Afghanistan war, launched on October 7, 2001, to try to find Al Qaeda's leader, Osama Bin Laden.

3D and Neil had to patiently wait until this wave of negativity and creativity started to make sense. D's creative process demanded long

149 In an interview with the author in Bristol, in March 2015
150 In an interview with the *Times*, published on March 25, 2006

hours of experimentations, doubts and sometimes exhaustion, hence a few more fights. Neil got stuck in with long days and long nights of recording and suffered from a feeling of solitude, when he had to end some arrangements on his own late at night. But this time, their work got much more coherent than in 2000. "I guess, when it's good, it's great," states Neil, "and I don't know how else to be other than in making music; without it I feel unimportant; it's how I take care of my children and give a meaning to my life[151]." D and Neil's relationship and friendship became their main source of comfort, as they were spending extra hours in the studio just to chat about their everyday life and joke around.

Inspired by their recent productions and newfound energy, Massive Attack officially released two new tracks in March 2002. The first one was out on a Lupine Howl single, 'Vaporizer', a remix of the song by 3D and Neil Davidge, written at the Ridge Farm studio in 2000. The other track, named 'I Against I', was out on March 19, 2002, featuring the American rapper Mos Def (aka Dante Terrell Smith, born in 1973). Written for the soundtrack of the film *Blade II*, directed by Guillermo Del Toro and inspired by a Marvel's comic book, it is a very dynamic and futuristic hip-hop track, extremely estranged from Massive Attack's recent productions.

When D played 'I Against I' to his friend Damon Albarn, who was working on the first Gorillaz' album at that time, the track had a direct influence on him. It was one of the directions Massive Attack could have gotten into in 2001/02 but D chose a more inverted route.

Massive Attack's fourth album finally emerged in 2002, in Bristol at the Christchurch Studios, and was mixed in July and August. It was written in only a few months. But in September 2002, 3D's preoccupations became once again more political when the music magazine *NME* published adverts for the military, just about a year after the attacks on the World Trade Center. D was outraged as he considered that the music world had by no mean the right to encourage war-going policies. He was willing to publish an alternative advert in

151 In an interview with the author in Bristol, in March 2015

the *NME*, in reaction, to stand against the idea of a war in Iraq, which now obsessed the American and British governments. And he hoped to get a few friends to join him.

Their advertisement was published in the *NME* on September 11, 2002, with two different messages: 'No War On Iraq' and 'Wrong War', slogans that Banksy suggested; they were written onto banners for marches. On September 28, Damon and Robert took part in the series of rallies in London against the bombing on Iraq, organised by CND and Stop The War Coalition with the former Member of Parliament Tony Benn and the journalist John Pilger, among many others. They handed out placards during the rally with Banksy's spray-painted stencils representing helicopters or a grim reaper. Two hundred thousand people marched that day from Parliament Square to Hyde Park. Among the few musicians to join the event, Damon and Robert were wearing T-shirt with their message, 'Wrong War', in capital letters.

"The idea is as an individual you say something, make a statement and other people who are like-minded join you," Robert told the *NME*[152]. "Eventually you create a force. Otherwise, how do you do it? It always starts with one person. That's how any political party starts, how any trade union starts, any force of protest starts, always with single voices. And to suggest that as musicians we shouldn't have a view is absolutely ridiculous because as musicians we're still British subjects who live within this country."

Massive Attack's fourth album thus took a more world-infused approach, more engaged, less detached. Even more when the songwriter 3D had chosen to work with came back to him with her positive response: Irish singer Sinéad O'Connor.

The hundredth window

Again, Massive Attack's project was nourished by the input of their collaborators. Among the nine tracks that this new album finally gather, two are sung by Horace Andy, three by Sinéad O'Connor and four by 3D himself. On the production front, D worked with Neil Davidge

---

152 In an interview published on September 25, 2002

and Alex Swift. Musicians included Angelo Bruschini, Jon Harris (on the bass), Damon Reece (drums), Stuart Gordon (violin), Skaila Hanka (harp) and Craig Pruess (strings direction).

This team entered the Christchurch Studios in January 2002 and recorded until April, composing the first notes of a new album in a few weeks, in the most spontaneous manner in the history of the band. After two years of detours and complicated research, trials and discarding, a monolithic piece came to fruition, as if the doubts and experimentations accumulated since 1999 were finally making sense.

Working without his two former band mates, 3D relied on his relationship with Neil. "I've worked with Neil for seven years now," 3D explained to the BBC, just before the album release, in January 2003. "He's the co-writer really. He's someone I trust. We have an intuition between each other and a communication process. It's important because, not being traditional musicians, lots of things need to be verbalised. Or even a look can mean, you know, let's try this."

Another significant change in D's way of working came from a radical decision: this album would not include samples from other musicians' songs. D worked with loops and samples of his own melodies and instrumental parts, produced by Massive Attack for Massive Attack, in a conscious decision. The album was conceived on powerful computers, with the newest technology and software, and 3D wanted to compensate this mechanical and electronic prevalence by a very strong human investment. And this was particularly audible in the lyrics, much more personal for D, and more politically aware in Sinéad's contributions. 3D progressively felt that using Pro Tools and powerful software allowed him to work more intimately, as it could record hours and hours of music and sonic experimentation.

He also started recording with the desire to produce an opus that he would find "less cold" that *Mezzanine*, less emotionally numbed. He often wrote his lyrics at night, after partying, getting drunk or using drugs, especially MDMA, which was very commonly used by electronic music producers at that time, and known for its euphoric effects and for enhancing sensitivity to music. That year, Massive Attack also invested in their own bar in Bristol, named Nocturne, where they organised events. D's way of life alternated from long, almost monastic days of work, and nights of heavy hedonism on weekends.

D was obviously looking for a way to connect music and emotions. "Too much music, these days, doesn't pay attention to what music should be about, which is communicating ideas and feelings," insists Neil Davidge[153]. If you get that bit right then you can write unconventional structures and melodies that work."

A few months later, 3D chose a title for the album, once he felt the direction it had taken. The "hundredth window" can refer to the title of a book published in 2000 by Charles Jennings and Lori Fena, on "Privacy and Security In the Age of the Internet". These security experts explained that even if ninety-nine of your windows open online are protected, if the hundredth window remains open, an invader can still get in... That hundredth window is the weakest. But Robert liked the phrase because he sensed a deeper meaning in it, as a metaphor for a place inside of us that we cannot completely block, and from which we could finally communicate freely, beyond speech.

"What I actually felt about *100th Window* when I saw it written down was that it's a more spiritual place," he told the BBC after the release[154]. "The third eye, the window to the soul, the whole idea of the place where you can communicate without thinking, examining the world without your personality being in the way." The *100th Window* is the one you don't close, he added a few days later: "It's the one you've got no real control over. It sounded celestial to me, almost Buddhist. It's a window in your head where people can look in and you can see out without fear[155]."

Working without Grant and Mushroom, the musician also felt that he would be scrutinised by critics, but his main concern was to renew the band's sound without betraying himself. "Because of Mushroom leaving and G being unavailable, people thought it was going to be a real guitar-fest," he told the BBC[156]. "Big and very dark, and very heavy. But, being stubborn, I didn't want to prove everyone right, so I did completely the

153 In an interview with *Sound on Sound* magazine, published in April 2003
154 In an interview broadcast in January 2003
155 In an interview with the weekly *The Big Issue*, published in January 2003
156 In the previously mentioned interview, broadcast in January 2003

opposite. Something a bit more gentle, more intricate and a bit more thoughtful, rather than just using power to convey emotion."

In the meantime, he worked with the photographer Nick Knight and the designer Tom Hingston on a series of photographs for the album cover, creating an impressive artwork made of glass human-shaped figures destined to be shot at. The pictures of the glass explosions perfectly epitomised human fragility. They were used for the record's sleeve and booklet.

"I was speaking to Marc Quinn[157], who was making amazing rainbow sculptures. We talked about working on something new but it never materialised," Robert wrote in the interview published in his art book. He felt Marc's work was too important to be reduced to a 12 by 12 piece off cardboard. "I began thinking about how we could make sculptures out of crystal and shine a light through them. Tom had shown me some pictures Nick had created shooting ballistics material through frozen flowers and catching their explosions. I started to imagine how the process would work with glass objects, but not on a miniature level. So 'let's make life-size glass humans and blow them up'. Luckily for me at the time *Mezzanine* had been such a success that the record company were totally cool with that. So we met a glassblower in Brixton and he agreed to make these nine different coloured glass figures and we went to a studio that Nick had set up to photograph with the shutter synchronised with the gun so it would capture the ballistic high points. We spent a day destroying these glass geezers. And it worked for the sleeve. It was the most fractious time in the band's history."

The album was mixed during the summer in London's Olympic Studios then in Bristol, with Mark 'Spike' Stent and the release was scheduled for February 2003. And by the end of that month, a first single was released, 'Special Cases'. 3D had decided not to rely too much on single releases or mainstream radio to promote the album. He found the music industry more and more commercially driven and felt appalled by record companies' pressure, especially as he was dealing for the first time on his own with the prospects of promotion. So only

157 Contemporary visual artist born in London in 1964, part of the so-called Young British Artists

one other single was prepared, an EP for the song 'Butterfly Caught', released on June 16.

100th Window is structured on a very free composition, away from pop albums' patterns, with long tracks (five to eight minutes), without chorus. Musically, it is impossible to categorise, defying genre distinctions. Guitars have now moved in the background; harps and violins are underlined. The lyrics are much shorter, excluding any rap, even more cryptic than before, ethereal or poetical. The album relies on a ternary structure, featuring three vocalists, and three types of songs: some engaging and universal ('A Prayer For England', 'What Your Soul Sings'), others more intimate ('Small Time Shot Away', 'Everywhen', 'Name Taken', 'Butterfly Caught') and a third kind almost apocalyptic ('Future Proof', 'Special Cases', 'Antistar'). The tracks sung by 3D himself come in between the others, giving a template and a rhythm. The opening track, 'Future Proof', and the last, 'Antistar', bring a dominant intention: they describe a quest to survive while facing an imminent external/internal collapse.

We can feel a musical trend in most songs, written verse to verse, with a slackening and a bridge, ahead of a new start. The whole album evolves from track to track in one forwarding movement, becoming the band's most coherent opus, with recurrent patterns and themes, from the opening to a climax, offering a journey through each song. The musical and lyrical atmosphere mimes the recent world events, dominated by fear and individualism, as well as surveillance and therefore mistrust. In front of this crumbling world, sole individuals feel they become even more fragile, even more isolated, and can only struggle to find peace. 'Butterfly Caught' and 'Antistar' offer a marriage between Western and Eastern patterns and sounds, even more than 'Karmacoma' on *Protection* or 'Inertia Creeps' on *Mezzanine*, as an attempt to bring the two worlds closer. All these themes and references became defining for the band along the year.

100th Window also offers moments of exquisite sensuality, allusions to love and sex, and suspended bubbles of redemption. It brings a spiritual dimension thanks to electronic loops and repetitive motives, along with the use of melancholic strings and some of the lyrics – in

Sinead's vocals (in 'What Your Soul Sings' of course, and 'A Prayer For England') and in 3D's lyrics (in 'Everywhen', 'Small Time Shot Away', 'Antistar'). A mysterious hidden track, without vocal and barely instrumental, closes the album.

Even if Robert Del Naja denies any will to create a "concept album", *100th Window* is a record of a rare kind, that listeners can rediscover at every listen, plunging more and more into its layers of a depth that is rare in popular music. The opus investigates the role of an individual in front of the collective, of anonymity and intimacy, in a more mechanical world, at a time when the internet started to change our reality. And it wonders how to resist in front of an increasing number of conflicts and such a level of acrimony between irreconcilable enemies.

Vocal transformations

With this fourth album, Massive Attack supported more clearly some of the values they had always carried with them, now expressed more openly. And their collaboration with Sinéad O'Connor brought a direct form of expression, with sincerity and engagement. 3D had for long been an admirer of her career. Born near Dublin in 1966, Sinéad became world famous when she sublimely covered Prince's song named 'Nothing Compares 2 U', in 1990. It was composed by the American artist in 1984 for a funk project called the Family and appeared on the band's only album in 1985, but remained relatively unknown. Sinéad included her version of the track on her second record, *I Do Not Want What I Haven't Got*, and the single became number one in the UK, the US and Australia. The track was produced by former Wild Bunch member Nellee Hooper. Sinead was influenced by Bob Dylan, David Bowie, Bob Marley and Siouxsie and the Banshees, influences 3D could only be sensitive to.

Sinéad was also well known for her outspoken social and political views. Massive Attack had already contacted her to try to collaborate in 1993, but the project had no time to even start. 3D had expressed his admiration for her directness and authenticity in some of his first interviews, especially for her raw presence on stage. They crossed paths in festivals and showed a mutual respect. Then in 2000, the Irish signer decided to take a break from the music industry, to learn the Irish language among other things. Only a few collaborations got her out of her silence until her comeback in 2005.

This time, Robert felt it was the right moment to work together. Sinead was an easy choice for him. They worked together on half a dozen songs. Three ended up on *100th Window*: 'What Your Soul Sings', 'Special Cases' and 'A Prayer For England'. Another, named 'Love Is Ours', was featured on Sinéad O'Connor's album, *She Who Dwells in the Secret Place of the Most High Shall Abide Under the Shadow of the Almighty*, a few months later.

Meanwhile, with Horace Andy, 3D wanted to explore new territories. They were looking for different vocal placements, on higher tones, less sung and more murmured, to suit the pieces of music D composed with Neil. Two tracks were finally kept for the album, the mystical and sensual 'Everywhen' and the dreamy 'Name Taken'.

3D described 'Everywhen' as the representation of a suspended moment of pure love, outside of time, in its very core fragility, a love we feel for a person but at the moment when it becomes crystallised as love itself, before it may sometimes disappear, when you change you mind... The lyrics are very minimalist, with sometimes a word by verse. *"My love, / Your Light / Incantations"*, *"The sequence ends / And begins"*... *"Everything / You think you know"*. The way D wrote the vocal parts let us think he could have sung it himself. On stage, D would later start singing the backing vocals for it.

For the first time, on this record, Robert Del Naja is actually singing. In what he likes to call "melodic whispers", more than real singing. "It's just a matter of challenging yourself to do something different," he told the press. "I just wanted to push the boundaries a bit. I'm very aware of my own restrictions, as I think everyone should be, but you've got to push yourself. Every time we start a new album there's a challenge to extract yourself from what you did before[158]."

One song composed in the first part of 2002 was 'Special Cases'. Sinéad O'Connor's lyrics deal with our world's tendency to replace

---

158 In an interview with the BBC, broadcast in January 2003

human relations by robots and machines. In very simple and direct words, she gives a harsh criticism on excesses behind computerisation, obsession with security, and the paranoia of our immediate post-September 11 western cultures.

Masses versus individuality

She makes a grim assessment: *"Take a look around the world / You see such mad things happening"*, but she also chooses to praise the beauty and the depth of meaningful relationships – *"There are few good men / Thank your lucky star that he's one of them / The deadliest of sin is pride / Make you feel like you're always right / But there are always two sides / It takes two to make love, two to make a life"*. The text praises the luck of being with someone you can trust in a frightening world, D would describe. These lyrics are working in a tense opposition with the music, which is slow and bewitching, but sometimes menacing. A delicate flow of strings is added to the beats and rhythms, an orchestral part recorded in London, which brings a feeling of breathing into the broody atmosphere. The title has many potential meanings, which adds to the mystery of its contrasts.

'Special Cases' became the fourth track of the album and was soon chosen to become the first single, scheduled to be released two weeks after the record, in February. It reached number 15 on the UK Singles Chart. The sleeve features a picture mirroring the album cover, with a yellow spark of broken glass.

The song was released with a video, directed by the French collective of filmmakers named H5, who had recently become superstars in the 'French Touch' electronic movement. The film was produced in two slightly different versions, edited in a different order. It shows the life evolution of two babies conceived in a laboratory, by researchers and scientists, a boy and a girl, who grow up in a special building where they are constantly scrutinised and studied, but who finally fall in love with each other. The first version shows the boy's story first; the second the girl's perspective, creating a subtly different impression. The result strongly emphasises the album's themes around dehumanisation and hyper obsession for technology.

189

Sinéad and 3D also selected for the album their collaboration named 'What Your Soul Sings', as the second track of the record. According to D, this song reflects Sinéad's optimistic view about the power of mankind to take their destiny into their own hands... It is a magnificent ballad, written as a hymn for personal growth and inner confidence, with a strong spiritual dimension. Sinéad starts with a sentence that comes again as the main pattern: *"Don't be afraid / Open your mouth and say / Say what your soul sings to you"*. And she develops: *"Your mind can never change / Unless you ask it to / Lovingly re-arrange / The thoughts that make you blue / The things that bring you down / Only do harm to you / And so make your choice joy / The joy belongs to you"*, she continues on soft notes of harps and subtle drum beats... The song has no chorus but long parts of layers of instrumental and electronic sounds. *"So make your choice joy / The joy belongs to you (...) You'll find you / Love you"*, she ends. Nothing could be further away from *Mezzanine*'s tortured guitars and anxious lyrics about gloomy corridors and half-awaken nightmares (as in 'Risingson') or traumatic dawns ('Group Four').

Developing the music for a third collaboration, 3D asked Sinéad to write a song that would almost feel like a prayer. She was quite to the point when she presented to him 'A Prayer For England' and Massive Attack thus unexpectedly produced their first real protest song. Sinéad powerfully declaims, as a wake up call: *"In the name of / And by the power of / The holy spirit / May we invoke your / Intercession for / The children of England"*... And she sounds like she is directly and courageously addressing Tony Blair's government, while they were starting to betray all their promises. A powerful gesture in the voice of an Irish woman...

Her lyrics get progressively more and more explicit: *"The teachers are representing you so badly"* (...) *"Beliefs kill children to / Feel the love of you and be healed"*. Then more personal: *"Let not another child be slain / Let not another search be made in vain"*. 3D was really impressed by her lyrics, that he found powerful without being too confrontational, especially on the subject of child's abuse. And he admired her capacity to denounce reality while leaving a note of hope. The song became the sixth track of the record and both wanted to release it as a single, but Virgin convinced them to release 'Special Cases' first, which had a potential everybody in the band agreed on. 'A Prayer For England' was in the end not released as a single.

The dark side of a world

'Future Proof' was one of the first songs composed for the album and became the opening of *100th Window*. 3D and Neil Davidge first worked on its guitar parts. From there, the construction develops in a snowballing effect, without chorus, opening on notes of synthesizers, followed by D's voice, the backing vocals, also done by D himself, then by more and more guitars in a crescendo that is growing until a climax, followed by a fall. After three minutes, the song almost stops half way through, then starts over with the synth notes, the voice, then the guitars, increasing slowly in intensity. It returns to calm before a slow instrumental and melodic ending. These effects are working magically on stage.

3D worked on minimal lyrics. *"Borderline cases / Reinforced glass / Absent friends / Passport photos / An elastic past / Empty pocket / They think it is all... / They think it's soul"* is the first verse, far from his long chatty raps from *Blue Lines* or *Protection*. He described the lyrics as a search for "this romantic notion of disappearance, the dream of becoming a ghost and escaping reality". The atmosphere can also relate to people's cold and distant behaviour in a paranoid and overpopulated world, in sharp, polysemous and intense phrases: *"Separate the leper / Hungry ghosts / Another imprint / In borrowed clothes / We can be numb / We can be numb / Passing through"*... It evokes sadness and loneliness, feelings mainly inspired by the absence of his former band mates.

The song often opened the band's show throughout 2003 and would never leave their set list. The crescendo effect and the major guitar solo in the middle add to its live energy and contrast sharply with the melancholic ending, in a powerful introduction to their performances.

3D's second vocal appearance on the album comes on the fourth track, 'Butterfly Caught'. His voice is also used to create the bassline, sampled as an instrument could be. Along with electronic sounds comes an orchestra of fifty strings recorded in London in June 2002. The musician wanted these violins to feel non-definable, exotic as well as familiar. "It sounds both oriental and western at the same time, as though it originated in Istanbul, when the Bosporus was still the limit between East and West," he described to the press[159].

The music elegantly and intriguingly marries two trends and produces a passionate effect, torn in between two cultures, bringing together elements that can sound irreconcilable in an exquisite manner. The *New York Times'* critic, Jody Rosen, praised it as one of "the most propulsive of the new songs" of the album, as "Mr. Del Naja can be an effective songwriter", both "as an existentialist and a nerd", and where the "violins play forlorn scales borrowed from Algerian rai"[160]. 3D himself described it as a love song though, celebrating the fusion of both bodies and beings, but the violins' melody infuses it with a tearing melancholy, while the beats reinforce a slightly menacing atmosphere.

These feelings inspired the director of the video, South African filmmaker Daniel Levi, to produce a particularly dark film, also brilliant and metaphorical, in which he shot Robert Del Naja metamorphosing into a moth, in a bleak room only lit by tired neon lights. His skin is getting covered with dark marks of make-up while his light blue gaze is turned into deep black. One more transformation for the artist who lengthily explained after the release of *Mezzanine* that he was obsessed with metamorphosis…

3D's next song on the album is named 'Small Time Shot Away', the seventh track. It is one of the longest – nearing eight minutes. After the first third, the track slows down and enters a different dimension, almost out of time, before starting again more intensely. Based on a Juno synthesiser's part and multiple layers of drums, it is one of the most original, brilliant and moving of all tracks on this fourth album.

'Small Time Shot Away' includes barely audible backing vocals from Damon Albarn, who was in Bristol for a day when Robert was working on the song; he was credited as 2D. His voice is more apparent on another version, a remix named 'Small Time Shot 'Em Up', which is featured on the band's compilation, *Collected*, released in 2006.

Inspired by the ending of a love story and the loneliness 3D felt deeply

---

159 In an interview with *Humo Magazine*, published in Belgium in March 2003
160 In a review published on March 16, 2003

that year, the song is also a metaphor for an internal struggle against doubt and against addiction, becoming one of the most personal songs written by Robert Del Naja, never sung on stage. It reflects a feeling of oppression, and a will to escape it. The words are deeply polysemous. *"Took her in / Dropped a line / Turned me on / We never leave each other cos we leave each other so cold"*, he begins. The song does not have a chorus but recurrent themes like: *"It's wartime every time / Small talk every time / It's my favourite chloroform"*. After the midway break, the cymbals start over and the melody mimes a form of rebirth, as the vocals go on: *"Ricochet / We're like identical twins / Sucking on the same teat / Spitting out the same things"*. And the last part of the song sounds like an ultimate effort not to abandon oneself to the appealing softness of disappearance, to refuse the temptation of the sedation, in a world dominated by this "wartime". A rare song about survival and redemption.

3D's last vocal appearance comes on the album's last track, 'Antistar'. Musically it was created from two verses based on the guitar parts, surrounded by percussions, layers of keyboards and the gorgeous strings, also recorded in London in June 2002. It can be read as the artistic declaration of a band that remained away from gossip and stardom. Musically, it is also inspired by Eastern music, like 'Butterfly Caught', and lyrically it is influenced by a novel by American writer Katherine Dunn named *Geek Love*, from 1989, which fascinates D. The book describes the tribulations of a family circus, in which a little fish boy with no limb inspires his fans to cut off their own fingers or arms. It attempts to raise questions about the rise of genetic manipulation and the effects of cults and fame.

'Antistar' explores the idea of living an entirely public life that only inspires horror in 3D, as the "stars" on magazines' covers seem nothing else than desperate to him. He strictly separates his artistic life from his personal life, in Bristol, where he has always behaved as a regular citizen. The lyrics depict the madness of fame via the story of Dunn's book, as well as the struggle to face an unfathomable, destructive world: *"Can you lick my wounds please / Can you make it numb / And kill the pain like cortisone / And grant me intimacy / How'll we split your chromosomes"*. Robert multiplies the references to sedatives and sedation. *"Yeah more*

sweet narcosis / Yeah more sweet narcosis / I'll turn a stone I'll find you"...
Ending on a raw statement: *"You look great in bloodstains".*

'Antistar' is the longest track on the album (8 minutes and 17 seconds).
For a while, Robert thought about producing a film to illustrate the
main theme, but finally abandoned the project, busy with the tour's
rehearsals. The song was regularly played live as one of the highlights
of the band's shows from 2003 to 2006.

A Massive Attack album? A Massive Attack album

100ᵗʰ Window was released on February 10, 2003 in the UK, and two
weeks later it reached number one in the Chart. The record was often
described in the media as Robert Del Naja's "solo" album, which the
musician deeply resents, as he has never worked alone. He described his
recording process and changes in collaborators as a natural part of the
band's evolution, predictable from as early as 1992, when Shara Nelson
left them.

Composed without Mushroom or Grant, the album was still
produced with Neil, helped by Alex Swift, with Sinead O'Connor,
Horace Andy, and Damon Albarn even, then of course the whole band,
Angelo Bruschini on guitars, Jon Harris on the bass and Damon Reece
on drums.

Grant, by that time, was about to announce his comeback for the tour.
"*100th Window* is just a Massive Attack album made by 3D," he told the
press. "It has a Massive Attack feel, but I think it's an album that sounds
the way D thinks Massive Attack should sound[161]." D had become the
band's driving force, it sounded more apparent, but this did not mean
that he wanted to work on his own, far from it. "What makes it *not* a
Massive Attack album?" he replied to a journalist in Australia. "Massive
Attack has always been a project and has always been ambiguous, and
we very rarely worked in the same room at the same time, anyway.
Obviously, Mushroom was never going to be involved in this project
from the start because he left the band. Grant's not the biggest lover of
studios. So for the last five or six years, I'm very used to working alone

161 In an interview with *World Magazine*, published in October 2003

with Neil Davidge. It's never really been an issue[162]."

The record company might have preferred a less risky album but was satisfied to have a new release from the band, which had millions of fans on the five continents. The album also became number one in the Chart in France and in Poland, for instance.

If the audience was still there, critics were polarised: some could not help looking for a link with *Mezzanine* and didn't understand the album; others were mesmerised, talking of a gem. In the *Observer*, Sean O'Hagan described it as "another masterpiece": it "is electronic in both the literal and generic sense of the word, dark, brooding, and possessed of a slow-burning cumulative power that is insidious rather than immediately arresting. A record that you have to live with for a while". O'Hagan also understood the evolution of the collective idea. "From the start, by design, they were never a proper pop group at all," he wrote, "more a loose, constantly shifting aggregation of like-minded souls who adhered around a core membership of three oddball Bristolians." 3D told O'Hagan in the interview: "To tell the truth, it feels like starting over every time we do an album. This time, it was me starting over on my own. It was terrifying, but liberating[163]."

The *New York Times* headlined "Bleak, Like Bristol, but Beautiful", and praised the new direction: "Mr. Del Naja is expert at ratcheting up musical tension. Many songs vamp on one chord for several minutes before opening up with a cathartic chord change," Jody Rosen wrote, adding that "*100th Window* is a rare thing" and that "Massive Attack has made that dark rumble into one of pop music's most compelling noises: the lowdown sound of troubled thoughts, bad times and great records[164]".

In France, in the daily newspaper *Le Figaro*, music journalist Bertrand Dicale wrote: "Everything is there: introspection and sharing, pain and relief, realism and compassion. Too difficult for FM's programmers, impossible to listen to on a car's CD player, it's probably the most stimulating album of 2003, the most intriguing and the most

---

162 In an interview with the magazine *The Age*, published in March 2003
163 In the *Observer*, on February 2, 2003
164 In an article published on March 16, 2003

important."

On *100ᵗʰ Window*, the long, looping, hypnotic songs come as interludes of beauty, stuck between hope and despair, and others, like 'Butterfly Caught' and 'Small Time Shot Away', expose the artist as never before, with raw emotions and retained, cryptic and poetical lyrics, as ambiguous as Massive Attack can be. Behind the powerful bass effects lie fragile human experiences, which can throw listeners off balance at first. But once tamed, very few records offer such a level of complexity and describe so well the feeling of surviving through a nightmare, to finally find beauty and sublime, in a cathartic manner.

The wrong war

If the three years that had come before this album release had been difficult for Robert Del Naja, 2003 woudn't be any easier. In February, while the band started the album's promotion – G reuniting with D, a new front opened that would dictate the tone of the rest of the year, as the war in Iraq was about to start.

Fiercely opposed to the conflict, Del Naja participated in another rally, on February 15, in London, which became one of the largest marches in the history of the UK, gathering about a million people. Again, he was one of the few members of the music industry, with singers Billy Bragg and Damon Albarn. More than one million people marched from Hyde Park to Westminster, along with Jesse Jackson, veteran socialist MP Tony Benn, playwright Harold Pinter and filmmaker Ken Loach among others, to protest what they name "the wrong war".

The events really echoed the lies dating from 1991 and the first Gulf War. 3D could not forget that the band had been forced to drop the word "Attack" from their name in 1991. And in 2003, he thought about dropping it again for this fourth album, as an anti-war statement... "But then I'd be buying into the whole notion that music and words and opinions are offensive," he finally decided. "And they're not. Bombs and bullets are[165]."

The musicians did not believe that the march would prevent the

165 In an interview with *Rock's Backpages*, published on February 3, 2003

war though, but that it could prevent future leaders to take decisions against people's will. In an interview given to Sky News during the march, Damon Albarn suggested a referendum. "Tony Blair would have no choice but to call off," he insisted. 3D added that most British citizens didn't even understand the clear reasons of the attack and claimed that "you cannot go into war without knowing what you're doing, it's absolutely crazy." Among the protesters were war veterans, British and American soldiers who fought in World War II, along with very young people, coming from all over the UK. Standing on Trafalgar Square by the end of the day, the group broadcast songs from the Clash and hip-hop tracks. British citizens clearly showed they were not in favour of this new war, but the government wouldn't listen.

The right-wing press described the protesters as supporters of Saddam Hussein. But Stop The War Coalition and the intellectuals involved worked hard to explain to their fellow citizens that the United Nations had no evidence that Iraq actually possessed W.M.D., Weapons of Mass Destruction, and that the question of the will of political leaders to ensure the control over the oil reserves in Iraq could not be avoided, as well as the history of the West's relations with the Middle East since the beginning of the twentieth century.

The themes and feelings raised in Massive Attack's fourth album soon appeared like a prophetic mirror to the surrounding chaos. Meanwhile, Robert's peers in the music industries were more interested in preventing their American sales from dropping than in political issues. And 3D felt even lonelier, thinking about musicians who, like John Lennon and Joe Strummer, had inspired his early convictions about social justice. Robert wondered where politically engaged artists had gone. His art and music, as he had just turned 38 years old, took a definitive turn.

At the end of February, as the new and completely redesigned Massive Attack tour was almost ready but still demanded a lot of final preparation, another event shattered Robert's life. On February 25, British police stormed his flat in Bristol looking for documents in the case of *Operation Ore*, put into place to fight children's paedophilia. They seized videos and computer equipments. A month later, on March

25, all his property was returned: Avon and Somerset police drop the investigation, having no evidence at all.

However, his name was leaked to the tabloid press. Though it was illegal, someone in the police office informed Rupert Murdoch's media group, News Corp., and his tabloid, the *Sun*. And the paper named 3D in an article. One of their journalists also apparently called the Australian and New Zealander Embassy, where the band's tour was about to start. Before even understanding that there was no affair, New Zealand cancelled the band's visas, only to apologise very soon afterwards. But their show had to be cancelled.

For Robert, it all felt like a nightmare. The feelings expressed on the record, the fragile glass figures featured damaged on its cover, the video of Del Naja turning into a moth filmed for 'Butterfly Caught', it all seemed suddenly like self-fulfilling prophecy... "Being accused of something you haven't done, when it's up there with rape and murder as a social taboo, was awful," he explained in an interview a few months later[166]. "I was suddenly living in a Kafka novel. I went back to the police station and asked why they leaked the story. They denied it of course, but I'm sure it was them. (...) Amazingly though, if they were trying to discredit me they failed. People from my past have gone out of their way to get in touch and let me know they didn't believe it. People were coming up to me in pubs. And the gigs have been the same. Fucking amazing, over the world. It was a big deal to me, but no one else cared. Every night we are printing emails being sent in to us at the show and we haven't had to censor a thing."

The only positive element was this solidarity reinforced around 3D. "It brought us back together in a way that music wouldn't have," Grant said[167]. And the band's tour started in March in Australia, as a proper machine to respond to the war-going policies, a wondrous and unseen show Robert had been working on for months with a collective of designers named United Visual Artists, known as UVA.

The *100th Window* Tour started on March 11. "Then, when they were in Melbourne, the war started and my problems seemed even

166 Published in *World Magazine* in October 2003
167 In the same interview with *World Magazine*, October 2003

more insignificant," Robert admitted a month later[168]. On March 20, the ground invasion of Iraq was launched by the American/British coalition. "I feel shattered, but you learn from it," Robert added. "When I wake up in the morning I get that sinking feeling, you know? But you have to deal with it; you have to go forward. It's given me a lot more resolve to do what I want to do[169]."

On stage: a new scale and a new stance

Massive Attack were on the road with Sinéad O'Connor – only for a few dates. The other artists included Horace Andy, Damon Reece, Angelo Bruschini, violin player Lucy Wilkins, Dot Allison who covered for Liz Fraser and Sinéad's vocals, and Deborah Miller.

Inspired by Japanese artist Tatsuo Miyajima, who used light installation and specifically light-emitting diode (LED) in his artworks, 3D co-designed with UVA a giant screen made of LED. It displayed pure data, statistics and factual details taken from the press about what was happening on the ground in Iraq – the death of civilians, Iraqi deaths, American death, the amount of oil being consumed, chemicals and weapons being found, as well as data from stock exchanges all around the world. All of these different facts and numbers were translated into local languages along the tour, including each time new input from local newspapers, to mix global with local information. A total of 36 languages was used over two years.

Every night, the line counting the number of Weapons of Massive Destruction found in Iraq read "0". Red and green lights alternatively dominated the screen, while the front stage remained in the dark. Progressively, 3D felt that the messages and exchanges of communication with the audience, able to send texts and emails to be displayed on the screen, brought a meaning to this dark period.

The show, most evenings, opened with 'Future Proof', followed by 'Everywhen', with Horace Andy. Then the set list moved to three songs from *Mezzanine*: 'Risingson', 'Black Melt' and 'Angel', before *100th Window*'s 'Special Cases'. 3D and Daddy G then performed 'Karmacoma';

---

168 In his interview with the *Guardian*, published on April 23, 2003
169 In the same interview with the *Guardian*, April 23, 2003

D continued with 'Butterfly Caught' and Horace Andy came again on stage for 'Name Taken'. The band added a few classics: 'Teardrop', 'Mezzanine', 'Hymn of the Big Wheel', 'Safe From Harm', and 'Inertia Creeps'. The end of the show was exploding in a ten-minute version of 'Antistar', before an encore of two songs: 'Unfinished Sympathy' and 'Group Four'.

The system of messaging varied across the set. During 'Future Proof' and 'Antistar', the lights evolved increasingly, in a dominant red colour. For 'Everywhen', Horace appeared as a shadow on a dark stage, the screen distilling a white light in a constellation on luminous spots. For 'Risingson', the LED screen resorted to three colours, yellow, green and white. The last part of the show brought in more political messages and quotes from newspapers, the last message asking: "Is the world a safer place now?"

3D came in every night in closed black clothes and remained on stage for almost the whole show, while Grant joined him for their duets. For 'Butterfly Caught' and 'Antistar', the violin player, Lucy Wilkins, was almost acting as a second vocalist, taking central stage and bringing a high level of emotion. After the show, the tour switched into long hours of partying, taking it to an even more hedonistic level that the *Mezzanine Tour*.

After Asia, the tour moved across Europe in April, including many festival dates, and on August 25, the band played in Queen Square, Bristol, in front of 20,000 people. They were sharing the line-up with many friends including Lupine Howl, Martina Topley-Bird, Goldfrapp, the Bees and the Streets. A few days later in Paris in the first edition of *Rock on Seine*, they crossed paths with PJ Harvey, Keziah Jones and Beck.

But while a second leg of the tour was scheduled to take them to America, the production of the shows unfortunately became increasingly expensive and almost bankrupted the tour. The band had to abandon their plan to travel to the US for a while. Fortunately, the following years made it possible.

The interruption of the tour, toward the end of 2003, seemed to define the year, a year of negativity and difficulty, but the band finally overcame the worst and transformed the dramas of the beginning of the year into an efficient response. Soon, for 2004, a second part of the tour was organised and the band was able to clear their debt. They toured in Latin America, then again in England, in Italy and in Central Europe. The band members were finally back home late 2004.

From darkness to daylight

In the meantime, Massive Attack had reached a high point in their career. Their fourth album peaked at number one in the UK and many other countries, selling more than one million copies. A few new tracks were released the last months of 2003: firstly 'Invasion', sung by 3D for U.N.K.L.E, on their album *Never Never Land*, released on September 22, and the two other songs interpreted by Sinéad O'Connor, 'It's All Good' and 'Love Is Ours', featured on her new own album. Massive Attack were also, first and foremost, at their best on stage.

As the magazine *Rock Backpages* noted, Massive Attack had become by far the most famous artists from Bristol since Cary Grant, born in the city in 1904, before moving to Hollywood in the 1930s. Yet, the band members remained, for many, two voices with no face, almost anonymous in their everyday life, despite their glory. Like his music in 2003, both melancholic and cathartic, expressing beauty and survival, Robert Del Naja in particular had successfully overcome a very difficult year.

In an interview he gave in Naples, Italy, in September 2003, Robert defined his music not as "dark", like most newspapers, but as mirroring our world. "The world in general is getting darker," he stated. "With the amount of surveillance we're under, the new American corporate century we're about to enter, it's a very frightening place. Media organisations are allowed to monopolise, they can own newspapers, radio and TV stations and all have political interests. It's dangerous especially if you're trying to put something out that's not just a hair product, a T-shirt or a chocolate bar, you're trying to do something creative. And that goes for writers, musicians, artists, filmmakers… It's gonna get much, much harder. The whole idea of our music getting darker is ridiculous. The issue is the media in general. The media's selling you a lifestyle, when the world is in a precarious position[170]."

However, inspired by the city he was interviewed in and where his family is from, 3D started to get into this attitude to life that was enjoy it while it lasts. Like Southern Italians, living under the shadow of the Vesuvius and the fact that it could erupt unexpectedly. And he emerged from these difficulties with an enhanced instinct of living in the moment. A lesson hardly learned, in a few months that might very well be the hardest in his life, but also the most eloquent.

170 In an interview with *Jack* magazine, published in September 2003

Chapter 11
Between War And Peace (2004-08)

After two busy years, by the end of 2004, Massive Attack were back home in Bristol. Grant was more focused on his family life, working mainly as a DJ on different sets when he could. On October 25, 2004, he released his DJ mix album, named *DJ-Kicks: Daddy G*, on the Studio !K7 independent record label as part of the *DJ-Kicks* series, featuring remixes of songs from Tricky and Massive Attack but also from American soul goddess Aretha Franklin as well as the Jamaican reggae and dub musician/producer Willie Williams.

Robert Del Naja and Neil Davidge, on their sides, were willing to work on new music. They were still pondering on the directions the latest album could have taken if the situation around him had been different. They were therefore looking for new directions in sound, away from the busyness of the tour, in Bristol. They were dreaming of a sound between gothic and soul, something like Siouxsie and the Banshees but sung by Beyonce...

But in 2004, the idea of returning to the studio to produce a new album was too heavy, and they received many other propositions that looked appealing, especially for film scores.

Bristol, from quietness to worries
Working on film projects brought an escape from Massive Attack to Neil and Robert. And calm could be felt in the music they produced in 2004 and 2005, for two films: *Danny The Dog*, created by French film star Luc Besson, and *Bullet Boy*, by the young British filmmaker Saul Dibb.

Danny The Dog, released as *Unleashed* in some countries, is a martial arts action thriller written by Besson, directed by Louis Leterrier, produced and interpreted by Jet Li. It tells the story of a young man, known as Danny, raised by a tyrannical landlord from his young age, in order to transform him into a "fighting dog" at his service. The man treats Danny as a master would treat a slave and uses him to threaten his business partners and get his money back. Soft and introvert, withdrawn from society, Danny manages to escape and befriends a blind piano teacher, Sam (played by Morgan Freeman), and his stepdaughter Victoria.

The film was released in February 2005 in France, in May in the US and in August in the UK. The whole score was written by Robert and Neil and distributed from November 2004 by EMI Music under the name Massive Attack. It gathers 21 instrumental tracks varying from dynamic electronic tunes (including 'One Thought At A Time', 'I Am Home', 'The Dog Obeys') to soft music pieces ('Red Lights Means Go', 'Right Way To Hold A Spoon' or 'Everything About You Is New') and eerie melodies (like 'Polaroid Girl', 'Danny The Dog', 'Montage' and 'Two Rocks and a Cup of Water'), in a very harmonious set. The film also featured a song entitled 'Aftersun', written in 2001 by 3D with Dot Allison, but not included on the record.

The soundtrack almost formed a new album from the band, described as "a fresh and remarkably listenable soundtrack" by the BBC, adding that "Massive Attack excel in creating a droogish urban soundscape full of eerie spaces and layers of saturated, ambient noise", offering "ample evidence that – should the charms of Bristol ever wear off" – Massive Attack's next destination might well be Hollywood." *Music OHM* magazine compared the song 'Montage' to the sound of indie rock Radiohead.

For the much more socially realistic *Bullet Boy*, a dozen instrumental tracks were written, plus the title track that was sung by 3D. The beautifully sad ballad is based on a slow and simple guitar part and layers of electronic percussions. Its lyrics are directly in relation with the film's story, set in Hackney, in East London, where a young black man is released from prison and comes home to his mother and little brother, but is soon endangered by the general climate of social violence and the prevalence of guns in his neighbourhood. *"Bruised from another place / Everyday takes grace / And the air's still warm / From a bullet in the wrong place*", murmurs 3D's voice, in one of the most touching songs composed by D and Neil Davidge so far.

The soundtrack was, this time, signed by "Robert Del Naja and Neil Davidge of Massive Attack" and released on iTunes in February 2005. The film received a prize at the *British Independent Film Awards* in 2004, for "Most Promising Newcomer" and Saul Dibb later gained more recognition with his next films, *The Duchess* and *Suite Française*.

Bristol's music scene, from the years of the Wild Bunch, had a strong link with cinema. It was therefore not surprising that Beth Gibbons' 'Mysteries' (from the album *Out Of Season*, composed by Beth and Paul Webb in 2001) was featured in *The Russian Dolls*, by French filmmaker Cedric Klapisch, in 2005. Beth, the same year, also wrote the score for the French film *L'Annulaire* by Diane Bertrand. After a lot of touring, Portishead decided to put any future band project on hold. Geoff Barrow worked on his side on his new label, Invada Records, launched in Australia and extended to the United Kingdom in 2003, with the help of producer Paul Horlick, known in Bristol as "Fat" Paul.

But by the end of 2004, Portishead and Massive Attack's members were reunited by more than a love for film scores. They decided to hold a charity concert for the victims of the tsunami in Asia, and, for the first time, shared the same stage.

United on stage

"I was talking to Beth on the phone," explained Geoff Barrow[171], "and she just mentioned what had happened and we talked about it, then I got off the phone and thought 'We've got to do something'. It was just before New Year. I phoned Ade and then rang Beth back – so we were all on for it. We didn't have a venue or anything, it was just an idea. Phoned up D, because it was the obvious next place to go, and D called me back, and said he was interested in definitely doing it."

A similar concert was organised for Oxfam, on January 22, in Cardiff, gathering 61,000 people, with Charlotte Church, Craig David, Goldie

---

171 In a long interview with the local magazine *Venue*, published on February 11, 2005

Lookin' Chain, Aled Jones, Badly Drawn Boy, Manic Street Preachers and Eric Clapton. Geoff Barrow heard from a friend that the DJ John Stapleton, a regular at the Dug Out in the 1980s, also a show promoter, had been offered the *Bristol Academy* to put together a fundraiser. Geoff called John, and the plan got on track. Two concerts were programmed at the *Academy* for February 19 and 20, 2005. Once announced in the press, all the tickets were quickly sold.

This Bristol show was meant to remain simple and straightforward. Adrian Utley from Portishead explained: "We didn't want a massive, full production with loads of gear. So the premise was we'd do it as acoustically as possible and add whatever electronics we need. It means 'not as we've done it before'. It'll be a stripped-down set-up, with shared equipment and shared musicians[172]." A choice appreciated by 3D. "We've toured for the last two years non-stop," he added, "and this is an opportunity to do something completely different – no production, no fucking 'concept'. The idea is to rearrange tracks, play them in a completely different way with different people[173]." He announced that he would be on stage with Daddy G and Elizabeth Fraser. The two bands were joined, for the rest of the programme, by Robert Plant, the Coral (a band produced by Geoff Barrow and Adrian Utley), Patrick Duff and Alex Lee of Strangelove, and Fuzz Against Junk.

The aim was to work with Oxfam not only for the benefit gigs but over the whole year, on their programme named "Make Poverty History", a campaign promoting fair trade and the cancellation of poor countries' debt. D wanted to produce another event for the following Christmas and to focus on aid in Africa.

Each show at the Bristol Academy lasted more then two hours, opening with Patrick Duff and Alex Lee, followed by Fuzz Against Junk, the Coral and Robert Plant. Then came a surprise guest: Damon Albarn, interpreting three songs including 'Tender' by Blur and a new track named 'Northern Whale', produced with his new project, the Good, the Bad & the Queen. He stayed on with Massive Attack when they performed 'Karmacoma', playing with Neil Davidge, Adrian Utley,

172 In a long interview with the local magazine *Venue*, published on February 11, 2005
173 Ibid

Angelo Bruschini, Damon Reece and the genius keyboardist John Baggott, often on tour with Portishead. The atmosphere, at this stage, was palpably joyful and warm. Massive Attack had rarely been seen so continuously smiley on stage. 3D introduced the instrumentalists after the first track, notably Neil, whom he described as a friend and a genius, and Elizabeth Fraser. She joined them for the first time in five years, interpreting divine versions of 'Black Melt' and 'Teardrop'.

3D came on the mic after her for 'Future Proof', in an entire rethought version, with Adrian Utley and Angelo on guitars, bringing a surprisingly folkish dimension to the recent track. D continued with the lyrics to 'Risingson', sung to the melodies of 'Glory Box', adding updated lyrics: *"Through alleyways and hallways, I love you always"*. This new version was progressively melted into Portishead's song.

Portishead took the stage to perform the rest of their song, then 'Wandering Star', 'Sour Times', 'Mysterons' and 'Roads', to a continuous stream of applause. Beth Gibbons was, as usual, intense in her voice, her face hidden behind her straight shiny hair, very simply dressed just like her close friend Liz Fraser.

This show constituted a very intimate set for both Portishead and Massive Attack, bringing a rare acoustic dimension to their complex music. Both Robert and Beth had just turned 40 years old in January and their humility was striking during the breaks, especially as they can be charismatic when performing. The local BBC station Radio Bristol described the sound of the shows as "airy and immaculate" and could not hide its enthusiasm: "Saturday at the Bristol Academy was unique in a number of ways. Portishead emerged from a seven-year recess to share the stage with fellow locals Massive Attack and both delivered a staggering, note-perfect, live set." In Bristol a lot of people were hoping to see them replicate the formula. Both bands will remain away from the stage the rest of the year, though.

In 2005, the United Kingdom seemed to have far grimmer preoccupations. On May 5, a disputed general election brought another but tighter victory for New Labour, yet in Bristol, where Tony Blair had widely disappointed, the party lost one seat to the Liberal Democrats. Then on July 5, riots broke out in Edinburgh, in Scotland, during a demonstration led by anti-capitalist groups against the G8 summit. The government responded with severe police repression, including helicopters and anti-riot guards. More than 350 people were arrested.

But much worse were the events of July 7: four co-ordinated terrorist attacks took place in London during the morning rush hour. Three bombs exploded in the underground (in Edgware Road, Aldgate and Russell Square); a fourth one was detonated on a bus near Tavistock Square. A group linked to Al Qaeda claimed responsibility for the attacks. A total of 52 people were killed, including two teenagers, as well as the four attackers, leaving the country terrified and the continent horrified. This had been the worst terrorist attack in Europe since the Paris' bombing in 1995 and it obviously echoed the September 11 tragedy.

The fear was palpable. Four other attacks were prevented by the police on July 21 but a young Brazilian man became the innocent victim of police panic the next day: Jean Charles Menezes, an electrician, was killed by seven bullets in the head, as he was wrongly taken for a potential suspect in the corridors of the underground. Tension was high. A trial was scheduled but postponed and the policemen finally paid reparations to his family in November 2007, but none of them were formally recognised as responsible for the killing.

The country faced many challenges as fright and paranoia grew in people's mind. Newspapers published investigations about Islamic extremism in the UK and especially in areas re-branded as 'Londonistan', in the northern part of the capital, near Finsbury Park. Many intellectuals, on the other hand, blamed Tony Blair for the consequences of his actions in the Middle East. Stop the War Coalition and the journalist/documentary filmmaker John Pilger were very critical of Britain's recent foreign policy. As a response, some writers and artists were also trying to figure out how to encourage unity.

Live and learn

Meanwhile in Bristol, this gloomy context shook some artists' deep pacifist beliefs and political involvement. But Massive Attack were also reminded by Virgin Records they had to fulfil their contractual obligations: to produce six albums and a compilation record. As the band were not satisfied with their current production to call it a new album, the time seemed right to agree on a compilation. For Robert, the only interest in participating in such a project was to include some new art and music. Robert and Neil started to think about an anthology.

The record was simply called *Collected*. It included two discs – the first one with a selection of tracks from the band's four albums; the other with new, rare or unreleased songs. Another edition included a DVD named *Eleven Promos*. The first disc comprised 14 tracks, 13 previously released, in this order: 'Safe From Harm', 'Karmacoma', 'Angel', 'Teardrop', 'Inertia Creeps', 'Protection', 'Butterfly Caught', 'Unfinished Sympathy', 'Risingson', 'What Your Soul Sings', 'Future Proof', 'Five Man Army', 'Sly'. The fourteenth track was a new song named 'Live With Me', written with the amazing American jazz and soul singer Terry Callier. *Collected* was scheduled for March 27, 2006, in the UK and a tour for spring and summer.

Robert and Neil chose 'Live With Me' as the new element to complete the list because the song represented a return to the band's soul and blues roots. The featured vocalist, Terry Callier, was born in Chicago in 1945 and was a legend of American blues, jazz and soul music. He was introduced to 3D in 2004, through a soundtrack project for a British independent film that was never produced. Neil and D wrote about five songs together with Terry for the occasion. 'Live With Me' was the most appealing.

It was composed in a very traditional song-writing manner compared to most of Massive Attack's work: the melody was first created on a piano, an additional part with strings and percussions was added and the music sent to Terry. The singer then came to Bristol to record the vocals with 3D and Neil; he sang 'Live With Me' in one take. The result was very different from Massive Attack's latest compositions for films and 3D was in awe of the singer, describing him as a man with a soul and a spirit as lovely as his voice.

Emotionally charged, evoking the pain of a separation, the lyrics are direct and honest, almost supplicating, in a very blues style: *"Gonna survive / You live and learn / I've been thinking 'bout you babe / By the light of dawn / And midnight blue / I've been missing you / I've been thinking about you baby / Almost makes me crazy / Come and live with me*".

It brings a strong emotional and direct impact that Robert wanted to see reflected in the video. 'Live With Me' was released as a single on March 13, 2006, with a film directed by Jonathan Glazer, who had already worked with the band on his first music video 'Karmacoma'. Shot in London around Caledonian Road, the film reflects on the role of alcohol on one fragile soul, a woman played by the Scottish actress Kirsty Shepheard. She actually really drinks until drunkenness for the role, showing a person at a moment of collapse, "between heaven and hell", according to Del Naja, who finds the film extremely touching, making us want to rescue the person and not judge her. An alternative version of the video features only a close shot of Terry Callier performing the song, Robert begging Jon to shoot Terry as he felt it would be a tragedy not to capture such a beautiful song being performed.

MusicOMH described 'Live With Me' as "not only a welcome return for the band but a hark back to their 'glory' days, circa *Blue Lines* and *Protection*; it is an aching, haunting love song... that beautifully evokes the pain and longing of failed romance." The song hit number 17 in the Singles Chart. Terry Callier sang it on stage with Massive Attack when their tour reached his hometown, Chicago, in September 2006.

And in 2009, Terry released two of the other tracks written with 3D and Neil, on his own album *Hidden Conversations*: 'Wings' and 'John Lee Hooker'. This collaboration easily added an entire chapter to the musical history of Massive Attack, a sound that could be qualified as "modern blues", extremely rare in Britain, where, according to Tricky, it is still hard to get any form of real "black music" produced.

Silenced voices and clueless blues

Collected reached number 2 in the UK Albums Chart. The artwork for the cover was created by 3D with Tom Hingston and Nick Knight, as for *Mezzanine* and *100th Window*, from intricate images of roses and guns. "I remember one of the albums I nicked off my mum, this Moody Blues album with a gatefold sleeve with these faces in the clouds like a James Bond-esque title sequence collage," Robert detailed in the interview added in his art book. "I wanted to turn one of these flowers into a collage and this sleeve that I stared at as a kid." The album also included a booklet with reproductions of some of his recent paintings, inspired by the French riots, which occurred late 2005, and by the recent attacks in Lebanon.

Collected's limited edition offered a second disc with rare versions of Massive Attack's songs: 'Incantations', 'Small Time Shoot Em Up', 'Black Melt', 'Danny The Dog' and 'Bullet Boy' from the recent film scores, 'I Want You' (with Madonna) and 'I Against I' (with Mos Def, aka Yasiin Bey). It also contained three unreleased songs: 'Joy Luck Club' featuring Debbie Clare (from the band Oom) on vocals, 'Silent Spring' sung by Liz Fraser, and 'False Flags', a track composed by 3D.

For the slow and original ballad that became 'Silent Spring', Liz is singing in an invented language to music that is almost acoustic, in what remains a demo version. She accepted that the band release it in this unfinished state. It shows the kind of music the band produced at this time, more natural, away from the refined productions of *100ʰ Window*. The touching track actually sounds more beautiful because it is imperfect and in an incomplete stage.

Apart from 'I Against I', all of the new tracks were credited without Grant Marshall. At this time, D seemed to have accepted and to enjoy working separately. "Everyone's still waiting for the sort of record G would make, aren't they?" said Del Naja in an interview with *The Times*, in March 2006. "You are defined by the work you do, not the work you don't do," he added. He particularly disliked hearing that Grant was soly responsible for the soul/hip-hop side of Massive Attack. "There's a lot of misconceptions about this band," Robert insisted. "Take the new single that we put on the compilation. Everyone said: 'Oh, you can tell G's back, it has the trademark Massive sound'. Well, G didn't have anything to do with it, it was me and Neil. The way we work now, me here and G over there, just suits us. We'll put it all together soon and see how it fits. We've even discussed making it an album of two parts[174]." He mentioned as an example the 2003 album by the hip-hop duo OutKast, named *Speakerboxx/The Love Below*, edited as two different records,

174 In an interview with *The Times*, published on March 25, 2006

created separately by the two members of the band, André 'André 3000' Benjamin and Antwan 'Big Boi' Patton.

When the press asked Grant if 'Live With Me' did display an influence of his passion for soul music, Grant reckoned he was very much less involved in the band than his partner at this time. "He has a drive about him. D takes care of all the details – I'm not so focused in that sense[175]." 3D explained it had not always been easy for him. "I think if I hadn't made the effort there would only have been a couple of Massive Attack albums. Part of me says I can't be tethered to this concept all my life; the responsibility is too great. The other part of me says that Massive is what I do. I don't have any family and the band is part of the reason for that[176]." Grant gave assurances that he was from then back for good in the band.

3D was also regularly asked about the melancholy in his music, to which he replied by speaking about the meaning of soul music to him, as a reflection about what was happening around them, closely, and more widely, in world affairs. In that sense, this type of sullen music is an inspiration to him and gives an energy, as it doesn't deny the reality of our world, unlike pop music and jingles punctuating news bulletins.

Since then and until now, D has refused to see music and art as entertainment, a distraction or a pure deviation from world's issues. Which is what he finds "dark". He expresses himself as a musician, but also as a citizen.

The last new song featured on *Collected* is a perfect illustration of this spirit. 'False Flags' was written at the end of 2005 at the time of the riots in France, erupted after the death of two teenagers near Paris, in Clichy-sous-Bois, on October 27. And it became one of the most political songs ever written by Massive Attack. Criticising the state of Europe, it recalls a series of uprisings that showed how some people, in Europe, refused political and social evolution that were not serving them.

"His city chews up clueless blues / Pays per views and no man's news / Blades will fade from blood to sport / The heroin's cut these fuses short", starts 3D's singing rap. *"Parisian boys without your names / Riot like 1968 again*

175 In an interview with *The Times*, published on March 25, 2006
176 Ibid

212

(...) And English boys without your names / Riot like the 1980s again", he continues, with references to the 1968 demonstrations in Paris, as well as the ones in Bristol in 1980 and 86, and in Brixton in 1981.

The second verse also takes a dig at the tabloid media: *"The ghosts you breed, the soaps that your write, the graceless charm of your guttersnipes."* And the rest of the lyrics present a list of social malfunctions in the urban sprawl: *"Ghetto stones instead of chains", "The flags are false and they contradict / They point and click which wounds to lick".* That, and wrong choices in foreign policy: *"Ghetto stones instead of chains / Hearts and minds and U.S. planes"... "The days of rage, yeah, nothing's changed / More pretty flames"*, 3D concludes, trying to seize the complexity of the most recent upheavals. The last part of the song is instrumental and ends with a short sample from the chorus of the song 'The Bends' by Radiohead, when Thom Yorke sings: *"Where do we go from here?"*

False Flags' was featured on the B-side of the 'Live With Me' single and a video was produced to illustrate it, directed by British filmmaker and photographer Paul Gore, showing flames surrounding a young protester as he is ready to launch a petrol bomb. The film's beauty resides in the choice of slow motion images, emphasising the act of throwing the bomb and perfectly matching the song's rhythm.

In August 2006, Massive Attack also released 'False Flags' on an MP3 format, broadcast online from iTunes, with another new song produced by 3D, named 'United Snakes'. The latter had been played live by the band from 2004. Written originally in 2001, as a potential part of the soundtrack for the film *Matrix Reloaded*, it was finally not used by the filmmakers. In 2008, a video was also produced for it, created by United Visual Artists.

At the end of April 2006, the band started the *Collected* tour and performed in the USA, for the first time in years, notably at the Coachella Festival in California, founded in 1999. Massive Attack toured until late September, crossing Europe in June, coming to Hyde Park in London and playing in many festivals. They had three dates in Paris in late August and returned to the US in September, then travelled to Canada. The personnel included Damon Reece and Andrew Small as the two drummers, Angelo Bruschini on guitar and Winston Blissett on bass;

Horace Andy, Deborah Miller and Elizabeth Fraser were the featured vocalists.

The show was centred on the band's political messages. It opened with 'False Flag', followed by 'Risingson'. D and Grant appeared close again while performing. Most musicians were dressed in black, except Liz, wearing a white dress, introduced by Robert with compliments on her angelic voice. Half way through, before 'Future Proof', 3D mentioned the band's work with UNRWA, the United Nations' branch for Palestinian refugees. The stage was illuminated in red by the giant LED screen. The last part of the show featured the band's hits, 'Safe From Harm', 'Inertia Creeps', 'Unfinished Sympathy' and 'Group Four'.

While Massive Attack were scheduled to play in Montreal on September 11, Grant showed his support for the political content of the band's visual show, interviewed by the Canadian magazine *Hour*. "The government is deliberately alienating the Muslims, saying that they're the ones to watch," he commented about the climate in England. "Ten, 15 years ago, it was maybe Indians and Pakistanis. Twenty years ago, it was black people. Even everyday laws, they're just not reflecting the England that we have. It's a multiracial society that we have." He concluded: "From the release of *Blue Lines*, 15 years ago, till now, there's been complete conflict in the world as we know it, and all these major disasters. So at the end of the day you can't help but take some of it in. We're quite politically motivated, in a way[177]."

The American leg of the tour was later postponed until October, but Daddy G had to go home, as his wife was about to give birth to their second child. The rest of Massive Attack performed in New York, on October 3, 4 and 5, at the *Roseland Ballroom*. The screen presented in enormous red figures the numbers and facts related to the Iraqi war to a bemused audience. Including the number of people killed and the cost of the war in different currencies, while Debbie was singing "*You can free the world, you can free my mind / Just as long as my baby's safe from harm tonight*".

The *Los Angeles Times* described "a remarkably dynamic and

---

177 In an interview recorded from France late August and published on September 7, 2006

involving 100 minutes that truly lived up to the creative standards that have been associated with the name Massive Attack." For the *New York Times*, "the spectacular light show was the real star, adding another layer of emotion to the band's enigmatic beatscapes." The media also announced that the band had been working on a fifth album, temporarily named *Weather Underground*, expected for 2007. And Massive Attack scheduled more dates in the UK, from February 2007, in Spain and Portugal in September.

Before the last part of the tour, Massive Attack were invited to perform in the legendary Abbey Road Studios in London, as part of a documentary series produced on British music, to be aired on Channel 4 throughout 2007. They performed a few songs, including 'Teardrop' with Liz Fraser – more convincing than ever, 'Mezzanine', as a duo, with slightly renewed lyrics, and 'Angel', with Horace Andy, in a very powerful set.

The performance was completed with an interview with the two band members, remembering the recording of the string parts of 'Unfinished Sympathy' and more recently 'Live With Me', in the very same studio. For 3D, the place, where the Beatles had recorded in 1969, remained iconic. But he mainly talked about his views on the world and the need to raise awareness on conflicts, as all human problems derive from war and conflicts, according to him. His goal was to bring about more light, analysis and debate on world issues with his music and art. Robert Del Naja mainly pursued it through his painting in the following years.

Art as a fight

Back from the tour, work continued in the studio on an ever-delayed fifth album. Robert Del Naja was painting regularly that year and involved in more of Banksy's projects. The street artist was by then mainly stencilling in the United States and in Palestine. From 2005, he was as preoccupied as Robert by the fate of Palestinians and displayed his murals on the world's most famous wall, in Jerusalem, all over the West Bank and even in Gaza.

To get into the Palestinian territories, Banksy had to go through the numerous security checks imposed by the Israeli army, and to arrive in Gaza specifically had to take the same tunnels from Egypt arms dealers and terrorists have to go through... Nonetheless in August 2005, his tropical landscapes appeared on the giant grey wall surrounding Jerusalem.

A few days later, back in London, Banksy entered the British Museum... in his own way. Placing on the art venue's walls his own reproductions of famous paintings, modified in his politically charged tastes. In Disneyland, in California, he installed a man-sized mannequin representing a prisoner from Guantanamo in the middle of a pond. Then on September 15, 2006, he was already the most famous street artist in the world when he opened his new pop-up exhibition – named 'Barely Legal' – in a warehouse in Los Angeles. His friends from Massive Attack were by then touring in California, reaching San Francisco on September 23. With their respective shows, they were addressing the same issues but in very different artistic approaches.

'Barely Legal' displayed for three days a series of art pieces, mainly three-dimensional creations, sculptures and installations, but also paintings and stencils. The main attraction was however a real elephant painted in pink and gold in a wallpaper styled pattern. 'The Elephant in the Room' was, according to Banksy, a symbol of the striking poverty still at stake in the world, which the wealthiest people chose not to see. All pieces were sold in two days, some for more than 50,000 dollars, a few of them bought by famous pop singers such as Christina Aguillera or Hollywood film stars including Brad Pitt and Angelina Jolie.

As for Robert Del Naja, back in England, a few weeks later, he was preparing an art installation for London's Victoria and Albert Museum, the famous V&A, museum of decorative arts and design opened in 1851 – one of the most prestigious and innovative art centres in the world. His installation is named Volume.

UVA were approached by the V&A after creating a successful light installation at the museum's Friday Late event named Transvision. "It had this mysticism about it," said Shaun Cole, the curator of contemporary programmes at the V&A. "It was one of the most popular pieces on the night." Signed by UVA and One Point Six, a company created by 3D and Neil for film scores, Volume was installed in the museum's John Madejski Garden, from November 24, 2006, to January 28, 2007.

The artwork was composed of an array of light columns positioned in the centre of the garden, "which react to human movement, creating a series of unique audio-visual experiences as one stepped through the light columns", according to the Museum. UVA described it as a "sculpture of light and sound", asking the visitors to "step inside and see your actions at play with the energy fields throughout the space, triggering a brilliant display". The installation later travelled to Taiwan, Saint Petersburg and Melbourne, and received the D&AD Yellow Pencil Award for Best Digital Installation.

Because art has always been for 3D mainly a means to share complex ideas and to act for a cause, he became more involved with organisations that he really admired: Greenpeace, the Red Cross and Red Crescent, Amnesty, but also and increasingly with smaller organisations, active locally and intensely, bringing a more direct and long-term aid. Since 2005, he had been working with the HOPING Foundation (Hope and Optimism for Palestinians in the Next Generation), helping children among the Palestinian refugees, funding programmes to enable them to learn music for instance. Early in 2007, D scheduled three benefit concerts for February (on the 6, 7, 8). The shows were scheduled to take place at the *Carling Academy* in Birmingham and in London's *Brixton Academy*. Before the second half of the *Collected* Tour.

3D invited an electronic music collective from Palestine, France and Tunisia, named Checkpoint 303, to join them as the first act in Birmingham and London. Created by SC MoCha and SC Yosh ("SC" standing for "*Sound Catchers*" or "*Sound Cutters*"), the collective worked between Paris and the West bank. Their name was inspired by an actual *checkpoint* in Bethlehem, one of the Israeli Army's many control points. Their music mixes sounds of the everyday life in Muslim countries with electronic loops and samples from luxurious Arab songs. Before those shows, the collective had only performed in small Parisian cafés. Each show attracted 5,000 people.

"The idea is to present something in between art and information to show that the Palestinians' daily life cannot be reduced to occupation,"

SC Yosh explained in an interview with the French daily newspaper, *Le Monde*. "There is a real civil society in Palestine, with normal people, living in a terrible and unfair situation but trying to get through it and to raise and educate their children[178]."

3D was aware of the difficulties that arose when dealing with such matters as an artist, and regretted the general lack of information on the conflict in the mainstream media. Massive Attack had been to Israel twice and enjoyed it, they had a number one album there with *Mezzanine*, but they also realised there was this problem with how people felt about the Palestine situation and couldn't suppress the problem in their minds. In Bristol, many are sensitive to the same cause. On Broad Street, near Nelson Street, in the city centre, a 'Palestine Embassy' even appeared in 2013 where exhibitions about art and history from Palestine are displayed.

To emphasise the issue, 3D gave interviews specifically on the HOPING Foundation, to the *New Statesman* and the *Guardian*, and discussed the matter on Sky News and the BBC. "It quickly becomes evident that Del Naja is unfashionably political, and not in the woolly way we have come to expect from our pop stars," wrote the *New Statesman*[179]. Robert explained: "We've been to Bethlehem twice, and to Lebanon, performing in Baalbek, which was heavily bombed in the last attacks. You see these places and you start to feel a connection, and to feel a bit more responsible for what happens there."

In the *Guardian*, he denounced what he called the "fear factory" of modern Britain. "Even before they found politics, politics found them", the journalist, Dorian Lynskey, commented, reminding the change in their name by their label in 1991. "We're not putting a flag up saying we believe in one side or another," insisted Del Naja. "We're saying we have to solve these problems, and they're manifold and complex, but let's start somewhere, please. Even if it is musicians acting like a bunch of idiots nobody's going to take seriously[180]." Grant intervened in a joke: "Someone's going to take us seriously. A few people. My mum and dad,"

178 In an interview with the French newspaper *Le Monde* in Jerusalem, published on April 18, 2007
179 Article and interview published on February 5, 2007, in the *New Statesman*
180 In the article and interview published on February 6, 2007 in the *Guardian*

adding: "I let D do most of the talking. I've got views, but they're more pub views. Give me a couple of drinks and you'll hear about Palestine and Israel and Robert Mugabe and all that stuff."

Robert mostly praised the work of Karma Nabulsi, who created and ran the Hoping Foundation, as well as Banksy's artwork in Palestine. He remained cautious to not alienate any views: "people end up bottling stuff up and saying, 'Oh fuck it, it's all Israel's fault'. People say that to me, and it's ridiculous. That's the danger when nobody deals with it on a proper discussion level. Unless people speak their minds openly about religion and politics and territory and economics, it's fucked."

Dorian Lynskey, who wrote a book about protest songs, concluded: "When musicians wade into political waters, even the most well-intentioned often seem inarticulate, ill-informed, simplistic or sanctimonious, but Del Naja may be the first musician I've met who is actually cleverer than he thinks he is." A serious compliment from the sharp and cruel British music press.

In the meantime, Robert was still working on projects for a fifth album, looking for the "gothic soul" sound that he had been dreaming about since 2001. D and Neil recorded a lot of songs with Horace Andy, Elizabeth Fraser, the American musicians Tunde Adebimpe and Dave Sitek from the band TV On The Radio and Damon Albarn. But they were not convinced yet by the shape it was taking.

Yet Robert's mind was more on art and politics. "Talking about how difficult it is to make a record is so trivial, isn't it?" he told the *Guardian*[181]. And it was not always possible to turn his deep interest for world affairs into music. "There's always inspiration in there but we've always been very cautious about how to write a song and a protest song is always difficult," he pondered. "When it works, it can be beautiful but when it doesn't, it can be quite feeble and patronising or silly. Instead, it can be about how you transmit ideas and share information on stage[182]."

Meanwhile, Robert and Neil composed music for more films that were related to important and engaging issues they cared for. The first one was a British documentary named *In Prison My Whole Life*,

181 Ibid
182 In an interview with the BBC, published on their website on June 20, 2008

directed by Marc Evans, filming Mumia Abu-Jamal, an American journalist and former member of the Black Panthers, unfairly arrested for the murder of Daniel Faulkner, a police officer on December 9, 1981. He was sentenced to death penalty in 1982 and had been imprisoned since. Mumia Abu-Jamal became a leader from death row, claiming his innocence and fighting against all injustices, a voice for the voiceless.

The film precisely followed his encounter with William Francome, a British citizen born on the day of Mumia's sentence, who decided to meet him and most of the former Black Panthers. The Black liberation movement, founded in 1966, was dissolved soon after Mumia's arrest, in 1982. The filmmaker also interviewed the activist Angela Davis, the thinkers Howard Zinn and Noam Chomsky, Steve Earle – musician and vocal opponent of capital punishment, as well as rappers Mos Def and Snoop Doggy Dog. Robert Del Naja and Neil Davidge created a new company to work more independently, 100 Suns, and composed a song to be rapped by Snoop Doggy Dog, 'Calling Mumia', in which the latter quotes the activist and musician Gil Scott-Heron, born in Chicago in 1949, and his famous line *"the revolution won't be televised".*

In Prison My Whole Life was shown at the Cannes Festival in May 2007 and nominated at the Sundance Film Festival in 2008 for 'Best Documentary', where it received the 'Grand Jury' award. It was released in the UK in October 2008 and won the Student Award and the Planet Award at the 2009 International Festival of Cinema on Human Rights in Paris.

Via 100 Suns, 3D and Neil mostly spent 2007 and 2008 working on scores for two other movies. The first one was *Battle in Seattle*, directed by Stuart Townsend, a political film on the protests that took place at the World Trade Organisation's Ministerial Conference of 1999. It premiered on May 22, 2008, at the Seattle International Film Festival. The other documentary was *Trouble The Water*, directed by Tia Lessin and Carl Deal, retracing the tragic events that occurred when Hurricane Katrina hit New Orleans in August 2005.

Then D and Neil decided to give themselves a break from soundtrack projects. Meanwhile, Robert regularly returned to his Bristol studio to work on the Massive Attack's potential fifth album, but was still unsatisfied. The most appealing collaboration he was offered by then came from his friend James Lavelle and included both music and art.

War paint

After inviting 3D to sing on his second album *Never Never Land*, released in 2003 (on the song 'Invasion', composed in 2001/02), in 2007, James Lavelle contacted him to compose, sing and create the artwork for his new record. U.N.K.L.E's album was named *War Stories* and featured many musicians including Josh Homme and Alice Temple. It was scheduled to be released during the summer of 2007 (on June 20 in Japan, July 2 in the UK, July 24 in the US). It was composed of seventeen tracks including 'Twilight', written and sung by 3D. And the record came with a 50-page booklet illustrated by D.

James Lavelle was working in a record store in London when he met Massive Attack, in the mid-90s, and could not be prouder of any friendship. He had been a fan of Massive Attack since *Blue Lines*. "I've never heard a record since that affected me as much as that did at the time,' he explained. "It was the basis of everything that I did with Mo'Wax. 3D was one of my heroes and everything about it, from the videos to the artwork to the style, the sound, everything, changed my life. 3D's now done the artwork for the new album and we have become very good friends. I admire him because he was an icon to me, but was someone that supported me. I admire his attention to detail, his stamina with it, what they've achieved musically and stylistically... I wouldn't be doing what I do now without them. I'm very proud of that relationship[183]."

It wasn't difficult for James to convince the artist. D gave to his new art pieces very strong titles: 'No Surrender', 'No Slogan', 'Unbelievable Truth', 'International Jihad', 'Peace at Last', etc. His main influences and themes were the so-called clash of civilisations. 'No Surrender' shows a crowd marching in a bright red background, holding white flags. 'Unbelievable' represents a skeletal figure with a defeated head posture and a red cross on its chest. 'International Jihad' pictures two Siamese figures holding an open Bible, with their head surmounted

183 In an interview with *One Week To Live* magazine, Issue 73, April 30–May 6, 2007

by a halo of five-pointed European flags' stars. 'Peace at Last', which was chosen for the album cover, represents two male figures in a sort of twin pair, painted in reversed colours, black and red, their head encircled with large halos. Other paintings were named 'Roadmap to Pieces', 'Renewable Fuel', 'Four Noble Truths', 'The Future Is Behind You', 'Beirut', etc.

Once he saw the pieces, James liked them deeply and they decided they should to be shown. They organised an exhibition with Steve Lazarides, at his gallery in Soho, London. 3D's artworks were reproduced as hand finished canvas prints. A run of limited editions was also printed and produced by PoW, *Pictures on Walls*, the online print shop created by Banksy. They all sold out in a few minutes.

The show was scheduled for March 25 – April 25, 2008 and named *War Paint*. It also featured art pieces by other artists including Warren Du Preez, Nick Thornton Jones, Will Bankhead and Ben Drury. The opening took place on March 20, five years after the launch of the war on Iraq… By then, Robert Del Naja was also starting his collaboration with Reprieve, an organisation founded by Clive Stafford Smith to fight the use of torture in prison, especially in Guantanamo, and he mentioned their campaigns in all his interviews set for the exhibition. The British attorney, specialised in the areas of civil rights, worked against the death penalty in the United States of America.

Still, in 2008, Robert Del Naja accepted one last proposition for a film score, coming from Italian filmmaker Matteo Garrone, for his upcoming movie, *Gomorrah*. The story was adapted from a remarkable book, an investigation by young Neapolitan journalist Roberto Saviano on the Camorra, Naples' mafia. The project had obviously a special resonance for Robert.

Gomorrah was released on October 18, 2008, in the UK and became one of the greatest recent successes of Italian cinema. On August 5, 2009, Robert Del Naja was awarded Best Original Song in a Film for the track 'Herculaneum', at the David Di Donatello Premi in Rome. In July, Massive Attack received the Q Award for Sonic Innovation in England, crowning the band's 20-year career.

More awards came in the following months. And in February 2008, the prestigious *Meltdown Festival* in London had named Massive Attack as curator for June 2008 – a special form of recognition in itself for the duo. It thus offered them an occasion to display their own history in sound and their numerous influences.

Chapter 12
The Spirit Of Bristol Is Still Alive (2008-09)

Since 1993, the Meltdown Festival had been organised in June around the Southbank Centre and nearby venues in London, as a reflection on the current state of British culture, seen by an artist named as its curator. In 2008, Massive Attack became the first band chosen to be curators. Before them, Tricky was invited to sing in Robert Wyatt's 2001 event and Lee "Scratch" Perry represented Jamaican culture as a curator in 2003, but they were the first artists to represent a part of the "black" British culture as curators of the Festival.

Clearly hoping to surprise and remain out of the box, 3D and Grant quickly announced they would not bring to London a representation of the "Bristol sound". Tricky, Roni Size or Portishead would not be featured in the event. Meanwhile, as they were getting ready, their fellow Bristol musicians were working on new albums.

Time to come back

Portishead took more than ten years to come back with a third album. While Adrian Utley was busy working on new musical projects, Beth Gibbons was composing solo and on other collaborations, but one of the main reasons for the band's silence might be Geoff Barrow's personal life: after his divorce, he moved to Australia and took a break. Adrian came to join him for a while, to compose a few new songs, but they were not enthused enough by the results to release them, and certainly not as an album. Geoff mainly worked on producing others bands, such as the Coral, with his label.

"I wasn't too busy with other things – I kinda quit music for a bit," he said later[184]. "There was the label (Invada, co-run by Barrow), but that didn't come along 'til much later. In '98 I just quit for about three years. I set up a little label in Australia too, with a mate – which is also called Invada, but it's more of a weird dance music label, but it's good. Yeah, I quit when we finished a tour, and I couldn't find anything I liked musically in anybody, in anything. I think it was a weird time, the late '90s, anyway."

Inspiration finally came back and in October 2007 Portishead announced that their new record, named *Third*, was mixed, almost ready and would be out in April 2008. Before then, they played and curated a series of shows at the All Tomorrow's Parties Festival, in Somerset, in December, where they tried some of their new songs: 'Silence', 'Hunter', 'The Rip', 'We Carry On' and 'Machine Gun'. This last song was released as a single in March 2008 and the band scheduled a European tour for the spring and summer, and were also booked for Coachella in California.

The album was released by Island Records on April 28 in the UK, the next day in the United States by Mercury Records, and on April 30 in Japan by Universal Music. It entered the UK Albums Chart at number two, number seven in America and was praised by the music press. It sounded less electronic and more folk than their two previous albums, raw and melancholic. 'The Rip' was released as a second single in June, followed by 'Magic Doors' in November.

While recording, Geoff Barrow was also willing to move away from the sound that got the band associated with the "trip-hop" label that Adrian Utley as well as Tricky have always hated. Adrian and Geoff were also looking into their early punk influences, including Mark Stewart's Pop Group.

"Tricky was absolutely that – he was more a punk than a rapper," Geoff explained to the media[185]. "I worked with him very briefly when I was much younger – I'm a bit younger than him – and he was brilliant. There was this sense of... It was like Public Enemy and PiL, never the lighter things in life. In that sense, Portishead was always lighter! So in

184 In an interview with the magazine *Drowned in Sound*, published on April 2, 2008
185 Ibid

Bristol, I think this 'sound' continues, but in some places it has become this affluent student town. It's very difficult to see the development of the 'sound' as lots of local bars and clubs are geared to getting the Sloane-y pound in. It's less about doing interesting stuff, although there are a few select venues – the Croft for example."

To compose *Third* differently, the band members swapped their roles: Beth played guitar on 'Threads', Geoff used keyboards, bass guitar and drums, and Adrian an acoustic guitar. They also worked with new and numerous synthesisers, with different beat boxes and an electronic organ for 'Machine Gun'. They collaborated with new instrumentalists including keyboardist John Baggott, Charlotte Nicholls on the cello, composer David Poore and saxophonist Will Gregory from the band Goldfrapp, who was born in Bristol.

The result still seems timeless and underlines the work of genius of the instrumentalists. Beth's voice sounds magically untouched by time and is powerful as ever on stage on 'Silence' or 'The Rip'. Their success was so intense that they soon promised to get back quickly to the studio and produce a fourth album for the end of 2010… But for months the trio was first immersed in numerous festivals.

Tricky returned to his Bristol roots with his new album. After years spent abroad, he decided to call the record *Knowle West Boy*, as a reference to the neighbourhood he grew up in. The record sounds both electronic and rock, qualified as "ghetto rock" by some music journalists. Very dynamic, with moments of rage, more sullen in other songs, it was inspired by his youth, according to Tricky, mentioning social housings, local crimes, queues at the dole office and a decadent environment, but also paying an homage to the ones who, like him, grew up there. "I'm not from Bristol, I'm from Knowle West," says Tricky straightforwardly when I meet with him in Paris[186], "which is a completely different thing".

Musically, he considered this album as a mix tape gathering his favourite sounds inspired by his memories of this "white ghetto", as he describes it. He listened to rap, as much as the Specials and Kate Bush to get inspired. Lyrically, he mentioned the gangsters' stories he also grew

---

186 In an interview with the author in February 2015, before a show at the Bataclan, in Paris

up with, stories of criminals and formers inmates, which explain why his music "remains so dark," he insists.

The first single, entitled 'Council Estate', surprisingly samples a song from Portishead's *Dummy*, 'Roads', and its lyrics are autobiographical. It is a duo with the mixed-race singer Alex Mills, from Leeds but based in London, merging a blues song on a rock rhythm. Alex was signed on Tricky's label, Brown Punk, created with Chris Blackwell. The album also featured the Californian musician Veronika Coassolo and the Italian-Icelandic singer Emiliana Torrini.

Knowle West Boy was scheduled for July 2008, by the independent label Domino Records, and reached number 63 in the UK Albums Chart. It was praised by the media; the *Guardian* even compared Tricky's voice to Tom Waits', just when the Bristolian was trying to collaborate with the American legend. He travelled to San Francisco, where Waits invited him. But we are still waiting to hear their music...

Soon, Tricky was working on another album, *Mixed Race*, digging into the same sources of inspiration. The track 'Ghetto Star' talks about the life of a gangster, while its promo video starts with the interview of a former prisoner. It is sung by Franky Riley, who was enrolled for Tricky's new tour. Two other tracks deal with the burdens of living in prison, 'Friend Went To Jail' and 'Bristol To London', which also featured Tricky's brother, Marlon Thaws. The album was released in September 2010. Then Tricky moved to Paris, visiting London regularly, where his daughter and her mom, Martina, still lived. But as he says himself, wherever he settles or travels, he remains a Knowle West Boy.

Meltdown: fusions and jolts

Virgin Records hoped to announce a new Massive Attack album for the end of 2008 – the band had accumulated more than fifteen tracks since 2005. But Robert and Grant were more focused on the organisation of their first festival. A year after Pulp's leader, Jarvis Cocker, succeeding to Patti Smith, Nick Cave and David Bowie, Massive Attack thus joined the prestigious list of Meltdown's curators. This was the first time a band and not a single personality were chosen for the role. Glenn Max, producer of contemporary culture at the Southbank Centre declared:

"Theirs is a world where psychedelia and punk align, where sensual sophistication and urban grit share equal ground. All this would be enough, but equally important... Few artists could throw a better party[187]."

The Festival took place from June 14 to 22, and after giving two shows themselves, opening and closing the festival, the band would go on tour. The term "meltdown" suited the band particularly well. D and Grant worked on a programme reflecting their first influences and their recent discoveries. They contacted their early heroes and firstly Mark Stewart. In 2008, his band, the Maffia, were pretty quiet, but Mark had always kept on producing music. He released a collection of his best work in 2005, on Soul Jazz Records, entitled *Kiss the Future*, and wrote the theme music for a BBC One drama named *Waterloo Road*, in 2006. His new album, *Edit*, had coincidently been released on the Crippled Dick Hot Wax! record label, in March 2008.

Also programmed were punk heroes from Stiff Little Fingers and Gang of Four, as well as Grace Jones, Horace Andy, the psychedelic rock band Gong (formed in Paris in 1967 by Australian musician Daevid Allen and English vocalist Gilli Smyth) and two American soul singers, Terry Callier and George Clinton.

Massive Attack also scheduled younger bands and music makers who inspired them more recently: the English band Elbow; the rappers Flying Lotus, Dalek, Cool Kids, Shape of Broad Minds; the British experimental folk band Tunng (formed by Sam Genders and Mike Lindsay in 2003); the young alternative pop outfit from London the Shortwave Set; the Americans from Seattle Fleet Foxes led by singer Robin Pecknold; the artist and experimental musician Georgina Pringle and the Los Angeles soul singer and rapper Aloe Blacc, from the band Emanon. The programme contained an exotic note with the Japanese electronica collective Yellow Magic Orchestra.

The poster created by Robert Del Naja for this 15th edition was a montage of two photographs of his and Grant Marshall's faces, mixed together in sort of surreal portraits. Robert particularly liked this

187 In an article published in the *Guardian* on February 15, 2008

curator's role. He also programmed visual artists and exhibitions for the festival, inviting Stanley Donwood of Radiohead's art fame.

Robert produced a series of art pieces representing alternative national flags, titled 'Favoured Nations', redesigned in grey, red and black, representing the United Kingdom, the members of the Commonwealth, the US and Middle Eastern countries in which the UK had had a colonial or political impact in the last century or so... The artworks were shown inside the Royal Festival Hall.

For Robert, Meltdown was an occasion to work collectively, with a wider spectre of artists, which he loves above all. "Art is so much more interesting when it's collaborative," he said[188]. "Curating the festival has been like a continuation of the events we put on when we were in the Wild Bunch: the warehouse parties and the jams on the streets in Bristol. It was a case of doing everything, from fly-posting to buying the beer, setting up the generator and painting the venue with graffiti. We've brought exactly the same approach to Meltdown."

Outside concerts and exhibitions, he also brought in a programme of films and events highlighting his passion for cinema. Most of them were documentary films, except a lovely independent British romantic comedy, *Somers Town* directed by Shane Meadows. It showed the summer holidays of two sons of working class parents in London, two boys who fall for the same girl.

Among the documentaries, *Taxi to the Dark Side*, by Alex Gibney, retraced the last days of imprisonment of an Afghan taxi driver, in an American penitentiary. This viewing was followed by a debate with Moazzam Begg, a British citizen of Pakistani descent who was detained in Guatanamo for years, and Clive Stafford Smith, founder of Reprieve, a non-profit organisation campaigning against the death penalty and representing the rights of prisoners of injustice.

On June 16, a screening of *The Night James Brown Saved Boston* was scheduled, a documentary about the evening that followed Martin Luther King's assassination, when Boston hosted a James Brown concert... which eventually prevented riots.

---

188 In an interview with the *Daily Telegraph*, published on June 12, 2008

Robert also proposed to recreate the soundtrack of Ridley Scott's 1982 cult film *Blade Runner* with an orchestra, as a live event. They commissioned the Heritage Orchestra for the performance and they put a lot of work into planning and arranging the songs and selecting the authentic synthesisers and instruments.

Then, for their own show, Massive Attack had a renewed set list, with eight unreleased songs ('Marakesh', 'Marooned', 'All I Want', 'Dobro', 'Kingpin', 'Red Light', 'Harpsicord', '16 Seeters'). Robert worked on the stage lights and messages with United Visual Artists and the artist Chris Levine. Grant expressed his enthusiasm this way: "I wasn't much involved with Massive Attack for a while. Now I'm back. We're going to be there all week. It's our show and we want to make sure everybody's welcome, that we see everybody. We don't take this lightly[189]."

The new songs were supposed to be a preview from the coming album. "We chose the tracks that we played live, because we felt that they were ready to perform," Robert explained[190]. "But there are another eight or nine tracks which aren't quite ready yet and we're not sure what shape to make of it yet. We're going to kick it into some shape in the autumn and we'll condense it by then. We're an album band and we always have been, so we have a purist idea what an album should be, as an experience like a movie or a book."

These songs were thus tested on stage, before any definite studio recording, but this time the band were playing the equivalent of an entire new album. Massive Attack's tour started before Meltdown in Estonia, on June 9, and after the Festival they were programmed in Glastonbury in late June, for the first time since 1997. The band performed with Horace Andy and new vocalists: American folk singer Stephanie Dosen and Bristolian soul/punk artist Yolanda Carter, leader of the band Phantom Limb, created in 2005.

Their visual show was dominated by a LED screen and thirty mobile lights, and aimed at synchronising the sound and the images. The messages displayed were created with Reprieve and Clive Stafford Smith, refering to the American army's secret surveillance flights and

---

189 In an interview with the *Daily Telegraph,* published on June 12, 2008
190 In an interview on BBC Radio One, on June 20, 2008

arbitrary detentions in the name of the fight against terrorism. Further messages mentioned quotes from political leaders and campaigners, from the Burmese opponent Aung San Suu Kyi to the Mexican-American farm workers' leader Cesar Estrada Chavez, including humanist American poet Edwin Markham, civil rights activist Susan B. Anthony and journalist Horace Greeley, who founded the *New York Tribune* and fought for the abolition of slavery in the United States. The screen also occasionally displayed, in a sharp contrast, quotes from Josef Stalin and Augusto Pinochet.

These words were followed by extracts from newspapers, notably during 'Inertia Creeps', flashing in an intense green light – grim headlines about current wars were followed by frivolous details on minor celebrities' daily life, underlining their absurdity. A list of basic human rights was also showcased ("right to protest", "right to privacy", "right against torture"...).

Other songs were played with only simple lights on, without written messages. Later on, some sentences came as pure life advice or mantras, encouraging people to "say what you think", or "make your voice heard". The general goal was to create a world of ideas, in constant evolution. All great music is political, estimated Robert and told the *Observer*: "I think it's more of a recent phenomenon – since maybe the Sixties – that people tend to separate art and politics or music and politics[191]."

Weather Underground – music and politics

This show was taken on tour. Massive Attack were playing with Angelo Bruschini, Winston Blissett, Damon Reece and Andrew Small (on drums), and John Baggott (on keyboard). Their classic songs got a new feel with new guest vocalists: Stephanie Dosen sang 'Teardrop', while Yolanda Carter performed 'Safe From Harm' and 'Unfinished Sympathy'. Both of them had recently composed songs with the band, bringing completely different directions. Stephanie worked with 3D on the soft and psychedelic 'Kingpin', the sublime and melancholic 'Red Light', and 'Marakesh' on which they both performed. Yolanda wrote

191 In an interview alongside Clive Stafford Smith, published on May 18, 2008

with Grant the tracks 'Harpsichord' and 'All I Want', which he duets with her. D sang solo on two other tracks: the powerful 'Dobro' and 'Marooned', a love song about abandonment. They added to the set list 'Karmacoma', 'Risingson' and 'Mezzanine'.

In July, 3D invited again the Middle Eastern collective of soundcatchers Checkpoint 303 to join them in Lyon, France. They share his view on the links between music and the real world. "The sound artwork of Checkpoint 303 is a call for human rights and, above all, for justice and the right to freedom and self-determination," Checkpoint 303's leader, MoCha, explains to me[192]. "Musicians and artists are often closer to the truth and reality on the ground than politicians will ever be. In addition, activist artists can describe the situation as it is felt/experienced by civil society, without getting stuck into mind-numbing political correctness or worse, electoral political tactics. The reactions of politicians, be it in the Arab world or in the west, following terror attacks in their respective countries, is often very similar. The mix of rhetoric calls for 'unity' in the face of terror and vows 'to destroy those who hate us and our way of life' is a stance that we have seen over and over again. It stems from a sad combination of short-sighted vision and egocentric individual political ambitions, and generally leads to dramatic failure."

In September, Massive Attack's tour arrived in the United States, in the middle of their most passionate political campaign in decades, Barack Obama representing the Democratic Party against the Republican John McCain. The Bristol band displayed their criticism of George W. Bush's regime. Then the tour ended after a date in Copenhagen in Denmark, and the band went home feeling like their mission was accomplished. The time spent on stage was definitely feeding the bond between the members.

Mid-2008, 3D still had in mind to call this next album *Weather Underground*, inspired by the American social movement founded in 1969 in Chicago, regrouping anti-imperialist and anti-racist activists. He was thinking that the youth in the late 2000s needed to be more

---

192 In a phone interview with the author in January 2016 between Montreal and Paris

politicised, to open their eyes on what was happening in the world.

Before the tour, D and Grant were thinking of mixing the album in the autumn and releasing it before the end of the year. When asked in May: "What point are you at with it? Are you at a terrible and crucial time?" Grant replied: "It's always a terrible and crucial time with us. That's Massive Attack[193]." D started working on the songs further once back in Bristol. Some reached a third or fourth versions, 'Marakesh', 'Dobro' and 'Marooned'. 'Red Light' was recorded again with a male voice, Guy Garvey, instead of Stephanie Dosen. But 3D was still not satisfied.

He wanted to be inspired by something new and was looking to tell a new story. He and Grant went back to New York to compose with the band TV On The Radio. "When we got to Brooklyn for the first time, to Williamsburg, when me, G, and Neil went over, it was really apparent that there was a proper scene and in Bristol unfortunately that scene has kind of evaporated a little 'cause the city has changed, like every city. The old-school areas are more gentrified. (...) When I went to Brooklyn I felt that the Bristol scene in the '80s with Roni Size, the Portishead guys, and with Tricky, that was what Brooklyn felt like a little bit. There were a lot of people hanging out at the house and the energy felt really good," he explained[194]. He was looking for that type of energy.

TV On The Radio had indeed a lot in common with Massive Attack. The band formed in New York is composed of various evolving members, mainly David Sitek, guitarist and programmer, Tunde Adebimpe, a Nigerian-American singer with a wonderfully deep voice, Kyp Malone, a multi-instrumentalist, the drummer Jeleel Bunton and the bass player Gerard Smith.

In November 2008, 3D announced to their record company that the album was definitely not ready. The songs that could have formed *Weather Underground* therefore disappeared. Some of them were partly reused or transformed, sometimes drastically. 3D still thought, as their website stated by then, that "If a thing's worth doing, it's worth doing slowly". The band took another year to explore a new path of research.

193 In the *Observer*, May 11, 2008
194 In an interview with *944 Magazine*, in 2007

And as D was working with collaborators from diverse horizons, he was also inspired by political considerations and by the social evolution of his very own city, Bristol.

Facing Bristol

The same year, 2009, another herald of Bristol's culture returned home... Banksy was discretely preparing an exhibition for his hometown. Both superstar and anonymous, Banksy remains a paradox and built for himself a unique status. He managed to keep his event secret until the opening, at Bristol Museum, on Queen's Road, in June 2009. Even Bristol's council, which is financing the free museum, remained uninformed until the very last minute. "This is the first show I've ever done where taxpayers' money is being used to hang my pictures up rather than scrape them off," Banksy joked in a press release[195]. And he edited a trailer film to showcase the atmosphere of the exhibition, in which he appeared hidden under his hooded sweatshirt.

The show was entitled Banksy versus Bristol Museum and entry was free of charge. It opened on June 13 and would remain on display until August 31. It featured more than 100 pieces by the artist – stencils, sculptures, paintings and animated installations, in which humour prevailed. In the main hall was parked a wrecked ice-cream van, burnt down and surrounded by garbage, and a statue of a policeman playing on a child's seesaw. A little further, a replica of a Greek statue was holding shopping bags; another one had her head hidden under a tin of paint. Many of the canvas represented known paintings, slightly twisted, emphasising references to slavery and the Ku Klux Klan for instance.

Among the political pieces were monkeys in Parliament, rats in disguise, workers throwing anti-capitalist messages. Others showed child labour, or a punk young man tagging a sentence from Karl Marx's Communist Manifesto: "Workers of the world, unite!" Lots of his animated installations mocked the society of surveillance – video cameras being by then everywhere in British cities – the police or

---

195 See for instance the Guardian and the BBC's website, on June 12, 2009

monotheist religions. The show also displayed a suitcase full of his fake tenners featuring the late Princess Diana, created in 2004. "This show is my vision of the future, to which many people will say: 'You should have gone to Specsavers'..." added Banksy's press release.

The team running the museum admitted that none of them actually met Banksy, who only communicated via emails and phone calls. But they were all proud of the event. "He's a megastar," stated Kate Brindley, director of Bristol Musem and Art Gallery. "We're a gallery that wants to work with contemporary artists – he's our home-grown hero[196]." For an artist using tools still forbidden (stencils, spray cans, illegal pasting and spraying), generally considered as vandalism, it was quite a statement. The queue stretched far out of the Museum, up University Road and round the corner, for the entire duration of the show. Of course, the popular success of the exhibition did not prevent criticism from art experts. But controversies and endless comments on the value of his production suited Banksy perfectly. In the last room, the exhibition ended with a painting showing a bucolic landscape, defaced by an inscription in pink spray paint, reading: "Exit through the gift shop".

And Banksy chose this phrase as a title for his next project: a film. Presented as a documentary film, it was directed by Banksy himself and centred on the story of Thierry Guetta, a French art lover living in Los Angeles, obsessed with street art. Guetta soon decided to find Banksy and to document the street art movement, thanks to his so-called cousin, the French artist Space Invader. All through the film, Thierry was therefore introduced to other artists, including Shepard Fairey, also known as Obey, Ron English and Banksy himself. In the scenes where he appears, Banksy's face remains obscured and his voice altered; he is also one of the narrators. Surprisingly, Guetta soon developed the will to make his own art and showcases an exhibition in Los Angeles, as Mr Brainwash, which attracted an even more surprising popular interest...

Many of Banksy's friends were featured in the documentary: Swoon, Monsieur André, Sweet Toof, Borf, etc. The music was scored by Geoff Barrow and included a song by Richard Hawley, 'Tonight The Streets

196 Quoted on the BBC's website on June 12, 2009

Are Ours'. The film premiered at the 2010 Sundance Film Festival on 24 January 2010, and was nominated at the Academy Award for 'Best Documentary Feature'.

Banksy described his film as a "disaster movie" and it is hard to say if it has to really be taken seriously. The *New York Times* and the BBC launched many debates on its validity and interest. Guetta insisted in an interview: "This movie is 100% real. Banksy captured me becoming an artist. In the end, I became his biggest work of art[197]." The *Globe and Mail* probably nailed it when it headlined: "It might be a fake, but it's fun to watch", quoting Banksy himself on its commercial phenomenon: "Maybe there's something to be learned from it. Maybe it means that art is sort of a joke[198]."

When released on DVD in 2011, the film was completed with a 13-minute documentary named jokingly *B-Movie*. It featured a longer interview with Banksy, and interventions from experts and other artists, close to the man, including Damien Hirst and Robert Del Naja. The interviews retold how Banksy started in the world of street art, inspired by 3D's first graffiti, and was transformed by the choice of mainly using stencils. D confirmed that he has known Banksy since he started painting and praised his capacity to spray where no one had managed to spray before, "in the most absurd places"... and "getting away with it".

Some critics were also interviewed, and one of them, Waldemar Januszczak, from the *Sunday Times*, depicted Banksy's work as pointless and anything but artistic. Art collector Dennis Hopper, on the contrary, stated that Banksy was making declarations, shaking things politically, and going straight to the point by talking about real things. D and Banksy also reflected on the differences between authentic though ephemeral street art and rip-off for auctions. And Banksy both closed and opened the discussion by reminding us: "They say you die twice, once when you stop breathing, the second time when somebody says your name for the last time"...

---

197 In an interview with the *Los Angeles Times*, published on February 22, 2011
198 In an article published on May 7, 2010

Bristol's new waves

The end of the decade showed how much Bristol had changed in thirty years, since the first records of local post-punk bands from 1977, and since 3D's first graffiti in 1983. Few people in the rest of England would have bet on it in the early Eighties... And Banksy's own success proved how much 3D's first steps into what was later to be named "street art" had changed a part of our modern culture for good, putting Bristol on the map of the British history of art.

Late in 2009, Bristol was a city covered with murals and filled with new artists. St Pauls, Stokes Croft, Jamaica Street, and the Bearpit, officially known as St James Barton Roundabout, had become headquarters of the street art movement. On Jamaica Street can now be found the People's Republic of Stokes Croft, a gallery showing the work of many of the city's young artists. Nelson Street, in the city centre, also hosts some of Bristol's most well-known murals, including a marvellous piece by Irish street artist Conor Harrington.

North Street, in South Bristol's neighbourhoods of Bedminster and Southville, has become a nerve centre for street art by hosting, each July, Upfest, The Urban Paint Festival, created in 2008 by Stephen and Emma Hayles. Considered as Europe's largest street art & graffiti festival, it attracts each year over 300 artists painting in 35 venues throughout Bedminster and Southville. Artists include Bristol legends Inkie, Cheo, Oli-T, FLX and Lokey, sometimes Nick Walker, and younger artists such as Cheba, Andy Council, 3Dom, Angus...

Upfest also regularly receives guests from all over the world: the Londoner Cosmo Sarson (who painted in 2013 a giant *Breakdancing Jesus*, at the Hamilton House, facing Banksy's *Mild Mild West*), Dan Kitchener, also from London, painting impressive and modern urban landscapes, Columbian artist Stinkfish, or Louis Masai, inspired by animal and nature patterns. The three-day long festival hosts parties and DJs in the evening, at the Tobacco Factory, a former red-brick factory now transformed into a bar and theatre.

In the same way, in Bristol's city centre, many industrial dockside buildings have been transformed into art centres: the Watershed has been a vibrant spot for cinema and film production and a cross art form

237

venue since 1982, and the M Shed, built in 1878 along the harbour, was transformed into a history museum in 2006. In between the two still lies the vividly active Arnolfini Gallery.

Bristol's music scene has evolved even more quickly. Gig and club venues are countless, from Lakota to Thekla, the Louisiana, Motion, Black Swan, the Love Inn, Trinity Centre, Thunderbolt, the Fleece, the Fringe in Clifton, the Old Duke, and smaller venues such as Mr Wolf's, the Attic Bar, the Blue Mountain, the Canteen on Stokes Croft, the Exchange – Paul Horlick's club, etc. Paul is Geoff Barrow's partner in the Invada label and offering a special space for many new rock bands.

Among the major musicians, Sean Cook, formerly of Spiritualized and Lupine Howl, bass player, guitarist and singer, formed with Bob Locke and Tim Norfolk from the Insects the band the Flies, in 2003, in a fine mix of electronic folk and post-punk. Their first album, *All Too Human*, was released in 2007, and their second *Pleasure Yourself*, in 2014. They worked regularly with producer Andy Spaceland (from Alpha), and drummer Damon Reece (also working with Liz Fraser and Massive Attack).

"I came from a variety of influences, and the experience of the Insects on soundtracks gave us a more experimental, audio-visual feel," says Sean when we meet in Bedminster[199]. "On stage, I sing and play the guitar, and on the record I play the bass too. We treat each song like a project and try to remain as much as possible away from the mainstream and from the music industry." Their sound was described in 2007 by the *Guardian* as "David Lynch meets John Barry at a blues party in St Paul's", and praised for their "film composer's ear for arty atmospheres and dirty details: you can almost smell the sex and death."

In the rock scene, Australian musician and songwriter John Vistic created in Bristol the John E. Vistic Experience around 2010 and regularly played with Emily Breeze, from Candy Darling. Mike Crawford – singer and guitarist who was in the Spics in the late 1970s – has regularly been playing with them and Goldfrapp. Mike also performs as a solo act all over the city. The Blue Aeroplanes, Angelo Bruschini's first major band,

---

199 In an interview with the author in Bristol in April 2015

are also still active.

And Bristol's jazz scene has long been very interesting, with singers like Celestine and saxophonist James Morton among many others. In the mid 2000s, Jim Barr (on the bass) and Clive Deamer (on drums) formed Get the Blessing, a jazz rock quartet, teaming up with Jake McMurchie (saxophone) and Pete Judge (trumpet). Their debut *All Is Yes* won best album at the 2008 BBC Jazz Awards. To date, they have released six albums, *Bristopia* being the latest, out in 2018.

Meanwhile, for Massive Attack, 2008 and 2009 have been decisive years. Robert Del Naja and Grant Marshall were progressively finding the sound they were looking for in order to construct their fifth studio album. They took another trip to New York City to work in DFA Records with Tim Goldsworthy, known for his collaboration with LCD Soundsystem. The drum parts of many of their tracks were re-recorded there with Jerry Fuchs, who tragically died later that year in an accident.

And on May 21, 2009, the band received – from the hands of their friend Damon Albarn – the PRS for Music Outstanding Contribution to British Music Award at the Ivor Novello Awards, created in 1960. The duo reckoned that their decision to leave time to their creativity to develop slowly had probably been a key element in their longevity.

Just as they refused to let the music industry rush his creative process, the band want to keep on working more deeply on artistic projects reflecting their convictions. *Heligoland* would come to marvellously illustrate this effort.

Chapter 13
Grey Rainbows And Promised Lands
(2009-2012)

Smith & Mighty, Massive Attack, Tricky or Roni Size have come to represent a part of the black identity in British culture, a complex identity inherited from a troubled colonial and post-colonial history. This culture had for a long time waited to express itself fully. And by deepening their openly conscious discourse on these issues, Massive Attack have forged an additional dimension to their creativity. They are no longer obliged to express themselves as a culturally mixed entity on the issue of diversity only, but they have mastered the art of commenting on the state of the world, through their art, from a different viewpoint, complex, profound and rich.

In 2009, Massive Attack were preparing visual ideas for a new tour and working on their forthcoming album. After their recent artistic developments, they wanted to give their next album an even stronger visual aspect. "I've got a low satisfaction threshold for things", 3D commented in early 2010[200]. "I can spend weeks working on something and hate it, and the same goes for other people's work. I can take us all on a journey and then go, 'It's not working'. Which for everyone is really frustrating." They were increasingly intrigued by the idea of dealing directly with Britain's colonial history, rightly, and specifically by Bristol's past.

Continuous creativity and reflexivity

The first months of 2009 saw the return of Grant Marshall to Massive Attack's studios. The coming album was from the start defined by an

---

200 In an interview with the *Sunday Business Post*, published in Ireland, on January 31, 2010

even larger number of collaborators, spanning continents. In Brooklyn, 3D and Grant had been working with TV On The Radio. Grant contacted the singer from the band Mazzy Star, Hope Sandoval, born in Los Angeles in 1966 in a Mexican American family. And D thought about collaborations with the American singer-songwriter Tom Waits and Mike Patton from Faith No More, whom he produced demos with.

"Tom Waits, I spoke to on the phone... I think something died in translation between my Bristol accent and his drawl," he later said[201]. "He kept calling me Steve, and I kept going 'no, it's D'. He'd say 'what Steve?' And in the end it just didn't work out, we didn't even get beyond the fucking introductions."

In England, Grant wanted to work with Damon Albarn, while D composed with Guy Garvey. In Bristol, Grant also started composing with Stew Jackson, a musician and producer known as 'Robot Club' who worked for Phantom Limb. "You change your perspective as you go along," 3D described. "You're not necessarily destroying lots of pieces of music, you're just building on top of it and stuff is getting buried as you go. I wouldn't say we're perfectionists – I think we're imperfectionists. Because we look for the imperfection in everything[202]."

Massive Attack were simply looking for a warmer sound and a more collective atmosphere. Grant and 3D always had very different rhythms. D and Neil also recruited a young sound engineer named Euan Dickinson, introduced to them by the Insects, after Alex Swift left. "I was interested in music from a young age, and always aware of the big acts in the city like Massive Attack and Portishead," Euan tells me when we discuss his first steps into music. "I originally picked up the guitar aged 10, and quickly became obsessed. I played in little bands with my friends at school, but became quite interested in recording and studios. I started using the home computer to try and make a more complete sound, which was the start of my passion for recording, producing and using technology[203]."

Neil Davidge's role remained central too. "In 2009, the recording was

---

201 In an interview with the magazine *The Skinny*, published online on February 2, 2010
202 In an interview with *The Big Issue*, published in February 2010
203 In an interview with the author between Bristol and Paris in March 2016

much warmer and more fun," describes Neil, "but I still remember me and D having some serious arguments! D and I were in a relationship in a way that I've not been with anyone even romantically. We know each other very well and I do miss him. We can't see each other enough[204]."

A new album, soon-to-be named *Heligoland*, emerged from all these differences and influences, born from new ideas that made it a very hybrid opus, with multiple dimensions.

Tower of Babel

To reassure the record company asking about their new schedule, the band announced that their plans included working with an old friend: Damon Albarn. After his huge successes with Blur, Gorillaz and side projects like his first opera, *Monkey, Journey to the West* in 2007, Albarn was widely regarded as one of the most gifted musicians of his generation. He was also an admirer of Massive Attack's work, deeply influenced by their music.

Grant felt very comfortable in his 13 Studio, in West London. Damon asked Robert to promise he wouldn't be taken into a two-year "Bristolian vortex", but to work in the frame of a two-day session, with a clear timetable. 3D trusted Damon's ability to follow them into new territories and to explore things sonically. "He's already taken himself away from his own comfort zone so many times anyway," 3D said of Damon[205]. Albarn also hoped to make them work on major keys instead of minor, but that would be a bigger challenge... They launched their recording session in January 2009.

Robert started by writing the long and intense lyrics for a song that became 'Splitting the Atom'. The backing track was created spontaneously with Damon, playing on a blues chord arrangement on a Farfisa electronic organ. Horace Andy was soon added to the trio, to record backing vocal parts for 'Splitting the Atom' and later for a reinterpretation of his old song, 'Girl I Love You'. Grant and Stew Jackson also composed a backing track for another song for Damon to sing; the latter chose to add his own lyrics to it, calling it 'Saturday

204 In an interview with the author in Bristol in March 2015
205 In an interview with the *Big Issue*, published in February 15-21, 2010

Come Slow'.

After this fresh start, the album began as a new journey. A journey through different locations and different voices. The main female voice on the album is Tricky's first muse, Martina Topley-Bird; she co-wrote 'Babel' and 'Psyche' with the band. "They invited me to tour with them and we started writing together at the same time," remembers Martina[206]. "It was good timing for me since I had just ended the promo for my second album, *The Blue God*." And Grant sent a new version of 'Harpsichord' to Hope Sandoval, in California. Guy Garvey and 3D wrote a demo entitled 'Bulletproof Love'.

Massive Attack also worked with new instrumentalists: the drummer Jerry Fuchs, the keyboardist John Baggott, Portishead's guitarist Adrian Utley and the bass player Billy Fuller. Billy had just founded a new band in Bristol in January 2009 with Geoff Barrow and Matt Williams, named BEAK>. Extra contributions came from David Sitek, Tim Goldworthy, Dan Brown and a series of brass players, in the middle of this wide array of influences in between Bristol, West London and Brooklyn.

3D also reworked parts of songs from the *Weather Underground* project: '16 Seeter', fused with the music of 'Girl I love You'; 'Harpsichord'; and 'Marakesh', which evolved into a whole new song to be named 'Atlas Air'.

The album's release was first announced for October 2009, then postponed to February 2010. An EP came out instead on October 4, with a first single from the coming album, 'Splitting The Atom,' and a series of remixes. A special vinyl edition included a remixed version of 'Bulletproof Love' (by Van Rivers and the Subliminal Kids), a remix of 'Psyche' (by Christoffer Berg), and the album version of 'Pray For Rain'. The band started touring again in the autumn 2009.

Divisible particles

'Splitting The Atom' was first broadcast on BBC Radio 1 in August 2009. It would be challenging to choose a better-suited track to represent the coming album. The song features three voices, for the first time since

---

206 In an interview with the author in November 2018

Blue Lines: 3D, Daddy G and Horace Andy. Based on a clapping hand rhythm and a synth melody, it starts with a rap written by 3D and voiced by Daddy G, underlined by backing vocals from D performed on a Vocoder. The song evolves increasingly in emotions, from Grant's cold, menacing rap to Horace's warmer part, followed by a longer, melodic rap and harmonies by 3D. Hypnotic and touching strings reinforce the last section of Vocoder vocals.

Musically, the song was inspired by reggae and ska bands 3D and G used to listen to as teenagers, such as UB40 and the Specials. The result is very mysterious and dreamy. The lyrics contribute to the building of an atmospheric and worrying world: *"The baby was born / in Nettles and Ferns / The evening it chokes / The candle it burns / This disguise covers / Bitter lies / Repeating the joke / The meaning it dies"*, starts G, pursuing a while later with mentions of the social and economic downturn in the west, a few months after the sub-prime crisis shook the world: *"The jobless return / The bankers have bailed / The mighty retreat / The pleasure it fails / At the end of the week"*. Horace's voice intervenes, in a lower tone that usual, with a repeating pattern: *"It's easy / Don't Let It Go / It's easy / Don't Let It Go (...) Don't lose it"*.

In a series of prophetic metaphors, 3D describes later: *"The needle sticks and the penny drops / The summer's gone before you know / The muffled drums of relentless flow / You're looking at stars that give you Vertigo / The sun's still burning and dust will blow"*... concluding with an image echoing the title: *"A kiss of wine we'll disappear / The last of the last particles / Divisible invisible"*.

The references to banking bailouts are mixing "cod-politics, but in a more subtle way", 3D explained to the press[207]. "That was more of an ironic title, I guess. I find that people are constantly arguing about the same thing and it was a metaphor for that kind of constant debate and the fact that nothing ever changes. The lyrics were just like a very short poem that was just saying, 'here we go again', from the 1980s with Thatcher's Britain, to the start of the 1990s with our first album, with the political climate and the background of the Middle East crisis,

---

207 In an interview with the *NME*, published on January 16, 2010

recession, boom, bust, the whole thing, you know[208]."

2009 was an electoral year in the UK. In June local and European polls were marked by the rise of the far-right BNP, the British National Party, until then quite weak in the British political representation. The next general election took place in May 2010, and most parties were going through a process of decomposition in between.

The song was also "a reference that D made to splitting us," added Grant a few weeks later. "The way that we've moved and taken our ideas since our incarnation as the Wild Bunch, then Massive Attack and how things have split away from the main source. People have fallen away, we've split off into different factions – it's just a metaphor for how we work[209]." The lyrics, with many possible meanings as usual, thus mix personal and political references.

'Splitting The Atom' was played during the encore in Massive Attack's new tour, launched in September 2009 at Bestival, on the Isle of Wight. A promo video for the song was broadcast a week later. Directed by Baillie Walsh, responsible for the band's first videos from *Blue Lines*, it features a violent bullfight and was online on September 25.

"When Baillie Walsh suggested the idea of filming a bull fight, it was obviously an issue we found difficult and troubling, because we don't agree with that sort of torture or cruelty," said 3D in the Promo EMI Interview for the album. "So watching it was hard work and it was very far from an enjoyable experience, but we were suddenly in the same voyeuristic place as everyone else watching, removed from the song and feeling the same emotional response everyone else was getting from it, which was quite strange."

A second video was produced a while later, and broadcast in February 2010, a slick black and white film, directed by French filmmaker and animation creator Edouard Salier, depicting an apocalyptic world. Salier described it as a "committed" film, to lead the viewers in an eye-opening experience, shake them out and make them question their environment.

Meanwhile, the band's tour continued until late in November in Switzerland, with 46 dates, before another leg in Asia and America

208 In an interview with *The Independent*, published on February 12, 2010
209 In an interview with the magazine *Clash Music*, published in October 2009

in 2010. Most nights, these shows were opened with a brand new song, 'Hartcliffe Star', a powerful punk track inspired by Bristol's neighbourhood of the same name, south of Knowle West. The song was not selected for the album however. The band also tested 'Babel' and 'Psyche' with Martina Topley-Bird on vocals – wearing gorgeous colourful and bright dresses – as well as 'Girl I Love You' with Horace Andy, giving a sense of the new direction to be found on the coming album.

"I was really inspired when working on 'Psyche' and there was a real ease and simplicity writing 'Babel'," Martina told me. "Since our first sessions in 2009, I worked in their studio with D and Euan Dickinson. G also sent me songs written by other artists to sing, one or two tracks I reworked from home and sent back." Martina also sung 'Paradise Circus' on stage with the band, as Hope Sandoval couldn't tour with them. "This song is much closer to my style of singing and register," confessed Martina, "it was easier but I also covered 'Teardop', which is a big song for Massive Attack. And Liz is so revered… I felt I was walking on eggshell! But I enjoyed singing both[210]."

Reunion of different worlds

With *Heligoland*, the band wanted to work on telling a story. One of the first songs completed for it became the opening track: 'Pray For Rain'. The lyrics were written by Tunde Adebimpe and Robert said he could completely relate to the words. "Lyrically, it's like a parable and it kind of reminds me a bit of Cormac McCarthy's *Blood Meridian*: a kind of crazy apocalyptic Western with a sense of connection to the spiritual world as well, which I really dig," he told the press[211].

"*In deepest hollow of our minds / A system failure left behind / And their necks crane / As they turn to pray for rain / And their necks crane*", sings Tunde, supported by a series of percussions and drums, "*Dull residue of what once was / A shattered cloud of swirling doves / And their eyes change / As they learn to see through flames*"… In the United States, the *New Yorker* described the song as "filled out by a complete melodic line and easily

210 In an interview in November 2018
211 In his interview with *The Independent*, published on February 12, 2010

audible lyrics", adding that "the emphasis here is on a slow build and a lack of horizons"[212].

With the second song on the track list, 'Babel', Martina Topley-Bird introduces a different energy. She described her lyrics as those of a teenage love song. Her vocal performance immediately charmed Grant and 3D, who had wanted to collaborate with her for a long time, probably ever since Tricky's *Maxinquaye*. She brought a touch of soul music that they had been looking for, but in a very personal and unique way. As much as on *Mezzanine*, on this album, male voices create the anguishing background atmosphere and the female beautiful chants are more hopeful. The song's quicker tempo gives a lighter dimension too.

'Splitting The Atom' is the third song on the album, followed by 'Girl I Love You', sung by Horace Andy. Musically, this track evolved from the band's 2008 song '16 Seeter', especially the drum parts, and lyrically it samples Horace Andy's own song, already named 'Girl I Love You', produced in 1973. The original tune has a joyful reggae flavour. Massive Attack's interpretation lays on a strong percussive rhythm, reinforced with the anger of a punk guitar, amplified by oriental sounds and by a series of brass instruments, recorded live and multiplied by electronic brass-sounding elements.

"It's a song of cultural confusion and disorientation," said Robert, "which is always great if you can capture that[213]." Horace interpreted the song live with the band during a mini-concert for the KCRW radio in Los Angeles, in February 2010, and gave one of his rare interviews with them, explaining how much he enjoyed working with Massive Attack. "It's amazing. I never knew I could do this. In my heart, I wanted to do this a long time ago. With 3D, we've been married for twenty years," he laughed. "3D, he's the man behind all this, really, a real genius, he's blessed", Horace stated straightforwardly, praising Daddy G's voice too and the creative way 3D managed to push him to sing in increasingly unexpected manners.

The fifth track of the album is a shorter song, 'Psyche', featuring Martina again. Musically, it was produced by 3D and Neil Davidge,

212 In an article published in February 15, 2010
213 In an interview with NPR Music radio in the USA broadcast on December 31, 2009

inspired by the American modern composer Steve Reich, born in 1936 in New York. When they played the instrumental part to Martina, she fell for it and added her lyrics. *"I'm looking for you in the woods tonight, I'm looking / Looking for you in my flashlight, I'm searching / From in the high or down the ocean / And I face myself in reason"*, she starts…

"To me," Robert later said, "the song is like when you close your eyes and you've got that strange shimmer of water or sunlight going through trees and it creates a strobing effect over your eyelids. You instantly get taken back to every single summer you've ever experienced, all in one collage. And you have that really weird sense of immortality, and then a deep melancholic sadness about things that are lost and things that haven't happened yet[214]." There he refered to the core melancholy so often attached to Massive Attack's sound… "And it's that weird moment where you actually recognise… I know this sounds really profound… you recognise that everything will end, and for a brief moment you're happy with it."

'Psyche' is followed on the album by 3D's collaboration with Guy Garvey, 'Flat Of The Blade'. The melody of the song comes from a piece of music D and Neil composed when they were working on the UVA installation for the Victoria And Albert Museum, *Volume*, in 2006. Once reworked as a song and completed with Guy's lyrics, it became a track temporally named 'Bulletproof Love', performed on stage from 2008, and transformed again in 2009.

Guy's lyrics join the general theme of the album launched by 'Pray For Rain':

"I'm not good in a crowd, I got skills I can't speak of / Things I've seen will chase me / To the grave"… *"How does it feel / The weight of the steel? The weight of the steel / The flat of the blade"*, finally adding a touch of hope: *" I will build for my family a bulletproof love"*. The rhythm mimes noises that echo the sounds of soldiers and wars that the lyrics come to match.

Nourished by these many foreign and external influences, *Heligoland* is also a very Bristolian album. And this is very apparent in the last four tracks.

---

214 *The Independent*, February 12, 2010

Bristolian crescendo

The seventh song on the album, 'Paradise Circus', started as a composition by Grant Marshall when working with Stew Jackson and Yolanda Carter in Stew's studio in Bristol. In 2009, it was interpreted live in an almost acoustic version. The romantic ballad, based on compelling keyboard notes and a seductive female voice was recreated in the studio later in 2009 with 3D. The latter reinforced the drums with double-time percussion and human handclaps to create a more "conspirital but also spiritual feel", as he described it to me.

This second version was finally sent to a new singer, Hope Sandoval, in Los Angeles, via email. She recorded her vocal parts in her studio and sent them back electronically to Bristol. The result is one of the highlights of the album, probably enriched by the confrontation of so many levels of creativity and inputs from different composers, also melding directly D and G's approach for the first time since *Mezzanine*. 'Paradise Circus' was released as an EP in October 2011.

The eighth track on the record cuts short the atmosphere and brings the audience back to the post-punk/electro experiences of the band. On 'Rush Minute', 3D's voice is much more familiar than in 'Splitting The Atom', where he modified his vocals. His earliest influences are also more present: Bauhaus and Public Image Ltd, for instance. Familiar themes in the lyrics include obsessions, the fight against any form of addiction, a search for a more balanced state of being, between high moments of creativity and emptier, calmer times… "*I wanna be clean but I gotta get high / It's good to be here so hard to come by / You bring pain cause you got game / And needles and pins a man can't take*"… Ending with "*Got more highs you and me / And deluxe rooms in recovery*".

The lyrics also mention the general context, the "wars on gasoline", and "Marshall Amps into broken homes", evolving around the central character trying to connect with himself. "It's not a battle with addiction so much as it's just about trying to moderate everything," D explained to the press in 2010[215]. Surprisingly, he confessed five years later that it was Grant who insisted on keeping 'Rush Minute' on the album.

---

215 *The Independent*, February 12, 2010

From then, when working on his vocals for a track, Robert started recording his voice himself, alone in the studio on Pro Tools, to be more relaxed, recording up to six or seven takes, as close as possible to the microphone, to sound more intimate. He sometimes modifies his original lyrics slightly while recording, often late in the evening. He later listens to all takes one by one, on headphones then on speakers, selects the best parts and leaves notes for Neil or Euan to listen to the whole song after him, the next day, to get an outside opinion.

'Rush Minute' is followed by 'Saturday Come Slow'. Composed by Stew Jackson and Grant musically, Robert and Tim Goldsworthy added new drums and guitars to it. The lyrics came from Damon Albarn. *"Lost in the magic / From the last time / This town turning / My rose to desire"*... And they pay a little homage to his friends' city: *"In the limestone caves / In the south west lands / One sound in the kingdom / Believers understand"*.

It also sounds like a tearing love song, Damon begging repeatedly *"Do you love me...?"* Music journalists described it as one of his most sensitive songs. "His cracking voice implying he's been up for half the night, Damon Albarn lays bare the vulnerability that his public air of self-confidence conceals," wrote Paul Mardles in the *Observer*[216].

The album ends with an epic and intense track, sung by 3D, which took many detours and evolved into half a dozen versions over three years. 'Atlas Air' merged two original songs. One of them was the track called 'Marakesh' that D wrote with Stephanie Dosen. Lyrically, the new version ends up referencing rendition, secret flights and torture... D being inspired by his work with Reprieve.

"I know the drill, got cells to burn, I'm dressed to kill / A mortal coil and time is still on secret soil / Yeah, pay the bills, cells to burn, mouths to fill / On Boeing jets in the sunset make glowing threats". Lyrically and musically transformed, the song brings in ambiguity. Going from *"it took all the man in me / To be the dog you wanted me to be"* to *"My heart was big and like my pride / Let them feast on my insides"*.

"It's not really something that's easy to sing about," 3D explained. "Some of it's actually sung from the point of view of those who actually empower themselves and actually are the perpetrators of these crazy situations. It's like stepping into different shoes. It's obviously ironic, 'let's go on a holiday to a secret prison we've got lined up for you as a package deal'. The track was meant to be slightly schizophrenic[217]."

This ambiguity of the song is enhanced by the Middle Eastern drum parts and the slightly Turkish feel of the organ, played by John Baggott. The song ends in a long apocalyptic instrumental part that works brilliantly on stage. Atlas Air is the most passive aggressive song of all, it's all about aggression and anger and cynicism, according to Robert[218]. It was distributed on a vinyl EP, in November 2010, and the profits sent to the War Child charity.

The release of *Heligoland* was finally confirmed in November 2009 for February 8, 2010, with a definite list of the ten tracks. Grant even promised that the next EP would feature unreleased songs. "We've got over twenty tracks left," Robert also revealed, "that we might bring down to a workable amount. There's some more Hope Sandoval tracks, some material that Damon's done for us, Guy Garvey stuff and Martina's done a bit. There's loads of stuff in the vaults really and hopefully we'll be releasing another EP further down the line, around June or July[219]."

The album was mixed with Mark 'Spike' Stent in between Los Angeles and Massive Attack's studio in Bristol, and mastered at the Metropolis Studios in London.

A historically charged archipelago

Robert Del Naja was obsessive about bringing coherence to the album project, when they finished mixing it. He suggested the title for it and started creating art for the cover. Each track has its own story to tell but the whole album brings them together. They need to belong to their own time and location, he thinks[220]. He chose a name that was different from the tracks' titles, the name of a place.

"I was watching *Shadow Of The Vampire*, which was partly shot or partly based on the Heligoland Islands, and when the word came up

217 In the *Independent*, on February 12, 2010
218 In Bristol in February 2015
219 In an interview with *The Skinny*, published on February 2, 2010
220 In a conversation with the author in April 2017

on the screen I thought: 'Wow! I love that!' Then, when I was doing my research, I realised that the place had quite a lot of really weird and wonderful history," he recalled[221]. The film, starring John Malkovich and Willem Dafoe, was directed by Edmund Elias Merhige in 2000 and inspired by the 1922 version of the vampire myth, *Nosferatu*, directed by German filmmaker Frederich Wilhelm Murnau.

Heligoland is the name of a tiny archipelago in the North Sea. Now a German territory with just over 1,000 inhabitants, it has a surprisingly troubled history. It was exchanged many times by European empires in the nineteenth and twentieth centuries: Danish from 1714 to 1807, it became British and was used to spy on Napoleon's troops. In 1830 and in 1848, during times of revolutions, it served as a haven for dissidents fleeing European conservative powers. It hosted artists and poets including the brilliant Heinrich Heine, and later evolved into a spa resort. In 1890, it was at the centre of the Heligoland – Zanzibar Treaty, between recently-formed Germany and Great Britain, which enabled an exchange of possessions: Heligoland became German and Britain gained the island of Zanzibar, one of the jewels of Indian ocean.

During World War II, the archipelago also played a key role: as Germany turned it into a submarine base, it was bombed by the British Air Force in their raids against the Nazis. British soldiers surrounded its waters with mines and the local population had to be evacuated on April 18, 1945. Two years later on the same date, the Royal Navy used the territory to test its explosive devices – 6,700 tones – in one of the most powerful non-nuclear explosions in history, nicknamed by scientists as the "Big Bang". It was so violent that the main island was heavily affected and its fortifications exploded. The islands were used for bomb tests until 1952. Nowadays, the archipelago hosts a new German spa retreat and has the special fiscal state of a free zone – ironically. But, according to some experts, it could still be mined...

The name of the archipelago comes from old German "Heylige Land", meaning "sacred land". It was associated to a myth from the Frisian tribe of Northern Germany, stating that the islands were the home of the god

---

221 In the *Independent*, February 12, 2010

Forseti, incarnating the values of justice and reconciliation.

The accumulation of history and symbols around the tiny territory immediately sparked Robert Del Naja's interest. From the colonial past to the military insanity, added to the mythological elements, the name seemed very rich to him. The word also sounded like a play on the words "Hell Ego Land". The sound of it is indeed surprisingly telling in English, as "Helig-" – from "Heilig" in German, which means "holy" – is so close to "hell"... With a simple name, Robert's references went from the Holy Land to Limbo. Also bringing a spiritual dimension to the album, like for *100ᵗʰ Window*. The artwork then came to deepen these meanings even more.

Messages beyond the rainbow

Heligoland is possibly Massive Attack's most interesting album in regards to the artwork created for it. To deepen the sense of this complex universe built up over a couple of years, Robert painted a whole series of images, which would illustrate the album cover, the singles' sleeves and an additional booklet, bringing a heightened coherence to the symbols and references he put into the music and the title. And this series came to explain more deeply his relationship with Bristol.

What inspired him was the dialogue in the press in Bristol about the slave trade, the Colston Hall, the idea of race, and the cultural identity of the city, of its inhabitants. He thought he would play with that as a motif for the album, also because he was getting this sense that Massive Attack and Bristol had grown apart, in the sense that Bristol had been changing.

The Colston Hall is Bristol's main auditorium and for a city that has been so enriched by its Caribbean musicians, it feels odd, to say the least, to have it named after a slave trader, Edward Colston. Among the series of images that Robert created, the one that became the cover art for the album represents a figure of a "blackface minstrel", inspired by the eighteenth and nineteenth century caricatures produced in the United States, through actors using black make-up to mock African people in comedies, adverts and shows.

Robert's painting represents a half black/half white man with a bleeding eye on a bright orange background, surmounted by a grey rainbow. It can also be seen as a composite of 3D's and Grant Marshall's heads. The Wild Bunch first experienced the blackface stereotypes when they performed in Japan in 1986. The local party promoters had designed a poster in an old-fashioned "racist" way, according to Robert. His new image is a representation of Bristol's past and its disorientation regarding its own history.

For all these reasons, 3D still refuses to play in the Coslton Hall. "They've spent £18m on it, and our point was, if you're going to rebrand Colston Hall, don't you want to think about changing its name so it's not named after a slave-ship builder?" 3D wondered just before the release of *Heligoland*. "You could just alter it, so it's called the Colston Hall and the Sierra Leone Centre, or the Freetown Centre. You don't have to erase Colston, you just add something about the African slave trade to the equation, so when people come to Bristol, it's not hidden. We're just trying to address some of these things, un-Tippex them, so that it changes the way people look at the city[222]."

With this mature album, produced both in Bristol and outside the comfort of their homeland, which has changed as much as Massive Attack have changed, Robert was questioning their relationship with the city. He painted 30 to 40 pieces for *Heligoland*. Some are sketches, deliberately left unfinished.

Another painting represents two minstrels, a tall one painted in white, the other in black, on a bright yellow background. A duo that resembles 3D and Daddy G, in reversed colours, as an appeal to look beyond the stereotypes, but also to stop rewriting history to airbrush the parts disturbing the mainstream and the powerful. And that is the meaning of these representations of the band as two troubadours travelling and two polar opposite artists, as the stereotypes on the band often described them.

This painting was used to illustrate the band's 'Atlas Air' EP. The figure of the minstrel, circus clown or troubadour, is also a way to discuss the modern role of artists and musicians in our days, travelling

222 In an interview with the *Guardian*, published on September 10, 2009

on roads to meet their audience. The goal is to question their role in an extremely merchandised world, in a culture dominated by disguise and lies, in entertainment but also in politics, where reality is recreated in altered versions to fit a persuasive subjective discourse.

Robert's minstrel on the album cover is wounded and overshadowed by a colourless rainbow, created with spray paint, as a response to the abuse of colours in advertising, as a promise of happiness linked to the purchase of a product. The shiny shade of orange used in the background comes to produce a sharp contrast.

"I was trying to paint in lurid, bright colours for this series," 3D told the press a few years later, "taking quite obnoxious, dark imagery and making it day-glo. I remember this from when I was buying antagonistic punk music, which was always pressed onto to this brightly coloured vinyl. Angry music with really bright colours. Provocative and ugly images painted in a bright garish way, with a theme of bad cultural stereotypes[223]."

Robert worked with Tom Hingston to finalise the visuals for the sleeve, on vinyl and CDs, and created a 28-page booklet for a limited edition version of the album. The images were later shown on pop-up exhibitions along Massive Attack's next tour dates in 2010.

The other images in the series show human figures with skull-like faces, with exposed vital organs, especially lungs and hearts, but also bones and guts, as if scanned by a piercing gaze. An illustration depicts a faceless sailor piloting a ship; another (named 'Cruel Britannia'), a plane filled with slaves. A series declines rainbows in different sets of pale colours. One, called 'Believer', resembles his 'Unbelievable' canvas from the *War Paint* series and is painted in negative, with a colourless figure on a bright yellow and light blue background. And another is inspired by Aztec patterns, depicting some sort of shamanic icons and skull masks, as twins or in a mirroring effect, channelling "the idea of being both at the beginning and at the end simultaneously", 3D explained[224]. This one was be used as the cover of the 'Splitting The Atom' EP.

In a bizarre twist, the *Heligoland* posters were forbidden in the

---

223 In an article published in the *Guardian*, on August 7, 2015
224 Ibid

corridors of the capital's underground by Transport For London, claiming that "street art" is forbidden on the tube... TFL even asked the band "to remove all drips and fuzz from it so it doesn't look like it's been spray-painted", Robert confessed. "It's the most absurd censorship I've ever seen[225]." TFL was worried about the spray paint and not about the reference to the British Empire's use of slavery.

All these efforts to merge art, music and a historical perspective were meant to open a debate on the world the artist lives in. Bristol was changing indeed, has been increasingly since 2000. The university attracts young middle class students from all over Europe; Bristol house and rent prices have rocketed, especially as London is only 90 minutes away by train and many people leave the capital because of sky-high house prices. Bristol's suburbs are growing and newcomers are often not interested in Bristol's history or complex social mix. The local authority want to attract more tourists and tend to market one side of the city's history as represented by the Suspension Bridge, the harbourside and its maritime history, without acknowledging the role that sea trade played in slavery and how so much of Bristol's wealth was built on the proceeds of the slave trade.

Many artists from the city are still waiting to see the diversity of Bristol's music scene get more recognised nationally. Historian, writer and poet Edson Burton underlines that "Bristol had its role to play in the cultural evolution of the United Kingdom, precisely by displaying its diversity[226]".

For the centenary of World War One (1914-1918), curators tried to correct this effect, and the M Shed museum, on Bristol Harbourside, organised an exhibition on the role of African, Caribbean and Asian soldiers in the Great War.

But if history was made of mistakes, the country's present is not ideal either, according to Robert Del Naja and Grant Marshall. Their unreleased song 'Hartcliffe Star' depicted police helicopters flying over South Bristol to track cannabis' dealers in Hartcliffe, Knowle West, parts of St Pauls or Totterdown. This is the experience of many of the

---

225 In an article published in the *Guardian*, on February 6, 2010
226 In an interview with the author in Bristol's M Shed Museum in February 2015

poorest families who are not benefiting from the gentrification and enrichment of the city.

All the issues referenced in *Heligoland*'s music and artwork, about the UK's inaction on injustice, social inequalities and mishandling of the foreign policy, proved to be particularly topical. In November 2009, the results of the Chilcot Commission were announced, a commission put into place to investigate the relations between the UK and Iraq since 2001 and to evaluate the government decision to invade the Middle Eastern country. Its first conclusions left no doubt about the absence of weapons of mass destruction in Iraq in 2003. Tony Blair appeared guilty of having lied to his fellow citizens on the real causes of the war. But the final report of the commission wouldn't be published before another six years.

On the road, with a mission

Massive Attack continued their tour, begun at the autumn 2009, with a light show created by Robert Del Naja with United Visual Artists. In this evolved stage show, he started using a VP55 Vocoder synth to play, harmonise and augment his own vocals. The band installed a Moog Voyager for basslines and two control keyboards running native instruments patches as well as multiple "space echo" effect pedals. Visually, on top of optic panels for the display of information, they added an enlightened and revolving map of the world in three dimensions, made of lights, when the stages they played on allowed it.

The screen was used to project lists of data, from newspapers, the internet and from the audience, forming a snapshot of the world at a precise moment, a series of fragments of our reality. For instance, while touring Italy, the case of Stefano Cucchi – a young man who died in prison but whose death was not investigated – was mentioned on their screen. The reference was taken from a short report in a local daily newspaper. The very next day, the national press commented on that part of the show and the story became a headline.

When in Paris in November, an old friend came to visit the band and Martina Topley-Bird: Tricky. He was living in the French capital at the time, working in a residency at the cultural centre named Le

Centquatre. He came to say hello backstage, for the first time in years, burying the hatchet. The same night, Robert Del Naja had dedicated their song 'Teardrop', sung by Martina, to the organisations promoting women's rights and to all women in the world, and 'Safe From Harm' to women and children living in conflict zones.

In December, while the United Nations' Environment Summit in Copenhagen turned sour, D mentioned in an interview his work with Greenpeace, but explained that he had recently chosen to concentrate more of his efforts on raising awareness for the children living in refugee camps and for civil rights. Some of the profits from the show were sent to the Hoping Foundation in Palestine and in Mali; they send musical instruments to the children in displaced people's camps, among other things, and build recording studios to organise music lessons.

After the tour's winter break, *Heligoland* was released on February 8, 2010, entering the UK Albums Chart at number 6, number 2 in France and in the top 5 in many other European countries. It was dedicated to the memory of Jonny Dollar, *Blue Lines'* producer, who had just passed away. And the same day, Massive Attack started the second leg of their tour, in Wales. It took them to Australia, New Zealand, the United States and Brazil in November, where it ended after 88 dates. Most of the shows opened with the song 'United Snakes', before presenting five songs from the new album, as well as the unreleased 'Invade Me' – a duet between 3D and Martina, 'Teardrop', 'Safe From Harm', 'Inertia Creeps', 'Risingson', 'Unfinished Sympathy' and 'Atlas Air'. While Martina radiated in gorgeous colourful gowns, Deborah Miller appeared in an elegant long black dress.

When in the USA, Robert met with the members of the People Speak organisation, created by young activists and inspired by historian Howard Zinn's work, notably *A People's History of the United States*, the first scholarly work to tell America's story from the point of view of and in the words of American women, factory workers, African Americans, Native Americans, working poor, and immigrant labourers.

"I think musicians have a major role to play," Del Naja said in an interview. "I find the more I get involved, the more the movement becomes something tangible. I remember going to 'Artists Against

Apartheid' gigs, and 'Rock Against Racism' gigs around the same sort of time. Bands like the Clash and the Specials had a lot to do with influencing the minds of the youth in those days[227]."

He sometimes had to explain the meaning of the show to American journalists. "The internet has placed the impetus on live music, which is why there are so many more festivals now," he told the *Los Angeles Times* when in California[228]. "We're a communal people, a migratory race; music is what keeps us going. One of the things that we've always strived to do is communicate with our fans via a visual performance onstage capable of matching the music. Sometimes, it takes us longer to do our stage show than it does for the music itself. Of course, artists don't live in a vacuum un-impacted by life and politics, so we talk about the Arizona immigration law, the BP oil spill, the Greek riots."

Asked whether it was still possible to write protest songs, he replied: "Things have certainly changed, but I think that we're going through a substantial period of change at the moment where people are seeing the effects of capitalism failing people on a catastrophic sense. I think people are waking up to the way we've been living. Change doesn't necessarily need to start at a federal or state level, but it can start at groups on Facebook and Twitter – they can have a very large influence and it's important[229]."

These comments came as surprisingly timely, just a few weeks before the start of the Arab Spring in December... In Britain, a new Tory government was elected on May 6, led by David Cameron. And in April 2011, in Bristol, there were riots in Stokes Croft in protest against the opening of a Tesco store in the fiercely independent area. The unrest was soon followed by protests in London, in August, after the death of Mark Duggan, a black man killed by a policeman in Tottenham. Part of them turned violent and extended to other cities, including Birmingham, Wolverhampton, Nottingham, West Bromwich, Lincoln, Manchester and Salford.

Just like Robert Del Naja described in his song 'False Flags' in 2005,

227 With the *New Statesman*, published on September 3, 2010
228 In an interview with the *Los Angeles Times* published on May 18, 2010
229 Ibid

and just as the lyrics of 'Splitting The Atom' underlined, the United Kingdom was at a turning point, watching the history of the Thatcher years repeat itself. But the musician still hoped that music and art could help to open a dialogue on all these issues.

Visual and sonic variations

Finally, *Heligoland* also gave the band a platform to express themselves even more than before through the art of short films. Eight films were produced between 2009 and 2011, with small budgets, giving directors complete independence. Only three songs from the album weren't be the subject of films: 'Babel', 'Girl I Love You' and 'Rush Minute'; while 'Splitting The Atom' got two, one by Baillie Walsh, the other by Edouard Salier. The latter also created the video for 'Atlas Air' as a sequel of 'Splitting The Atom', black-and-white animated films representing an apocalyptic war-torn universe. In the second one, for 'Atlas Air', a giant beast wildly runs through the same apocalyptic environment, surrounded by lightning and firing.

The band members appeared in none of the films. In the video for 'Paradise Circus', the director, Toby Dye, imagines an adventurous scenario where he mixes extracts from porn films from the 1970s with an interview of the starring actress, Georgina Spelvin. The video actually starts with Georgina confiding that she used to be a prostitute and describes her motivation to work in the porn industry: "I love the camera"… She later comments on the porn scenes, with sharp and precise descriptions, admitting how humiliating it could sometimes be. Puzzling, extremely explicit and bluntly honest about an absolute taboo in Western culture, the film is rarely shown on television or even on YouTube, but questions our obsession with fame and television.

The film created for 'Psyche' couldn't be more different. Directed by John Downer, it delightfully pictures a wild nature blossoming, with insects, light flashing, tree leaves in the wind and water flowing, including clips of metamorphosis, from daylight to night-time, from caterpillars to butterflies, matching the song's quick rhythm and psychedelic feel. For 'Flat of the Blade', British photographer Ewen Spencer follows a young rapper from Birmingham named Deeze in his everyday life. And

Ridley Scott's son, Jake, directed the video for 'Pray For Rain', filming the blur of a middle-aged man's morning in an enigmatic and dreamy cinematography.

The eighth film is among the most strikingly powerful. In an eight-minute edit directed by Adam Broomberg and Oliver Chanarin, the sound specialist Michael Furman, from Cambridge University, is interviewed, as well as former prisoner from Guantanamo Ruhal Ahmed, to talk about the torture involving music used by the American army in the infamous prison. The film is set up with Clive Stafford Smith's organisation, Reprieve. The first minutes feature Ruhal reciting Damon Albarn's lovely lyrics in an anechoic chamber, before the music comes in. When his testimony later intervenes, the music stops... Even the most cynical music critics were speechless.

"Massive Attack are very committed to ending capital punishment. They started talking to us about the use of music in torture, they introduced us to Ruhal and it went from there," explained the director Oliver Chanarin in an interview[230]. "Music is something that we all associate with joy or pleasure. That transformation is so horrifying – that the beautiful thing becomes something intolerable."

Ending a very political couple of years, in November 2011, Robert and Grant travelled to Paris for the exhibition opening of French artist JR, named *Encrages*, collecting extracts from his series of photographs and pasting in urban areas all around the world. Born in the suburban city of Montfermeil, outside Paris, JR produces an artwork in between street art and activism. In 2010, Robert Del Naja participated in the score of his feminist documentary film, *Women Are Heroes*, shot on four continents.

And for December 2011, Robert suggested an "office christmas party" at the occupied UBS investment bank, with filmmaker Mark Donne. He invited Radiohead's Thom Yorke and the event became the end-of-the-year party thrown by the "Occupy London" movement, which had been very active since October. The benefits of the event, set in the unoccupied offices of UBS, were to be used to fight local social

---

230 In an interview with *World Magazine*, published on May 31, 2010

and economic injustice in the poorest boroughs of London.

Massive Attack also released in October 2011 a new song, 'Four Walls', in collaboration with the dubstep producer Burial. The producer actually had in mind to entirely remix *Heligoland*, in the way Mad Professor remixed *Protection* in a dub version... But never did. The 'Four Walls' EP was first released as a limited vinyl edition on October 17, 2011. It actually consists of Burial mixes of Massive Attack's previously unreleased track, 'Four Walls', with vocals and lyrical contributions by Hope Sandoval. The EP, housed in a gold glitter screen-printed sleeve designed by Robert Del Naja, also contains a remix of 'Paradise Circus'. A few weeks later, 3D released another piece of music via the band's Facebook page in celebration of the date 11/11/11. The track is simply named 'Vermona', like the type of German analog synthesizer used in the recording, and is voiced by D.

2011 was also an anniversary year for the band – 20 years since the release of *Blue Lines*, and they finally agreed to their record company's wishes to reissue the LP. It was available in 2012, in a remastered vinyl version. "We missed the 20th anniversary deliberately, because everyone does that 20 years thing, landmark nostalgia," Robert explained to *Crack* magazine, in an interview published in November 2012. "But we have this really great mix engineer, Bruno Ellingham, who suggested 'well, it'd be worth getting those tapes up, all those stems and putting them on the board again'. We're just putting it back out there, out into the world in a more dynamic fashion. With added volume! The fact that we're a year late is quite Bristol anyway." It was also an opportunity for 3D and Grant to reach out to Mushroom again... "We hadn't spoken for over 10 years," said 3D, "and that was a constant sadness in me. Life is too short to lose good friends and brothers, it's been like a happy dream communicating with Mush again."

As the band incredibly renewed their sound and image, their first album is still regarded as one of the most defining and revolutionary of the 1990s decade.

"Listening to Massive Attack's debut album, *Blue Lines*, 21 years after its initial release is like reading an old William Gibson novel that describes the then-near future, which is now the present, with unsettling precision," *Pitchfork* writer Miles Raymer penned on November 30, 2012. "Nearly every song offers a sound currently in use in music's taste-making leading edge," he added. "Post-*Blue Lines* music has never been the same," wrote John Robb the same month in *The Quietus*, "as a whole range of artists took the opportunity to enjoy the diverse influences and the sonic adventures offered up by this daring journey. Arguably the first album of the 21st century that arrived a decade early, *Blue Lines* remains a masterpiece – a serious record for serious times and a signpost to a future."

John Robb, a profound lover of anything punk, opened his article referencing Massive Robb described the "personal, symphonic and soulful" tones of the songs, capturing "a new multicultural UK, perfectly referencing Subbuteo and Studio One in the same song, as well as the rainy day reality of inner-city, urban life in expansive and imaginative songs," concluding strikingly by simply asking: "Could there be a more perfect record that sums up the cross pollination of ideas of the early nineties?"

In Bristol, success is not the key value though, sincerity is instead, and the musicians live at home like any other citizens, though very committed for their community and its future. Out of Bristol though, after such an epic and creative fifth album, Massive Attack have come to embody the rich, idiosyncratic sound of the city, and the complex history of a largely underheard part of the United Kingdom.

Chapter 14
Full Circle (2012-2018)

Bristol has a reputation for being an independently minded city, particularly when it comes to its artistic and creative community. This reputation was further enhanced in 2012 by the creation of a local currency, the Bristol Pound, managed by ethical *Credit Unions* in order to help develop an economy more based on local products and services. Many of the city's bars and restaurants use the Bristol Pound and some public employees are partially paid with it. Bristol also has the longest row of independent shops in Europe on Gloucester Road, which stretches from Stokes Croft to Horfield, and a few delightful urban farms, in St Werburghs and Windmill Hill notably, as well as many communal gardening spaces. The most radical expression of this independent spirit could be People's Republic of Stokes Croft, an organisation based in Jamaica Street, which has a philosophy of using art to change the way in which we view the urban environment. These are just a few examples of the city's openness I discovered while writing this story.

"Bristol always has been a really vibrant place," Robert Del Naja told Saatchi Gallery's magazine, in February 2012, and it can remain that way, he thinks, if the efforts are put into the new generation. "I know it's easy for me to say that, as I'm still a native of Bristol. But even now, there are new generations of kids making music and painting. It's always had its own feeling of independence. It's connected by the main artery of the M4 and now through the internet and data sharing. But it still has an independent spirit. And I think that really comes through in the music that the city makes and the art it throws up. It's the real blood essence."

In October 2012, when, after an electoral reform, Bristol's citizens had to choose their mayor through direct polls, Robert decided to write an open letter to one of the candidates, George Ferguson, as he was a well-known member of the Society of Merchant Venturers, created centuries ago by traders enriched by the slave trade.

Battlefields

His letter was published in local newspapers on October 9: "I read your campaign leaflet and am considering voting for you, so I hoped you might answer a few questions. As you are running for a public office, I thought an open letter appropriate. Can you truly describe yourself as an independent candidate, while being a member of the Merchant Venturers, an exclusive club that has many business interests in the city?" he wrote. "Even if you were to leave such an organisation, wouldn't your personal relationships with individuals and companies in the group present a potential conflict of interest? Considering that, if elected you would have enormous political influence over the future planning and development of Bristol."

In 2008, when a £500 million shopping centre opened in Cabot Circus, in Bristol City centre, Robert had already complained publically about this capitalistic non-sense and branded it as "absolute vandalism", which "captured that gripping 1980s shopping mall look of mid-America/the Midlands".

Socially, the city was quickly changing and facing gentrification, higher rents and a competitive real estate boom. With the arrival of students from all over the country and from many other European countries, Bristol's history was easily dominated by the tourist attractions, to erase the traces of the slave trade and effects of the colonisation of the Americas. Robert had these issues on his mind before the vote.

A day later, the independent candidate replied: "Why the hell am I a Merchant Venturer? In all honesty I sometimes ask myself the same question when I pay the annual donation, and I was encouraged by some to resign prior to standing for mayor, knowing this would be an issue. I am sure you know that I am not in any way an apologist for the appalling and deeply cruel slave trade, which was undoubtedly part of their history. I am proud to have played a leading role in anti-apartheid

265

campaigning in Bristol in the 1970s," George Ferguson wrote, "and deplored the council and chamber of commerce for being involved in a Trade Mission to South Africa, at that time citing the embarrassment of Bristol's role in the slave trade."

George Ferguson was elected a few weeks later, didn't have time to act on changing the auditorium's name though, and was replaced in 2016 by Marvin Rees, the Labour Party candidate, who is half Jamaican.

From then on, Robert judged that his social preoccupations would be better expressed directly through his art, and via his work with responsible, non-profit and non-governmental organisations. He didn't feel it was still necessary to be outspoken if his message was to be changed or deformed, and thought that all citizens should able to speak for themselves, as much as artists.

The same month, October 2012, a couple of Robert's art pieces were featured in Steve Lazarides' new collective exhibition, named Bedlam, inspired by the nickname used for the first psychiatric hospital opened in London, the Bethlem Royal Hospital, more than six centuries ago. For most Londoners, the word "Bedlam" had come to express an idea of chaos and madness. And Steve found it perfectly fitted our world, which had "gone mad", according to him… "Be afraid," he advised in his press release. "I really think of this as the complete antithesis of the Frieze Art Fair," he told the *Financial Times*, whose journalist described Lazarides as a specialist in "Outsider Art". "It is about chaos and pandemonium. Perfect themes for our time[231]."

The event was organised at the Old Vic Tunnels, in South London, near Waterloo Station, and ran until October 21. The incredible maze of tunnels hosted artworks by two dozen contributing artists including Conor Harrington, Doug Foster, the Artists Anonymous, Karim Zeriahen, Lucy McLauchlan, Antony Micallef, ATMA, Tina Tsang, Michael Najjar, Ian Francis, Kelsey Brookes, Klaus Weiskopf, Nachev, Tessa Farmer, Jane Fradgley, Tobias Klein, War Boutique, Dan Witz and 3D. They were all invited to reflect on the limits between reason and madness.

---

231 In an article published on October 5, 2012

By then, Steve Lazarides and Banksy had stopped their collaboration. Steve had opened his own gallery in London and featured younger artists, who also wanted to remain anti-establishment and refused the extreme merchandising of contemporary art. Their common goal was to conduct a message through their creation and to interrogate the world they live in.

3D created two pieces for the event, with UVA, containing LED and bits of mirrors. The first one was entitled Black Hole Information Paradox and assembled these elements in a triangle shape, with a six-pointed star at its centre, inspired by Islamic geometrical patterns. It also echoed the Bermuda Triangle, according to 3D, "and the myth of disappearance". It contained data about secret rendition flights and extrajudicial proxy detention victim testimonies, shared by Reprieve. The title refers to quantum physics and general relativity theories stating that physical information may permanently disappear in a black hole. "For me, it's a place where truth and information gets distorted, redacted and/or altered, and where law is total chaos, when it comes to truth and human rights in the so-called 'war on terror', which does look kind of mystic", 3D said at the show. The second piece was named Nevada Death Experience and featured data on activities of American drones in Pakistan.

At the end of 2012, Robert Del Naja also created his own label, Battle Box, for projects he was working on outside Massive Attack. He released a first track in December, 'Battle Box 001', distributed by The Vinyl Factory, featuring Guy Garvey on vocals. Three other singles appeared on the label the following years, remixing songs by Tunde Adebimpe's side project, Higgins Waterproof Black Magic Band, by Congolese musician Jupiter and by the very English Noel Gallagher, in the form of his new band, the High Flying Birds.

Two remixes of Noel Gallagher's 'The Right Stuff' were released on Battle Box in July 2015. "Originally released on Noel Gallagher's High Flying Birds' album Chasing Yesterday earlier this year, 'The Right Stuff' has been pulled apart and reassembled by Massive Attack's 3D and Euan Dickinson for two dark reworks of cinematic intensity," wrote Fact Magazine. "In 3D's words, 'it was a good opportunity to take a great song, slow it right down, remove the guitars and then scratch the clarinet backwards'..." the magazine continued. Speaking of the collaboration, Gallagher hinted that it had been a long time coming: "I remember being at The Brits in 1995 and D offering to do a Massive Attack remix of 'Cast No Shadow'. The idea was never followed through and it's something I've regretted ever since. It's nice to finally scratch the itch somewhat."

DJing too, 3D was invited by the DJ Damian Lazarus to participate in the Day Zero Festival, starting on December 20 at Playa del Carmen, Mexico, in honour of the end of a cycle in the Maya long count calendar, on December 21. "It's supposed to be the awakening of a new cycle," he told the *Guardian* on December 15. "And I think we are, globally, in a new information age where we communicate in a very different way than we did even five years ago. So perhaps it's something to do with a new cycle of human awareness." He cooked a special playlist for the cusp of the day. "You'd need a pretty good hi-fi to be heard above Armageddon," he added in the same interview, "the loudest soundsystem ever created, wireless and globally connected. You could play something gentle and choral, like Allegri's Miserere, so that a human voice was the last thing everyone would hear. Or maybe Burial reinterpreting Beethoven, something that spans the generations. It would be good to end it on our own terms; shake the world apart with bass before the asteroid hits."

D mainly worked with Euan Dickinson in his own 100 Suns Studio that year, as Neil Davidge finally left to pursue his own projects. "After *Heligoland*, I felt the need to explore other paths and other ways to work," Neil tells me[232]. Euan brought in a new energy to the studio. "So much changed about the music industry between 2000 and 2010," Euan underlines. "The traditional roles of producer, engineer in the studio had blurred, and I guess it was good timing having a young enthusiastic lad who could do a little bit of everything[233]."

3D and Euan worked on new soundtrack projects, the most striking one being for a documentary about tax evasion directed by Mark Donne, *The UK Gold*. It denounces the role of London's City as a world

232 In an interview with the author in Bristol in March 2015
233 In an interview with the author in Bristol in April 2016

tax heaven. The soundtrack also featured instrumental tracks created by Thom Yorke and Jonny Greenwood of Radiohead. 3D's parts are named 'Passive Fist', 'Dead Editors', 'Bullet Market' or 'Mission Creep', the most melancholic and hopeful track of the lot. The film was first shown in a preview in London in June 2013 and won an award at the East End Film Festival.

In 2013, 3D finally accepted Steve Lazarides' offer to organise a solo exhibition of his artwork. The show, entitled Fire Sale, was scheduled to open on May 23. "Like his music," Steve wrote for the show's presentation, "3D's art is modern and grounded, challenging and beautiful, industrial and ethnic. A vocal critic of the Iraq war, the conscious elements of the pieces are a reminder that Massive Attack have always been outspoken on social and international issues."

The exhibition ran from May 24 to June 20 and collected previously unseen pieces created for *Heligoland* alongside archival material from over twenty years, including graphic design, graffiti, painting and fine art. Some pieces were printed and hand-finished, some were on canvas. The show also displayed posters and illustrations created for Massive Attack's EPs and LPs, as well as 3D's two art pieces presented at Bedlam.

"I first saw 3D's murals when I was just 14 years old," Steve tells me a couple of years later[234]. "His graffiti were already way ahead of his time and his artwork still is. He's also very much interested in new technology. He is so respected as an artist but above all so unpretentious. It took me ten years to get him to do the exhibition."

Steve also announced that an art book would be put together after the show and that 3D was preparing "a monumental project" with the documentary filmmaker Adam Curtis, for the Manchester International Festival in July... The book, *3D and the The Art Of Massive Attack*, was finally rescheduled and released three years later and dedicated to Robert's father, Franco Del Naja, who passed away in June 2012.

"Monumental project" is an understatement in the case of Robert's creation with Adam Curtis. 3D got inspired at the Manchester International Festival in July 2011, while discovering Damon Albarn's

234 In a phone interview with the author in between London and Paris in March 2017

show, *Dr Dee – An English Opera*, directed by Rufus Norris. The festival's director, Alex Poots asked him if he would consider working on a show for a future event. 3D just said: "I'd love to do something with Adam Curtis", after viewing Curtis' BBC documentary *All Watched Over By Machines Of Loving Grace*. Alex texted Curtis the very same day.

In the sarcophagus of data

Born in Kent in 1955, Adam Curtis grew up in a liberal family – his father was a director of photography – and studied human sciences at the prestigious Oxford University, where he also started writing a thesis. He abandoned it later, disillusioned by the academic system, applied for a job at the BBC, to work on a film, and soon joined the team producing *That's Life!*, a series broadcast from 1973 to 1994, juxtaposing investigations with light-hearted content. He started directing a series for BBC Two in 1980 and one of his first films, *Trumpets and Typewriters*, shown on BBC One in 1983, retraced the history of war correspondents.

After many other daring films, Adam Curtis now introduces himself as a journalist aiming for objectivity but assuming his subjectivity. He covers very political issues, offering a personal analysis and a deep form of deciphering, but refuses to be labelled as "left-wing". His films *A Century of the Self* and *All Watched Over by Machines of Loving Grace* deal with the rise of individualism, the end of ideologies, and the obsession for risk-management theories.

He believes western societies have become pessimistic and backward-looking, constantly referring to the past, because they are too afraid to face up to a future, haunted by "ghosts", "suffocating in a sarcophagus of data", according to this expert in phrase-coining.

3D suggested working from one of Adam's films, to adapt it for the stage and create music for the soundtrack, in order to foster an experimental live performance. He focused on the kind of sensations he wanted to provoke in the audience in order to transport them in a "ghost story about now", that he would design with United Visual Artists.

Adam Curtis accepted the challenge but wanted to create a whole new film. He had already presented a show at the MIF in 2009, in collaboration with Damon Albarn and the stage company Punchdrunk, which specialises in "immersive theatre", where the audience is invited to take part. And despite their seriously different backgrounds, Adam and Robert found a lot of common interests, around using audiovisual media to transmit abstract messages and generate new emotions.

After months of preparation, Adam Curtis described it on his personal blog a few weeks before the show as "A collaboration between myself and the brilliant Robert Del Naja of Massive Attack. What links us is not just cutting stuff up - but an interest in trying to change the way people see power and politics in the modern world". Calling the outcome a "gilm", contraction of "gig" and "film", i.e. "a new way of integrating a gig with a film that has a powerful overall narrative and emotional individual stories".

The performance was named 'Massive Attack Versus Adam Curtis', with a subtitle: 'Everything Is Going According to The Plan'. It was scheduled to debut at the Manchester Festival, in 2013, from July 4 to 13, at the Mayfield Depot, a disused train station of gigantic dimensions. It was then programmed at the Kraftzentrale, in Duisburg in Germany, for the Ruhrtriennale Festival at the end of August, and in New York for early October, at the Park Avenue Armory. At the same time, from October 1, Banksy coincidently created ten pieces in New York City, as part of a sort of month-long residency titled 'Better Out Than In'. He actually unveiled one piece of art per day, sometimes more, mostly stencilled graffiti, documenting their apparition on his website and his Instagram account.

The three sites receiving the Massive Attack Versus Adam Curtis show had the capacity to host the nine monumental screens created for the show, broadcasting films' extracts, news archives, photos, texts and visuals. The main screens were also used periodically as transparent curtains, revealing behind them the band performing live.

Massive Attack's 3D and Daddy G were accompanied by Horace Andy and Elizabeth Fraser on vocals, Damon Reece on drums, Angelo Bruschini on guitar and Sean Cook on the bass and backing vocals. The images projected on the screens displayed archives from the Chernobyl nuclear explosion in Ukraine in 1986, the September 11 attacks and the war in Afghanistan, as well as extracts from popular films and television shows from the 1960s and 70s, all guided by Adam Curtis' commentary. At some point, the show juxtaposed extracts from fictional disaster movies – all produced before 2001 – depicting the fall of the Chrysler Building or World Trade Centre, such as Michael Bay's *Armageddon*.

In between Adam's explanations, texts and video extracts appeared on the screens, without any commentary, such as scenes from horror movies or Jane Fonda's televised gym class... Altogether representing the idea of a "sarcophagus of data", a metaphor inspired by the Chernobyl catastrophe. It refers to the mass of information under which citizens are now crawling; supposed to enlighten them, it only exhausts them.

Then at other moments came the music. The soundtrack was composed of a playlist, chosen by Adam and Robert. It included songs by Barbara Streisand, Siberian punk singer Yegor Letov, American punk band Suicide, Scottish alternative band the Jesus and Mary Chain, Bauhaus, Burt Bacharach, the Archies, Nirvana, and Massive Attack's own 'Karmacoma'. It was for Robert an opportunity to perform in a completely alien way, to sing covers of songs he's always loved, especially 'Bela Lugosi's Dead' and 'Just Like Honey', and to adopt new personalities and voices. 'Bela Lugosi's Dead' in particular has always been the centrepiece of Robert's DJ set. It was to him the desaturated gothic disco where punk met dub and rude boys ran the street. it was his first 12-inch, became the reason why he wanted a space echo, and was the track he most wanted to cover since 1979.

Adam Curtis saw the whole show as an opportunity to try to forge a new type of journalism, as an alternative to "boring and dry" mainstream reportage, he told the BBC on the day of the premiere. "I'm convinced that the future of journalism is a form of reporting that is as emotional as it is factually correct, that actually conveys to you what it's like to experience something." He wanted to underline that our civilisation's obsession with past and fixed cultures could sometimes inspire new creations but most of the time prevented any form of innovation.

For Robert Del Naja, the experience of the show should disconcert and disorientate, through a story that is sometimes scary, sometimes very human. The show's trailer promised to feature Massive Attack, Donald and Ivana Trump, Nicolai and Elena Ceaucescu, Jane Fonda and Ted Turner, Hamid Karzai and his brothers, as well as "Everyone in Goldman Sachs who made a killing in 2008", the neutron bomb, the Siberian punk movement, Bambi and "all your worst fears".

"At a certain point it's all about storytelling and the manipulation of imagery and then it's bang, look at the stage, and we are performing a song by Grob, in loud fake Russian, and then CUT and you're focusing on a real person that you never knew had such an influence on the world that you live in today," said Robert[235]. "And then it's back to chaos again. That way, it feels a bit like what it's like to be alive outside our comfort zone."

In August, he explained to German television that their goal was not to blame the audience, but to look for answers together. Which Adam Curtis confirmed. "I grew up thinking journalists and rock stars were heroes able to change the world," he told the press, "but I think that investigative journalism is now also part of the problem, because it's only trying to shock. However, I think that the role of journalism and of the politics, or of music as well, is to tell us what is wrong in the world but also to suggest – and not order – what we could do to change it[236]."

One of their main expectations was to take the show to New York, which can be seen as the centre of the world of power and struggles they describes through the "gilm". To open a dialogue.

Sean Cook, who is himself very politically aware, was playing bass during the shows and remains in awe at the initiative. "When we took the Adam Curtis project to New York, there was all kinds of fictional movie footage of the Twin Towers, there was a genuine concern that A) we would not get let into the country, and B) that somebody might take a pot-shot at us during the gig or something," Sean tells me in Bristol[237]. "And D took it totally to the bridge; we did the gig on Park Avenue, in the Armoury, in the richest bit of real estate in the world, right where September 11 was planned. We did the gig right there."

For Sean, such a goal is very rarely achieved by artists and when it is, nothing is more important. "This is the power of artists. A lot of

235 In an interview with BBC, published on the broadcaster's website on July 4, 2013
236 In an interview in Germany with the French daily *Libération*, published on September 1, 2013
237 In an interview with the author in Bedminster, Bristol, in April 2015

people think musicians should not get involved, and I don't understand that. Some bands don't know anything about politics; it's true. And to a large extent, the audience doesn't care, even with Massive Attack. Which is why you have to give even more respect to D; he's risking the alienation of his audience. The political side is all D. And this is what I like about Massive Attack. To me they're the modern equivalent of the Dead Kennedys. You don't get a much better compliment than that[238]." The American punk band formed in 1978 in San Francisco, known for their relevant, sarcastic, involved and progressive discourse.

"In Bristol", adds Sean, "D spends a lot of his time researching social and political issues. And if somebody is doing the research, then they do have a right to talk about what they've uncovered. Isn't it what journalists do? They go to places and research stuff and report what they've learnt. The thing that motivates me about Massive Attack is the political angle. Massive Attack is a cross-border phenomenon. And they still have a captive audience. D has provided another thing that we can do, that even some veterans, in 20 years in the business, cannot do[239]."

In between the performances in New York, on October 3, the Park Avenue Armory hosted a discussion about the show and the role of the media, streamed live on the internet, with four guests: Graham Sheffield, the Director of Arts for the British Council; contemporary philosopher Simon Critchley; Joyce Barnathan, president of the International Center for Journalists, a non-profit organisation dedicated to advancing quality journalism worldwide; and Alexis Goldstein, contributor to the *Nation*, the *Washington Post* and the *American Prospect*, as well as an Occupy Wall Street campaigner. They challenged the role of 24-hour news channels, like CNN, created by Ted Turner, who appears in Adam Curtis' film.

Simon Critchley is British and teaches at the New School in New York, working especially on the notion of political disenchantment and our society's need for more ethics. His input in the discussion was really rich and he underlined that music does have a nostalgic role, especially in our modern environments, "haunted by emotional ghosts". Songs like the cult 'Bela Lugosi's Dead' by Bauhaus or 'Karmacoma', in

238   In Bristol in April 2015
239   Ibid

which the lyrics refer to apathy, comas, as well as the spiritual eastern notion of karma, emphasise emotionally the ideas displayed, according to Critchley. He was fascinated by the idea of the sarcophagus, a place for "a passage to the afterlife", a tomb for those who refuse to obey the line between life and death, for the un-dead, the Egyptian gods as much as modern celebrities, still dancing on screens years after their disappearance, or our social media profiles...

The music also managed to highlight, in a contrast, the absurdity of the world as shown on television, for instance when Horace Andy sings the Archies' song 'Sugar, Sugar' – a very happy tune – over the images of Britain in the 1950's cut with a black and white minstrels American film... The scene made the audience see very strongly how unbearable the racist sequence from the minstrel film actually was, while for decades it was considered amusing.

To Simon, by working with Massive Attack, Adam Curtis replied to his own question about how to get out of the circle of ghostly data: by creating something new. "Bristol is a complex nexus of influences," added Simon, and, when they appeared, "Massive Attack was something new, music had never sounded like that before".

As a final statement, towards the end of the show, while Liz Fraser was singing in Russian 'Yanka's Song', a text was projected on the screen, which predicted: "*Outside our fragile cocoon, beyond the reach of the two dimensional ghosts, and the enchanted music of the dead, the future is also full of possibility. It is not predictable. You can make anything happen. You can change the world. Now find your own way home.*"

African detours and middle-eastern journeys

After more than a year spent working on this unique project, 3D returned from New York to work in his Bristol studio on more personal and small-scale projects. The band was on a break. In October 2013, 3D released a new track on Battle Box with a promo video, remixing Jupiter's song 'Congo'. He had met Kinshasa-born Jean-Pierre Bokondji, aka Jupiter, on a trip to the Democratic Republic of Congo in 2007, for the series of concerts uniting European and African bands, named Africa Express, created by Damon Albarn.

The song 'Congo' carries a strong political and anti-colonial message, also interrogating the way the country has changed since its independence, calling for democratisation, respect of some key traditions and right to modernity. Jupiter himself has an impressive story: born in 1963 in a village in his homeland, he lived in East Berlin where his father was a diplomat until the early 1980s, discovering European and American music in this environment. Back in Kinshasa, the promising son worked seven years in the national administration, then gave up his parents' career plans to become a musician. He had realised that he had inherited a gift for percussion from his grandmother.

In the song 'Congo', he sings in French: *"Nos ancêtres étaient des esclaves, on les fouettait trois fois par jour mais ils bouffaient trois par jour (...) Cinquante ans plus tard, les Congolais bouffent une fois par jour (...) Est-ce qu'on est indépendant ou dépendant ? Ca dépend, l'histoire nous jugera"* ("Our ancestors were slaves, they were whipped three times a day but they could eat three times a day (...) Now, fifty years later, the Congolese only eat once a day (...) So, are we independent or dependent? It depends. History will judge us."). He also sings in Lingala, one of the Congo's many indigenous languages, that Jupiter explores in his music. The song includes extracts from Patrice Lumumba's political speech, given on June 30, 1960, during the official Independence ceremony. Lumumba was then chosen as Prime Minister, a few months before his assassination, on January 17, 1961.

"My goal is to bring a new sound in the Congo," Jupiter tells me when we meet in Paris, "a country of 450 ethnic groups with thousands of different rhythms and musical styles. My music is the reflection of our people's rebellion too; but my messages can talk about politics as well as about our daily life, because it's often even more truly political. And working with Blur and Massive Attack also allows me to show the diversity in our music, mixing traditional sounds and modern experimentations[240]."

Robert's version of the song was named '3D on Jupiter - Battle Box 002'. It was "built with an unknown modular synth from Munich, a Moog

---

240 In an interview with the author in Paris, in June 2015

and a Vermona drum machine, with help from Euan Dickinson and Tim Goldsworthy", he explained in a press release. "I wanted to mirror the energy and message in the song without complicating it. The B-side is a more relaxed and melodic using a Prophet 5 and a Jupiter 8. It is the second release on the Battle Box label, which is made and distributed through the Vinyl Factory. Paul Insect has designed the covers and label art." A video was also produced with footage from Kinshasa nowadays and in 1960, including the Independence Day celebrations.

Robert also shared a few months later one of his paintings with Jupiter for the artwork of his second album, *Kin Sonic*, released in 2017. The artwork, entitled Double Heart, was created in 2015 and represents a darkened masked figure, inspired by an African theme, with a bright orange-red shirt. The character is surrounded by a blue and white background and four black airplanes, typical of the artist's favourite patterns. On his chest are two figurative hearts, one pink, one black. The painting was shown in London in January 2016 at Lazarides' ten-year anniversary exhibition, Still Here, A Decade Of Lazarides. Profits from the sales of Jupiter's album were used to help found a school for young children in Kinshasa.

A third track for Battle Box was mixed soon after, distributed for the label by the Vinyl Factory: 'Higgins in 3D', a remix of 'Mad Lifeline', by the Brooklyn band Higgins Waterproof Black Magic Band, led by Tunde Adebimpe. In 2014, D also worked with French electronic music pioneer Jean-Michel Jarre, on a track called 'Watching You', to appear on his double album, *Electronica*.

Later that year, Massive Attack toured again, without a new album. The band played many festivals from June to October, from Bulgaria to Latin America via San Francisco. The show opened with 'United Snakes' and a version of 'Battle Box 001' interpreted by Martina Topley-Bird, singing under a mesmerising array of colourful and hypnotic lights. It was followed by the rare and enchanting 'Everywhen', with Horace Andy on vocals, during which the screens displayed an array of questions and answers lifted from Google's search engine. Robert Del Naja was inspired by his work with Adam Curtis, looking to make the concerts evolve constantly. A lot of information displayed on the screens that summer informed about the situation in Gaza. The performance ended with 'Unfinished Sympathy' and 'Splitting The Atom'.

The tour brought the band to Glastonbury for the fourth time, then to Istanbul in June and in Lebanon on July 29, for a date at the Byblos International Festival. The organisers announced "a groundbreaking collision of music, visuals and technology!" The screen content listed the destruction in Syria by the "Islamic State" and called for solidarity with Syrian and Iraqi refugees. The band was acclaimed by a crowd that came out overwhelmed with emotion after such a moment of solidarity.

The profits from the show were sent to the organisation operating the ambulances in Gaza, which had just been heavily bombed by the Israeli Army in Operation Protective Edge, launched on July 8, following the kidnapping and murder of three Israeli teenagers by Hamas members. The Palestinians responded to the Israeli strikes with rocket attacks and ground fighting resulted in the death of thousands of people, the vast majority of them Gazan civilians. "This bombardment of an area that is one of the most densely populated on earth, where civilians aren't allowed to leave, is just beyond belief," Robert Del Naja told *Agence France Press* while in Lebanon, after he dedicated the band's gig to the children of Gaza. "In order to protect yourself, do you really want to massacre another people?" he asked in a rhetorical question…

Robert and Grant travelled with the Hoping Foundation, to meet the Palestinian refugees the organisation is helping. They went to Burj al-Barajneh, in the suburbs of Beirut, to visit a camp that was opened in 1948, as well as the Al Naqab Centre, hosting more and more Palestinian refugees arriving from war-torn Syria. They met the youth who participate to the centre's activities.

"We wish to especially mention three groups of Palestinian refugees today," Robert told the press. "First, those we just met, recently arrived from Syria who escaped death but are still living such harsh lives today. They have been made refugees many times – first in 1948, and again since the destruction of the Palestinian camps in Syria. Also it is important to bring attention to those Palestinians living in Lebanon since 1948: all the young people I met who weren't born in Syria were born in Lebanon, and all of them are waiting to go home. And today we want to show our love, solidarity and support for the Palestinian people in Gaza, indeed most of them are also refugees. All of them have a right to a life of dignity and beauty[241]."

Robert had wanted to come to the camp for years. Karma Nabulsi, director of the Hoping Foundation, set up the visit to one of the camps. Massive Attack refused to conveniently ignore the colonial past, for instance the Balfour Declaration signed in 1917 to support the establishment of a "national home for the Jewish people" in Palestine. An act that still has huge consequences.

On September 12, Massive Attack performed at the Fête de l'Humanité, near Paris, in France, posting on their screen slogans and quotes from Jean-Jacques Rousseau and Nelson Mandela. They travelled to South and North America in October, where Tunde Adebimpe joined them in Los Angeles to sing 'Pray For Rain' during the encore.

"If anything, Massive Attack's live presentation highlighted the here and now, particularly with the visual display that appeared later in the set," reported the American magazine *Consequence of Sound*. It "was ultimately a mirror of 2014 society, one that maybe was preaching to the choir, and chose to focus on the darkness of present society and technophobia, rather than the humanity and warmth that we each experience on a daily basis. It's hard to say we need more reminders of what is wrong with the world; maybe we need more opportunities to retreat from them? But Massive Attack made their position clear: that we retreat too much as is and that they had the opportunity with a captive audience to highlight their personal stance, which, at the end of the day, you can do nothing but respect."

Very timely, in 2015, Iraqi-French filmmaker Abbas Fahdel chose a song from Massive Attack – 'Hymn of the Big Wheel' – to be featured at a key moment of his film *Homeland (Iraq Year Zero)*, a documentary in two parts, retracing his country's recent history. An ultimate homage to their music, which had come to embody the soundtrack of an entire generation, with its bright moments and its tragedies.

Meanwhile, early in 2015, Banksy travelled to the Gaza Strip,

241 In the *Independent*, on July 30, 2014

adding his stencils to the region's walls, depicting children playing on a merry-go-round or with a giant kitten... He produced a five-minute documentary film on Gazans' daily life, posted online via YouTube, filming the tunnels between Gaza and Egypt used by smugglers, refugees and arm dealers, as well as destroyed areas in the territory.

Such a dismal world

A few months later, Banksy surprised everyone when he announced his return to his home region with a new attraction: a fake amusement park. Hosting three-dimensional artworks and an art gallery, it opened in August 2015 for six weeks in the resort town of Weston-super-Mare, in Somerset, near Bristol. The so-called "Bemusement Park" was baptised *Dismaland* and set in the former children's attraction named Tropicana, disused for years.

In his press release, Banksy said that "it's a theme park whose big theme is – theme parks should have bigger themes", and explained: "I loved the Tropicana as a kid, so getting to throw these doors open again is a real honour. I hope everyone from Weston will take the opportunity to once more stand in a puddle of murky water eating cold chips to the sound of crying children."

The whole event featured a lot of guests and was planned with artist friends, including 3D. One of the centrepieces of the attractions was a crumbling castle featuring an accident scene with a Cinderella's horse-drawn carriage, surrounded by paparazzi, in a representation of the death of Diana Spencer, the late Princess of Wales. It was described by the media as "something that is shocking, evocative and emotional".

Banksy also programmed Friday evening's events, with prestigious guests, including the hip-hop New York duo Run The Jewels, Sleafords Mods, Savages, the Russian punk heroines of Pussy Riot, the spoken word artist Kate Tempest and finally Massive Attack for September 26... The Pop Group was soon added to the list, with Geoff Barrow on the decks. All of them made an appearance at the very fancy opening party in late August. Tickets for the visit – costing between three and five pounds only – sold online in a few minutes and the queue for spontaneous entries didn't diminish any day in six weeks. At the very last

minute, Massive Attack finally cancelled their performance, however…
after a newly planned but eventually aborted film collaboration with
Adam Curtis, according to the band.

In the art gallery, indoors, were featured artworks from 58 artists
– and Banksy himself – including Palestinian painters Sami Musa and
Sliman Mansour; Paco Pomet from Spain; three Israelis: Amir Schiby,
Ronit Baranga and Neta Harari Navon; Tammam Aziz from Syria; and
many European, American and British creators – including Damien
Hirst.

Most of the outstanding pieces were three-dimensional installations,
like Banksy's pond, filled with replicas of refugee boats, and a Grim
Reaper as a bumper car attraction. Films were also on display as well
as an information desk, with data about Middle Eastern conflicts and
details from social organisations fighting injustice. It was hard not to
leave the park groggy. Humour was mixed with cynicism at every level,
in every corner. The media from all over the world rushed to the place
and the park brought an estimated £20 million to the local economy.

Once closed, some of the Dismaland structures were sent to the
informal refugee camps in Calais, in the north of France, baptised the
"Jungle", where thousands of Syrian, Afghan, Sudanese and Eritrean
refugees were waiting to cross the Channel to hopefully reach England.
Banksy travelled himself to the location to leave a few murals in
December 2015, including a portrait of Steve Jobs, founder of Apple,
probably the richest Syrian American in recent history.

Two years later, Banksy opened a controversial hotel in the West
Bank, in Bethlehem, the Walled Off Hotel, featuring a museum of the
region's history. The opening occurred at the time of the centenary of
the Balfour agreement, signed in 1917, which allowed the migration of
European Jews in Palestine, during the bloodshed of the First World
War.

Amid undocumented and persistent rumours suggesting that
Banksy and Robert Del Naja were the same person or at least a group
of artists united in all their productions (allegations they both denied),
Banksy nevertheless asked 3D to contribute musically, as well as Trent
Reznor. D proposed the purchase and modification of a Dislavier

midi player piano, offering international musicians the opportunity to perform remotely at the hotel without the need to actually travel. And the hotel created a piano bar where the mechanical instrument is still present to this day.

Back to the source

One month after their cancelled show in Weston-super-Mare, after intense rehearsals, Massive Attack announced new tour dates for 2016 and the release of a new EP for January. It would feature four unreleased songs, composed by 3D, including one with their old pal Tricky, written in 2012 in Paris.

Tricky was by then inspired to come back to his past again. With his album *False Idols*, released in 2013, and even more with the following, *Adrian Thaws*, out in 2015, he confided more memories. His eldest daughter sang on the record. And he even moved back to England for a while.

For his next project, Tricky worked with a friend from the early days: Miles Johnson, aka DJ Milo from the Wild Bunch. They wrote together in Berlin tracks to appear on Tricky's next album, *Skilled Mechanics*. "A city that makes me feel good," he tells me when we meet again in Paris in September 2017. "I do not go out to clubs or smoke here, but to walk, watch people bike, find some peace. Sometimes I spend days wandering without talking to anyone. I spend most of my time alone." Tricky mentioned in the album his mother's suicide, as well as the violence of his youth.

He soon after worked on his thirtheenth album, including a track with his first muse, Martina Topley-Bird. The sublime ballad, 'When We Die', became the last track of the new album, called *Ununiform*. "I have always had a strong link with the number 13," he tells me during our meeting in Paris, in a hotel with a cinematic look, which does not fail to make me think of the corridors of the 'Karmacoma' music video… "My uncle lived at number 13 on our street in Knowle West, Bristol, and his home was the happiest family place of my childhood." Thirteen tracks for a thirteenth album in 22 years of career, as heterogeneous as its producer. "I went from the street to crazy album promos overnight," recalls Tricky. "At first, it seemed obligatory to me, like I had to follow the rules, but I never liked promotions... Nowaways, I only advertise because I have my own label. I do what I love, that's all[242]."

Martina Topley-Bird admitted this collaboration was meaningful to her: "It's important to reconnect and remind yourself of your history," she told me. "I love Bristol and still have friends there. I still plan regularly on moving back... It's my musical hometown". She also started working on a new single, entitled 'Solitude' and released in 2018, to be followed by an EP (*MTB Continued*) and maybe an album.

Many other iconic Bristol bands were back in 2014/17. Alpha, launched by Massive Attack's label Melancolik in 1997, released a new album, *Loving Nobody*, produced by Corin Dingley without Andy Jenks. Andy was still producing the Flies, Sean Cook's band formed with Bob Locke and Tim Norfolk, from the Insects. Their second album, *Pleasure Yourself*, was released in the summer 2014. "To me", says Andy, "Bristol is more than a sound, it's a family, which is impossible to create in a city like London. It's a fantastic space of collaboration where all our bands and groups have been linked in a way or another[243]."

Andy also worked with Mark Stewart, who reformed the Pop Group in 2010, after performing at the All Tomorrow's Parties Festival in Somerset, along with Iggy Pop. Early 2015, they were back with their first album in 35 years, *Citizen Zombie*, and a tour. "*Citizen Zombie* is a declaration on our civilisation facing a technological turning point," says Mark Stewart[244]. "Nowadays, most citizens are suffering from the constant distraction that technology has brought about, with an obsession for consumption of renewed electronic products. I see my work as a musician as the one of a journalist. To me it's important to look at the world and question it, to help others to do so as well."

His lyrics for the track 'Nations' describe our modern societies this way: "*We're all addicted to something / Money / Sex / Television / Paranoia / Notoriety*"... And we have to free ourselves from them, he thinks. Mark is still close to Grant Marshall, Geoff Barrow and Banksy. And they

---

242 In an interview with the author in Paris in September 2017
243 In an interview with the author in Bristol, at the Christchurch Studio, in Clifton, in April 2015
244 In an interview with the author between Bristol and London in July 2015

still share the same views. "It's absurd to say musicians should stay away from politics," Mark adds. "Artists are citizens like any other and they have opinions to share. When Massive Attack are expressing their views, they act as an antidote to the 'zombification'. That's what we are here for, to launch new ideas, to look into the future[245]."

In 2015 still, the band Black Roots and the singer Janine Rainforth announced new albums for 2016. Even Portishead, who appeared in Glastonbury in 2013, were rumoured to be preparing a record... Adrian Utley was composing and the band scheduled more live events. "I often mention an album to the press," Adrian tells me when I meet with him in Bristol in 2015, "but it's just a way to give a simple answer to questions about the band. No, Portishead is not working on an album. A lot has been written about Bristol's pot smokers, about our slowness or our musical secrets, but it's all exaggerated and we have no rules. Each album was born out of lots of compromises and it was not always easy. Time is a precious value for us, that's all[246]." In 2015, Portishead played at the Latitude festival, with Thom Yorke making a guest appearance to the delight of the audience.

Meanwhile the 2015 and 2016's editions of St Paul's Carnival were cancelled, due to alleged mismanagement and a lack of funding by the city council, but the reggae and soul music scenes were still very vivid. One of their best incarnations is a young singer named Lady Nade, aka Nadine Gingell, who participated in the WOMAD Festival in July 2015. Inspired by jazz and soul singers such as Ella Fitzgerald and Nina Simone, she regularly performs in Bristol and beyond with her band, which include Seb Gutiez on guitar, Dan Everett on bass and Mike Cooper on drums. Nade released a first album, *Hard To Forget*, produced by Allan Keen, in the spring 2016, and started working on her second one in 2018.

Just like in the mid-1990s Bristol was an important platform for the drum and bass movement, and in the 2000s it became a catalyst for dubstep (nourished by influences from two-step garage, dub, techno, drum and bass, broken beat, jungle, and reggae), from 2010 Bristol

245 With the author in July 2015
246 In an interview with the author in Bristol, in September 2015

became a hotspot for grime music, mixing electronic sound with drum and bass, hip-hop and garage/jungle influences. The Young Echo collective are pioneers in this movement in Bristol, including a wide array of DJs from diverse horizons: DJ Kahn (aka Joseph McGann), rapper Jabu, Gantz who is from Istanbul... They are regularly associated with bands like Vessels, from Leeds, pressing their own EP's on vinyl and performing in Bristol as much as in New York or Japan. "When we began," explains Kahn, "we didn't want to live in the shadow of Bristol's famous bands, as we knew we were part of the birth of a new form of music. But soon, we did play with Portishead on stage and with Rob Smith, who programmed us in Glastonbury. But we do work much more with the younger DJs[247]."

Then of course hip-hop is also a major influence for a lot of Bristol's acts, such as Laid Black, QELD, K*Ners and Slackjaw Trait. DJ Chris Johnson is also still active, now under the name of Kinsman, and released an album in 2016. "According to me, Bristol is a real magnet!" Chris insists when we meet in Stokes Croft. "I lived in the United States and in Ireland, but I came back. It is the most creative city in the world[248]." Mixing hip-hop, electronic music and powerful female voices, Dr Meaker is one of the upcoming acts of the city. Their debut album, *A Lesson From The Speaker*, and their single 'Bad Boy Calling' were both released on November 17, 2008. Their main producer, Clive Alan Meaker, names Massive Attack as his main influence.

In 2017, the band Idles released their debut album, *Brutalism*, inspired by the term coined by architectural critic Reyner Banham to identify the architecture that emerged following the Second World War. The press welcomed the record as the best thing that happened to post-punk in years. The band emerged from nights spent in the Bat-Cave nightclub in Bristol, run by singer Joe Talbot and bassist Adam Devonshire, who met at college in Exeter. They decided to start a band in 2011, joined by guitarists Mark Bowen and Lee Kiernan, and drummer Jon Beavis. In September 2018, they came back with a second album, *Joy As An Act Of Resistance*, debuting in the UK Albums Chart at number five, selling

247 In an interview with the author in Bristol in February 2015
248 In an interview with the author in Bristol in May 2015

11,000 copies in its first week.

"I think words are the most powerful and important thing we have," singer and lyricist Joseph Talbot told the *Guardian* in June 2018, referring to his lyrics often described as honest and politically aware. "I don't like to sit back and be a spectator. So I was not necessarily going to be a frontman, but I was definitely going to be involved. I've got no patience and I couldn't learn an instrument. That's why I became a frontman." Joe said singers like Thom Yorke or Kayne West inspired him because "they open discussions, not close them, and that's what I want to do. I'm not going to dictate my ideas to people and ram things down their throats. I just want to paint a picture that's a slightly abstract, expressive picture of something but let the listener finish it off[249]."

Yes, "Bristol has a very active scene," confirms Euan Dickinson, "but I think the best music comes from those always looking outside the city's boundaries! I have great pride and affection for my home city, but I think I would have had a passion for music wherever I had been born. Saying that, I am definitely influenced by the concoction of sounds and genres Bristol has created over the years, and I am lucky to live in a place with so many creative people[250]."

With a vibrant street art scene too, Bristol is shining bright out of its walls. The Aardman Studios also made the city an important hub for animated films, just like the Arnolfini and Spike Island galleries rival other cities' art centres. With only half a million inhabitants, compared to eight million in London, its cultural scene is impressive. In November 2017, Bristol's reputation as a leading film centre was underlined with the announcement that it has been named "a UNESCO City of Film". The bid included the input of places and groups like the Watershed, Knowle West Media Centre, Calling The Shots, Aardman Animations, BBC Bristol, Encounters Festival, Bristol Festivals, the Old Vic Theatre School, the department of Filmmaking at University of West England – Bristol, and many more.

249 To *Clash Music* in March 15, 2017
250 In an interview with the author, between Paris and Bristol, in April 2016

Rebirth and reiterations

While finishing the tracks that could become part of Massive Attack's potential sixth album, Robert Del Naja was also working on various audiovisual projects, especially in Italy.

At the same time, James Lavelle was releasing an album called *UNKLE Sounds – Naples* and asked Robert to contribute to the project. "We have all made careers out of borrowing and sampling, and James is the king of the borrowers," Robert wrote on social media. "He pursues you relentlessly when he wants something – art or music – you are eventually assimilated. The strangest one for me was the 'Global Underground' album *Naples* that he was curating. He asked me to do some sketches, I was initially curious and the record company sent me the art, which was essentially a photo album that captured the 'spirit of Napoli'. There were photos of all the places I had taken him to, the backstreets, the bars, the stadium, my old friends, but civic pride and nostalgia were soon replaced by feelings of surreal discomfort. I had been replaced by James in all of the pictures! Assimilation is one thing, being edited out of your own personal history is quite another." After seeing the result, many found James' approach quite manipulative.

Unlike this experience, with his Neapolitan friend and fellow artist Giancarlo Neri, Robert created a sound and light performance for the centenary of the Italian painter and land art artist Alberto Burri, to be held in Gibellina, Sicily.

Born in 1915 in Umbria, trained to be a doctor, Burri was forced to enrol the Italian army during the Second World War and captured in 1943 in Tunisia by the American army. He was sent in a prison in Texas and became a painter while in jail, creating his first pieces from the limited material available to him at the camp, converting them in an art marked by his experience of turmoil and violence. Transformed by this two-year long dramatic and painful experience, he never practised medicine again. After his release in 1946, Burri moved to Rome to pursue a full-time career as painter. He was invited to the Venice Biennale in 1952 and the following year to the Young European Painters exhibition at the Guggenheim Museum in New York, being the only artist to represent his country. In 1960, he was invited to have a solo show of his art in at the Venice Biennale, where he was awarded the Critics' Prize. He worked with the American painter Robert Rauschenberg. Later, Kooning, Matta, Rothko and Twombly came to visit him in Rome.

From 1985, he was invited to create a piece of land art in a small Sicilian town, Gibellina, which was destroyed by a severe earthquake in January 1968. With Il Grande Cretto, he built up a gigantic artwork to completely recover the old destroyed village with white cement... The magisterial piece took decades to get finalised and was finally completed the autumn 2015, for Burri's centenary, with the help of new funding.

Giancarlo Neri had already been invited to the city for performances where he created light installations. In 2015, to celebrate the completion of Burri's Grande Cretto, Gibellina's city councillor in charge of art, sport, and tourism, Giuseppe Zummo, invited Giancarlo Neri to create a new form of audiovisual performance. And Giancarlo asked his friend from Bristol to work on a soundtrack for it.

Audioghost68 was a light and music event scheduled for October 17 and invited the inhabitants of the entire village of Gibellina to come back to the destroyed site and walk through Burri's Grande Cretto, at night. Carrying electric torches on their forehead, the dwellers illuminated the Cretto's alleys from the inside, while two hundred radio sets broadcast the soundtrack created by Robert, as an archival score. The radio sets were placed all around the 27.4-acre site acting as a distributed audio network, via a local radio station. The 3,000 people walking in were fuelled with sounds from 1968: songs from Ennio Morricone's soundtracks, the Beatles' 'Revolution', extracts from Italian opera, news programmes commenting on the invasion of Prague, events from the Vietnam war, the Apollo spaceship reaching the Moon or Paris' Mai 68. The year of the earthquake seemed to come back to life, just like the site itself.

"Alberto Burri's Grande Cretto, remembering but also hiding the tragic event under concrete, represents a return to life through art," said Giancarlo Neri. "We would like to pay homage to this great piece, and to the great artist who created it, with a 'collective' work that would further underscore its greatness: tonight, it will take a thousand of us[251]."

Meanwhile, in Bristol, on the purely musical front, Massive Attack wasn't sure of the relevance of the album format in 2016, because playlists and streaming sites came to dominate listeners' habits. They decided to release a couple of EP's before any form of new record. Grant worked with Stew Jackson in his studio on the second EP, to be released later in the year.

Looking for new, young voices, 3D collaborated with the Londoner Azekel, for a track named 'Ritual Spirit'. D also worked with Run The Jewels, Ghostpoet, Roots Manuva, Jack Barnett from These New Puritans, Cameron McVey and Neneh Cherry, and Young Fathers. The Scottish trio won the Mercury Prize for Best Album in 2014 for *Dead*, mixing hip-hop and electro with a punk-rock energy. Among the members, 'G' Hastings is from Drylaw, near Edinburgh, Alloysious Massaquoi was born in Liberia in a Ghanaian family, and Kayus Bankole was born in Edinburgh to Nigerian parents and also lived in the United States for a while. Young Fathers' second album, *White Men Are Black Men Too* was released in 2015.

3D co-created 'Voodoo In My Blood' with Young Fathers. It was interpreted for the first time on stage by Massive Attack in Dublin on January 19, 2016, first date of the band's new tour. Irish press described it as the highlight of the show. Another of their demo songs, 'He Says He Needs Me', remixed by Forest Swords, was at the centre of a short film conceived by Mark Donne, *La Fête est finie (The Party Is Over)*, on our oil economy, shown in Paris in December 2015 during the United Nations' Climate Conference. A new, shorter version of 'He Says He Needs Me' was featured at the end of 2016 in the movie *Assassins Creed*, and on its soundtrack album in January 2017. 3D and Young Fathers also co-wrote a song named 'Way Up Here', which would be performed live in 2018.

At the same time, 3D composed a soundtrack for French artist JR, for an art film directed with American filmmaker Darren Aronofsky, *The Standing March*, shown in Paris too, during the time of the Climate Conference, but outdoors, on public buildings. "The consequences of

---

251 In his speech before the performance in Gibellina, Sicilia, on October 17, 2015

failure are absolutely catastrophic, but that didn't prevent the previous twenty Conferences of Parties doing precisely that," 3D and Mark Donne wrote in a joint statement about *La Fête est finie (The Party Is Over)*. "As with any party, the skill is in knowing when to leave. For decades, fossil fuel extracting by transnationals and Western governments have continued to dance and partake long after the bright lights of climate science evidence were switched on and the deafening music of denial had its plug pulled."

In January 2016, Bristol, which was the 2015 European Green Capital, also hosted a large number of environmental-friendly and activist events. Artist and filmmaker John Akomfrah, founder of the Black Audio Film Collective in 1982, chose the Arnolfini Gallery to premiere his new film *Vertigo Sea*, created for the Venice Biennale the previous summer. Shattering reflexion on slavery, migration and conflict, the film was projected on three large screens, delivering a sensual, poetic meditation on our relationship with the sea, exploring its role, both mesmerising and tragic, in human history, using television archives and images from the BBC Natural History Unit, based in Bristol.

"I haven't destroyed this country," wrote John Akomfrah in the *Guardian* at the time of the screening, "there's no reason other immigrants would[252]," offering a vibrant plea in favour of human rights and solidarity. A week later, he was in Bristol for a public conference in the gallery and reminded the audience that "it is not possible to immerse the past for good and expect it to disappear[253]," in front of dozens of people who opened a debate on Bristol's past in slave trade and raised again the question of the naming of the Colston Hall.

Ritual and virtual

The ghosts of the slave trade are still haunting Bristol and a few artists have chosen to confront them and therefore transcend them through music or creativity. Fittingly, in January 2016, Massive Attack released their new four-track mini-album produced by 3D and Euan Dickinson named *Ritual Spirit*. It includes four new songs: 'Dead Editors' (with

252 In an article published on January 7, 2016
253 In Bristol's Arnolfini Gallery, on January 16, 2016

Roots Manuva), 'Ritual Spirit' (with Azekel), 'Take It There' (rapped by 3D and Tricky for the first time since 1994) and 'Voodoo In My Blood' (with Young Fathers). In March, the vinyl version entered straight to number one in the UK Vinyl Singles Chart, ahead of PJ Harvey's new song, 'The Wheel'.

As *Pitchfork* magazine underlined, it is "noteworthy that *Ritual Spirit* features entirely black collaborators and engages significantly more with rap than *Heligoland*[254]." The journalist added: "Feverish 'Ritual Spirit' hangs somewhere between meditative and heartsick, Azekel's vocal like a smoke curl; meanwhile, 'Voodoo in My Blood' captures its collaborators' best impulses: a more driven version of Young Fathers' polyglot rock, a more dynamic version of Del Naja's often-of-late meandering work. Massive Attack were always equally as good producers as they were curators; it's promising that, as much of their old sound as they've retained, they've kept this as well."

Drowned In Sound was even more seduced: "Wait until you hear Roots Manuva on 'Dead Editors'. Jesus, man. The prodigal grime rapper of Ninja Tune infamy comes in slick as a hot blade through butter, and steps deep into woofer-shaking beats that bounce heavy through MA's eerie choirs and intricate gadget ensembles," wrote the reviewer, Lee Adcock[255]. "Add the mystery of Manuva himself – when he says *"what would it take to get back to the blackness,*" he could refer to the night sky void, or the hole in our eyes, or the more obvious racial connotation – and you've got MA's most beguiling urban ode since the gritty soliloquies of *Blue Lines*." About 'Take It There', Lee Adcock stated: "Tricky and 3D interweave like – like – fuck it, like two voices that know exactly what powers they possess to infiltrate and captivate, that Tricky's strength is to stagger and 3D's is to glide. Like this is their turf, and it's always been theirs, and it's just taken 20 years to reclaim it together."

Tricky and 3D continued working together and a track created by 3D with Euan Dickinson appeared on Tricky's next release, *The Obia EP*, in September 2016. This song named 'For Nothing' features London singer Lyndsey Lupe and was credited to Euanwhosarmy, as Massive

---

254 In a review published online on February 5, 2016
255 In a review published online on February 4, 2016

Attack wouldn't use their name on Tricky's label, False Idol.

To offer the audience a new means by which to discover music, Massive Attack also co-developed a phone application baptised Fantom, which remixes extracts of these new songs, employing the user's phone sensors. Described as a "sensory remixer", Fantom helps create "your own versions of the duo's sounds", taking into account variables like movement, time of day or night, location and what the phone's camera can capture. Inspired by the theme of his 'Hungry Ghosts' since *Protection*, Del Naja dreamt of creating a new form of shows, including holographic elements and joined forces with Andrew Melchior and the US-based company the Magic Leap. It uses a 3D computer-generated imagery that can be superimposed over real world objects, by projecting a digital light field into the user's eye, to create new forms of entertainment.

On the cinematic front, 'Take It There' was accompanied by a promo video directed by the Japanese filmmaker living in Los Angeles, Hiro Murai. It illustrates the dark ballad with a sort of dance of the living deads, around a main male character played by American actor John Hawkes. A second video was broadcast online in February 2016 for 'Voodoo In My Blood', directed by Ringan Ledwidge, and starring British actress Rosamund Pike, in a mad and demonic choreography involving a futurist flying object, borrowed from the move in cult movie *Phantasm* from 1979, written and directed by Don Coscarelli. It is also a homage to Andrzej Zulawski's film *Possession*, with Isabelle Adjani, released in 1981.

A third film was shared in March, illustrating 'Ritual Spirit', directed by Robert Del Naja with the collective Medium. It features his friend Kate Moss, dancing in the dark with an illuminated light bulb that she's twirling around herself. The project started spontaneously as an artistic endeavour, Robert told me, in a fun day out in a photo studio that unexpectedly delivered a pop video. The final result, hypnotic, nonchalant and sensual, once edited, seemed to fit 'Ritual Spirit'. As a result, these three films explore the art of choreography, which Massive Attack had rarely embraced in videos, only for 'Be Thankful For What You've Got'.

Meanwhile, the band went on tour around Europe with Horace Andy, Martina Topley-Bird, Azekel and Young Fathers at the beginning of 2016. They unveiled five tracks on stage, including the unreleased songs 'He Says He Needs Me' and 'Clock Forward', sung by Martina Topley-Bird. Their stage show was centred on a hub with the drum machines, the keyboards, 3D's chaos pad and keyboards, including a Yamaha Roland VP330 and a Vocoder for manipulations on backing vocals.

But for the first time in their whole career, during the ten first dates, they didn't play any song from *Blue Lines*. Because every time they performed 'Unfinished' or 'Safe From Harm', Robert felt a sense of guilt and betrayal towards Mushroom, he told me after the shows, something he never publicly admitted... In February, Massive Attack were joined by Deborah Miller and finally added 'Safe From Harm' to their set list, and, some evenings, 'Unfinished Sympathy'.

In Berlin a few weeks later, Tricky joined the band on stage to sing 'Take It There' with 3D, while simple and powerful messages appeared on the screens: *"learn"*, *"cure"*, *"protect"*, *"connect"*, *"trust"*, *"accept"*, *"join"*, *"open"*... Obvious references to the persuasive power of social media. Flash forward to 2018: In the same spirit, the band temporarily removed themselves from Facebook and cut direct connection to three million followers the week of the full exposure of the Cambridge Analytica data theft scandal.

The band's light show remains a way to deliver a very strong and emotional message, which mostly represents their own interrogations about our world. Still working with UVA on LED screens, Massive Attack also teamed up with the photographer Giles Duley to showcase his visuals documenting the refugee crisis, from Syria and Iraq to Europe. During the song 'Girl I Love You' for instance, the pictures were passed at an intense speed on the screens, following the rhythm of the percussions. While the band played 'Splitting The Atom', the photographs were shown more slowly and lengthily. And the end of the show was left to the screen with the photographs, without music. "Like a dangerous country," wrote the *Guardian*'s music critic mid-January, "Massive Attack is interesting to visit, though you wouldn't want to live there." Remaining confrontational and unorthodox is obviously one of their goal.

Giles Duley was commissioned in 2015 by the United Nations' High Commissioner for Refugees. The details to help the UNHCR appeared at the very end of Massive Attack's last slideshow. Giles, who was severely wounded in the Afghan War, first worked as a fashion and music photographer. He moved to Bristol at 19 years old in the mid-1980s. "When *Blue Lines* was out in 1991, it so fitted my mood… I was a big fan of the graffiti scene too and since then, I had always wanted to work with Massive Attack," he told BBC Radio Scotland in June 2017. "I met Rob back in the day and he told me to show him my work. But I knew I wasn't ready. It took me 25 years to be ready… But I did contact him again."

The band pursued their tour all over Europe. "You can revel in Del Naja, one of the best rappers this country has ever produced," commented Ben Beaumont-Thomas in the *Guardian*, after seeing the show[256]. "His monotone moves like an arachnid Fagin, stepping with malevolent care around his syllables, and he lends 'Karmacoma' and 'Safe from Harm' their earworms and edge," Beaumont-Thomas continued, adding that "the dub effect that Horace Andy gives his own voice – as if applying echo to his singing on the fly – remains exquisite; the guitars that suddenly flood him on 'Angel' are euphoric."

The band being on the road, they didn't take part in BBC Radio 6 Music's Festival in Bristol that year; included on the programme were Mark Stewart and the Pop Group, Janine Rainforth, DJ Krust, Tricky, Geoff Barrow and Roni Size. Massive Attack still wouldn't play in the Colston Hall anyway, where most of the 6 Music events were staged. In February 2017, British Nigerian historian and writer David Olusoga insisted in the *Guardian*: "I know black Bristolians who refuse to set foot in Colston Hall while it carries the name of a slave trader and to their enormous credit, Massive Attack, Bristol's most innovative and successful band, have for years refused to play there. (…) We are better than this. As part of a mixed-race, multicultural Bristolian crowd, I

256 In his review of the show published on February 4, 2016

hope to finally watch Massive Attack perform in their home city – in the venue formerly known as Colston Hall[257]."

Massive Attack still have a singular voice, sometimes discreet for months, sometimes hard-hitting.

Social change in the making

In May 2016, surprising everyone in town, the band announced they would be back on stage in Bristol for the first time since 2005 for "something made in Bristol, with a truly international reach", Massive Attack said in a statement, announcing a day-long festival on the Downs, in Clifton, scheduled for September. On top of their guest vocalists, Deborah Miller, Horace Andy, Azekel and Young Fathers, the festival invited Primal Scream and Savages, spoken word artist Kate Tempest, the grime rapper Skepta, and a lot of local acts. "We will also use the project to engage with the important social and political issues of the day," Massive Attack added. On May 20, they sold out 27,000 tickets in only 90 minutes.

On July 1, the band were scheduled in London's British Summer Time Festival in Hyde Park, with a fabulous programme, closing the show after the first performance of Patti Smith in the famous park. A few days before, in late June, British people voted to exit the European Union. In echo, Massive Attack performed 'Eurochild' for the first time in years, announcing before their iconic European-themed song: "We are all immigrants... Born of immigrants". This song is to them a "requiem" for the European Union, written prophetically in the mid-1990s.

"Over the next 90 minutes we're bombarded with hysterical Brexit newspaper headlines, slogans from leave and remain, consumerist logos and moving images of refugees. It's like Twitter, after a particularly trying week, has invaded the stage for a very public breakdown", wrote the *Guardian*. "It ends with a full orchestra adorning 'Unfinished Sympathy' beneath pictures of refugees and the slogan: 'We are in this together', a sour national mood brilliantly bucked."

257 In an column published on February 25, 2017

UVA's collaboration with Massive Attack has spaned 14 years since the *100ᵗʰ Window* Tour and never stopped evolving. "The distribution of information in the digital age and its consequence has evolved in ways that no one could have imagined since we started working with them," Matthew Clark of UVA explained in an interview with Bristol's *Crack Magazine*. "Our work has really been an observational commentary of this phenomenon[258]."

For Massive Attack, the challenge is to enable this approach to evolve even further with their time and via technology, to embrace the current changes in our society in an artistic, compelling and creative way. "The idea is to eventually try and get the show almost working as independent intelligence, using deep learning computation," 3D said. "I'm wondering if the light show could start to create itself not unlike Fantom as it starts to remodel music with its software: can the light show start to remodel itself from the inputs we give it, and if so what form will that take[259]?" His main preoccupation evolved around the idea of 'the post-factual society'. "The truth is rewritten as it's shared," he stated. "It's an interesting but scary time we live in; we can see from the misinformation that was spread around the time of Brexit as a very recent example of how precarious that is. (…) Ultimately, our aim is to question information, the sharing of information and our role in it[260]."

The Bristol homecoming event was scheduled for September 3, a month after the release of Daddy G's EP, late July, named *The Spoils*. The song is a sublime and melancholic ballad featuring Hope Sandoval. The B-side features a dark and hip-hop track, 'Come Near Me', written by G with Stew Jackson and Ghostpoet. A choice unanimously acclaimed by the music press.

The two songs were released with two powerful videos. 'Come Near Me' was directed by Ed Morris and shot in a day, in Hove, starring Kosovar actress Arta Dobroshi and British actor Jonathan Aris, in a dark dance showing a couple drifting away, in a destructive relationship. The powerfully visual narrative encounters a sudden jolt halfway through

258 Published in September 2016
259 In *Crack Magazine*, in September 2016
260 Ibid

the film, when the lady unexpectedly crosses path with a friend in her car, her radio loudly playing Massive Attack's own 'Unfinished Sympathy'… The song "brings such nostalgia and love with it," Morris said to *Dazed & Confused*, "it's basically the 90s showing up in a present day promo." For 'The Spoils', Australian director John Hillcoat filmed the Oscar-winning actress Cate Blanchett's face, undergoing a series of impressive technological transformations.

In September, Massive Attack announced that a new single, 'Dear Friend', would be pressed on 12-inch vinyl, via Battle Box and the Vinyl Factory. A wider vinyl and digital release was planned for later. Robert Del Naja and Euan Dickinson wrote the track, which features poet and vocalist James Massiah, with amazingly powerful and contemporary lyrics, dealing with *"Academic underachievement, social separation and a desire to fit in"*, describing the everyday life of a young black man in South London.

The one-day festival in Bristol featured different acts playing on three stages. Discussions and parallel events were also organised. Giles Duley was invited to give a talk on his work with the UNHCR (United Nations High Commissioner for Refugees). "In recent years I've been collaborating with poets, writers and musicians, seeking opportunities to reach new audiences and tell stories in innovative ways. Massive Attack were one of the bands I'd been talking to, and working together to highlight the refugee crisis seemed like a perfect and timely collaboration," Giles Duley told the UN body in an interview for their website, in November 2016. "I was deeply moved by the pictures he was sending me," Robert added to the HCR. "What's really shocking is that you could be looking at photographs from any time in the last 100 years of a crisis involving refugee migration and war. And what's terrifying is you think 'Nothing's changed,' and that is what we have to engage with because this is not the past. This is now."

With the pictures, the shows gained a new dimension, mixing images from the real world, portraits of people affected by real wars, with data, words and symbolic images. "There's a track during the show where we use all the flags of the various factions fighting in Syria," described Robert, "and you see that these ideological struggles are being sponsored by foreign powers, thus creating a perpetual state of civil war, and ever intensifying violence. In the light of that you understand why people would be fleeing for their lives, it's not a matter of choice, it's a matter of necessity and I think we often forget that. It's editorialised and in a sense you lose touch with the fact that it's actually life or death. It's on a completely different level than how we're actually thinking about it, we've lost touch with that idea[261]."

After his talk on one of the smaller stage areas, I caught sight of Giles Duley by chance in the rain... His appearance on stage was a special moment for him, after years of hard work to display refugees' stories, his pictures were finally out there on a wide scale, via the Bristol band's performance. Later in the evening, he watched Massive Attack's show from a corner of the stage. "I sat on the stage to see my images on the screen," he told journalists in June 2017. "And it was one of the most beautiful days of my life".

Massive Attack closed the evening under torrential rain, bringing a surreal light on the main stage. The show's visual effects seemed even more magical under the raindrops... Just as they did through all Europe in summer festival, they perform 'Eurochild' as a response to the Brexit referendum. Towards the end of the evening, Tricky also came up on stage to sing 'Take It There' with 3D, jumping in all the members of the collective's arms at the end. While introducing Tricky, 3D declared in answer to the persistent press and social media stories on Banksy's identity: "Rumours of my secret identity are greatly exaggerated... We are all Banksy!"

The local website Bristol 24/7 reported: "Massive Attack were undoubtedly, and deservedly, the highlight of the main stage. Massive's music has always been dark. It's evocative of real lives in the 21st century – lives a million miles away from reality TV; the hardships and inequality resulting from unfettered bigotry and rampant capitalism and exposes the malaise that lurks beneath social media and feel good culture. That said, it's powerful and uplifting and the band aren't afraid to kick back, challenging and informing and with music that is empowering, moving

261 In his interview with *Crack Magazine*, published in September 2016

and really rather unique (who else sounds like this band?)[262]." In the year of the "Brexit" vote in the UK and Donald Trump's election in the USA, they have never appeared so relevant.

2016 was also an anniversary year for the band. "Massive Attack's *Blue Lines* Just Turned 25, But It Still Feels Ahead of Its Time", headlined *Vulture* magazine in America, in August. "The genius of the album lies in the casual precision with which it discovers lyrical and sonic counterparts for the experience of socially marginal second-generation immigrants — for their displacement and bewilderment, to be sure, but also for the curiosity that emerges from displacement and for the perceptiveness at the core of bewilderment," wrote critic Frank Guan. "The lyrics in *Blue Lines* aren't about getting rich, but getting by; being grateful, as opposed to greedy; loving one person constantly, instead of juggling several; holding back from firing the gun rather than firing it. Now that a quarter-century dominated by Trumpian belligerence and declarations of self-worth has all but run its course, it makes sense that hip-hop has come to resemble the state of *Blue Lines* more and more." An album, which announced the end of an era and the beginning of another. 25 years after 1991, Massive Attack have shown how much they have changed Bristol and therefore England.

Suddenly, seven months later, the Colston Hall announced its decision to finally rename the auditorium, following a campaign supported by Massive Attack against its continued use of 17th century slave trader Edward Colston's name. The statement on the venue's website read: "The name Colston, and its associations with the slave trade, does not reflect our values as a progressive, forward-thinking and open arts organisation."

George Ferguson had actually promised privately to Robert Del Naja in 2012 that he would help change the name of the Colston Hall if Massive Attack got behind his election. And just before the end of his five-year term, they were invited to a meeting at the Colston Hall to discuss the issue.

On April 26, 2017, in her official announcement, Louise Mitchell, the

262 Published on September 4, 2016

chief executive of the Bristol Music Trust – which operates the 150-year-old Hall – publically described the Colston name as a "toxic brand". The building closed for refurbishment in 2018 and is due to reopen in 2020 with a different name. A move that reflects social change in the making... A new era of difficult but necessary discussion on unresolved history wounds is beginning in the whole United Kingdom.

But the announcement also provoked negative reactions from numerous inhabitants, denouncing political correctness. "The perverse reality is that if Colston Hall had been named after a merchant from any other trade, the renaming would have been a mundane and uncontroversial affair," replied British Nigerian historian and writer David Olusoga in the *Guardian*[263]. "But the defence of Edward Colston has become a proxy battle: for a defence of a form of history in which uncomfortable facts can be airbrushed, and the views and histories of other peoples are dismissed as irrelevant, or as pandering to 'political correctness'." He concluded: "The question facing Bristol now is this: is the city willing to fully confront the darkest chapter of its past, or are there those determined to enter into a fourth century of denial?"

Relevant and powerful, Massive Attack are still working on new music material, maybe not in the form of a long-awaited sixth album, but on more personal projects, soundtracks, featuring, art events. They have been recording from 2015 with the English experimental music group These New Puritans, American punk-soul and very politically aware American band Algiers, Congolese percussionist and vocalist Jupiter, and many more, in their typical secretive atmosphere... They went on an Asian tour in the autumn 2017, performing in Hong Kong and Tokyo, and on a European summer tour in 2018, which took them up to Istanbul, Kiev and Moscow. In July 2018, 3D's song composed for Neneh Cherry with the producer Four Tet, was also released: 'Kong' is a statement in favour of migration and tolerance, and remarkable musical return for the singer. While the Massive Attack crew were touring Europe through the summer 2018, their shows became increasingly anti-Brexit and anti-fascist.

---

263 In a column published on April 27, 2017

Meanwhile, Banksy also painted murals about the lack of solidarity in Europe and towards refugees, in Hull and in Paris, France, notably. This produced multiple ripple effects in the media, every day more obsessed with uncovering his identity. The artist only replied with more provocation. In October 2018 for instance, a piece of his Girl With Ballon (subtitled There Is Always Hope) shredded itself at an auction at Sotheby's in London, just when it reached more than £1 million. Banksy posted a video on social media to reveal that the device was secretly built into the painting "a few years ago ... in case it was ever put up for auction".

Alex Branczik, Sotheby's head of contemporary art for Europe, commented the following day: "Banksy didn't destroy an artwork in the auction, he created one. Following his surprise intervention on the night, we are pleased to confirm the sale of the artist's newly titled Love Is in the Bin, the first artwork in history to have been created live during an auction." The *Guardian* described the move as the "latest anti-establishment statement by the elusive street artist, who has travelled the world etching progressive messages on to unlikely canvases." The BBC Arts editor Will Gompertz simply wrote: "When I said a couple of weeks ago that for the past century artists have failed to outwit and outdo Marcel Duchamp (the French conceptual artist who placed a urinal in a gallery in 1917), I hadn't realised that there was an artwork hanging on the walls of a London auction house which was about to do just that[264]." Robert Del Naja described it to me as a genius shredder stunt, and maybe the most important art piece of 21st century?

Meanwhile, in Bristol, 2018 was also the year celebrating the 50th anniversary of St Pauls' Carnival and the 20th of Massive Attack's third album. "*Mezzanine*'s impact rumbles on", wrote *Fact* magazine in 2013, for its fifteenth anniversary, "it's an obvious precursor to the Weeknd's dysphoric R&B, and we'll bet a pack of croissants that Yeezus' savage industrial rap wouldn't have sounded the same without it either." Rock-lover *Pitchfork* conceded in 2017 that the band laid down their "definitive paranoia statement with *Mezzanine*[265]" and that "it's hard not to feel the

264 On the BBC's website on October 13, 2018
265 In an article published online on January 8, 2017

album's legacy resonating elsewhere."

To celebrate, the band prepared a special reissue on vinyl and CD of the album including unreleased dub versions recorded with Mad Professor in 1998. They also worked on a special show dedicated especially to the record and... to the songs that inspired it. The shows scheduled for late January, February and March 2019 were prepared with Liz Fraser and Horace Andy, and the visuals included material from Massive Attack's very own virtual machine, conceived through artificial intelligence with engineers from King's College, London. They designed a brand new visual show, working once more with Adam Curtis and with a new collaborator, Mario Klingemann, a German artist working with algorithms and data to investigate the possibilities that machine learning and artificial intelligence offer in understanding how creativity, culture and their perception work. They wanted the show to be a deconstruction of *Mezzanine* itself, Robert explained to me, but also of the last 20 years.

Exploring cutting-edge technology, from artificial intelligence to neural net sampling and DNA Storage, the band worked with Professor Robert Grass and his team at ETH Zurich, to have the album stored in DNA molecules. It was the first time that an entire record had been saved in this way. In October 2018, a limited batch of aerosols each containing the DNA of one million copies of *Mezzanine* were produced.

Massive Attack are increasingly involved in collective multi-dimensional projects and in August 2018, Russian filmmaker Ilya Khrzhanovsky revealed that they participated in his gigantic and hyper-ambitious film /performance named *DAU Freiheit* (*DAU Freedom* in English), created over more than twelve years and inspired by the life of Soviet physicist Lev Landau. They worked on the long-awaited project along with Brian Eno, opera director Peter Sellars, Nobel prize-winning physicist David Gross, mathematician Shing-Tung Ya, and artist Marina Abramovic... The film should be shown in art installations featuring performances and live interventions in Berlin, Paris and London in 2019. 3D is also creating his own opera, inspired by the Marcel comic *Elektra*, created by Frank Miller.

Awarding the Nordoff Robbins O2 Silver Clef to the band in July

2016, Lucy Noble, Director of Events at the Royal Albert Hall, said: "Throughout their career, Massive Attack have continually pushed the boundaries, exploring the incredible possibilities of music through pioneering experimentation, exceptional songwriting and a complete contempt for the restrictions of genre. They are as exciting, dynamic and original as ever. We still have fond memories of their magnificent headline show in 1998 – a highlight of the band's famous *Mezzanine* Tour - and are delighted to announce that they are the winners of this year's Royal Albert Hall Best Group."

Changing music through a strong social awareness, the band has also managed to change society through their strongly creative and powerfully innovative music and performances. The fulfilment of a virtuous circle.

Chapter 15
Phantoms Of The Past, "Faithful Mirrors" Of Our Present And Visions Of The Future

Why would artists leave a city that they have almost reinvented? Since the development of a reggae hub in St Pauls in the 1960s and the formation of a genuine and active post-punk scene in the late 1970s, Bristol has generated many musical and artistic movements, in continuous waves, after decades of near silence. And specifically after the years of experimentation led by the Wild Bunch and taken beyond the city's walls by Massive Attack, Bristol has come to embody another part of Britain's culture, enriched by its diversity and revolutionised by the energy that came from hip-hop in the 1980s.

After exploding into a multiple and diverse scene, the Bristol sound and its emerging type of street art have found other paths to evolve and transform themselves. Massive Attack's history, and these of some of their counterparts from the city, has been made of metamorphosis and enrichment, building many links with the outside world and crossing many bridges. From Britain to the Caribbean, from England to the United States, from Bristol to Istanbul, Gaza and Beirut, from Europe to Africa, their hometown has grown to become an evolving world and a language in itself.

In five decades, Bristol has deeply evolved. Its population is nowadays English, European, Caribbean, Asian as well as East African, and it is estimated that more than ninety different languages are spoken in the city. It has a reputation for being a culturally open and friendly city. Away from the clichés about England's monarchy, traditions and homely comfort. While the United Kingdom has chosen to retreat from the European Union, in the Brexit vote of June 2016, 62 per cent of Bristol voters were in favour of remaining in Europe, making Bristol the English city most in favour of remaining.

When they were facing Thatcher's blocks and restrictions, Bristol's artists chose to believe in their own values, to display a spirit of novelty, to break cultural barriers, and to share with each other their opportunities and success. Values inherited from the ethos of both punk and reggae music. And they did so despite crises, riots and political disappointments. Bristol, through the years, saw new artists emerge and remain authentic, building up a counter-culture that would never bow under the weight of consumerism.

This evolution owes a lot to the pioneers from the Sixties and Seventies, the first reggae DJs in Bristol and bands such as Black Roots and the Pop Group. They all incarnated the hope that art and music, even in our era of multinational companies, tax havens, obsessive anti-terrorist fights and climate change, still have the power to transport complex and deep ideas and values, to help us understand our world and our humanity.

After travelling the world, most of Bristol's artists came to meet their audience back home in recent years. Because as much as Bristol is evolving and facing new social challenges, their engagement for their hometown remains intact, as well as their recognition of the opportunities the city gave them in their youth.

The emergence of this multicultural scene forced the city's inhabitants to look into the eyes the country's past and to digest it, a complex and sometimes ugly past that the voices from *Blue Lines* as well as the stencils from Banksy have made visible but also transfigured. Like an alchemical process, the melancholy of their sound, the darkness in their music, and the cynical humour or visible pain present in their art, have turned the darkness into a truer light.

Bristol's cultural history has taken a new stance since 1990, full of powerful messages, creativity, legitimate fights and discourses. These have enriched an urban subculture and an underground movement to the point that they could elevate them to venues and stages all around the world, using them as springboard for their ever-evolving creativity, following the changes of the environment. This music and art have therefore managed to embody its era and to sound timeless at the same time, to overcome social and cultural barriers, to reunite opposites, and to foster revolutions.

It is the main strength of an avant-garde movement, to be able to incarnate their era and to think beyond it at the same time. The themes of ghosts and phantoms, of light and darkness, have been very present in Bristol's music, lyrics and art, just like the theme of mirrors. From 'Hymn of the Big Wheel' (*"The wheel keeps turning / The sky's rearranging / Look my son the weather is changing"*) to 'Risingson' (*"I see you go down to a cold mirror… Check it by the signs in the corridor / You light my ways through the club maze / We would struggle through the dub daze"*) and 'Teardrop' (*"most faithful mirror, fearless on my breath… / You stumble in the dark"*). Also in 'Antistar' (*"I turn a stone I'll find you there / Into reflected light I'll stare / You blind me with flash bulbs / And puzzle me with syllables"*) as much as in 'Dead Editors' (*"Flashing light years / What would it take to get back to the blackness / Up there out there / Wanna gonna be like stars / Constellations in installations of my fixation of so sensational oh / What would it take to know / With a viewing of the night sky /Taking a peep at the history /Messages in the mystery"*).

Most of them being self-taught artists, they never needed to follow anyone else's lead. That was at the core of the beauty of this artistic journey. Open to new horizons, geographically and culturally, Bristol artists are faithful to their origins and remain anti-establishment.

As their creations renew themselves this way, in different directions and dimensions, open to the world and enriched through it, this scene seems to have captured a charm fighting the effects of time. As the early twentieth century French philosopher Henri Bergson would say, isn't art a powerful means to overcome our own limits? Limits in time and space. Limits of the mind itself, and limits of our perception's capacities. One thing is sure when we look at this art and music, in and out of Bristol, it is that the artists involved succeeded in doing so by constantly getting themselves out of their own comfort zone.

--

Bibliography

Primary sources

3D And The Art of Massive Attack, by Robert Del Naja, Vinyl Factory, July 2015

Art and Sound of the Bristol Underground, by Chris Burton and Gary Thompson, Tangent Books, Bristol, 2009

Children of The Can: Bristol Graffiti and Street Art, by Felix 'FLX' Braun, Tangent Books, Bristol, 2008

Straight Outa Bristol, by Phil Johnson, Hodder and Stoughton, 1996

Historical references

Black and British, A Forgotten History, by David Olusoga, Pan MacMillan, 2017

Richard Ameryk and the Name America, by Alfred Hudd, 1908

Britain and the Slave Trade Hardcover, by Steve Martin, Channel 4, 1999

Remembering slavery and abolition in Bristol - Slavery and Abolition, by Madge Dresser, 2009

The Black Presence in a slaving port: Bristol 1688-1835, by Madge Dresser

Pero: The Life of a Slave in Eighteenth-Century Bristol, by Christine Eickelmann and David Small, Redcliffe Press Ltd, 2004

Black 1919: Riots, Racism and Resistance in Imperial Britain, by Jacqueline Jenkinson, Liverpool University Press, 2009

Black and White on the Buses, Bristol, by Madge Dresser, Bristol Broadsides, 1986

On Music

Indie & New Wave Music, by Colin Larkin, Guinness Publishing, Enfield, 1992

Reggae and Caribbean Music de Dave Thompson, Backbeat Books (*Third*

Ear: Essential Listening Companion), 2002
Nine Lives, by Goldie and Paul Gorman, Sceptre, 2003

On street art
Subway Art, by Martha Cooper and Henry Chalfant, Henry Holt & Company Inc, 1984, then 1st American Editions, 1996
Banging Your Head Against A Brick Wall, by Banksy, Weapons of Mass Distraction, 2001
Wall and Piece, de Banksy, Random House, 2005
Banksy – The Man Behind The Wall, by Will Ellsworth-Jones, St. Martin's Press, 2012